PRIMAL
INTELLIGENCE

You Are Smarter Than You Know

ANGUS FLETCHER

Avery
an imprint of Penguin Random House
New York

AVERY

an imprint of Penguin Random House LLC
1745 Broadway, New York, NY 10019
penguinrandomhouse.com

Image on page 227 by Sudowoodo/Shutterstock

Book design by Angie Boutin

Library of Congress Cataloging-in-Publication Data

Names: Fletcher, Angus author
Title: Primal intelligence: you are smarter than you know / Angus Fletcher.
Description: New York: Avery, [2025] | Includes bibliographical references and index.
Identifiers: LCCN 2024053849 (print) | LCCN 2024053850 (ebook) |
ISBN 9780593715307 hardcover | ISBN 9780593715314 ebook
Subjects: LCSH: Genius | Intellect | Creative ability
Classification: LCC BF412 .F64 2025 (print) | LCC BF412 (ebook) |
DDC 153.9/8—dc23/eng/20250516
LC record available at https://lccn.loc.gov/2024053849
LC ebook record available at https://lccn.loc.gov/2024053850

ISBN (international edition): 9798217176847

Printed in the United States of America
1st Printing

The authorized representative in the EU for product safety and compliance is Penguin Random House Ireland, Morrison Chambers, 32 Nassau Street, Dublin D02 YH68, Ireland, https://eu-contact.penguin.ie.

For my father
Who read me *tyger tyger*

CONTENTS

PART III: PRIMAL SCIENCE

Nobody noticed the colonel on the campus green. The spring day was busy, students rushing to class, absorbed in their phones. And anyway, it was the colonel's job to go unseen. With his standard shoulders and colorless clothes, he'd parachuted onto a thousand targets, from coconut Pacific reefs to concrete Persian palaces to moonlit bullet alleys. Wherever he went, he vanished.

It was March 2021. The colonel had dropped into Ohio State—a rambling public university built of brick and brick and brick and glass—to investigate a rumor. During the colonel's twenty-year U.S. Army career, he'd investigated rumors about psychic spies, aura cameras, and faster-than-light flying machines. But it had been a while since he'd probed a tale as unlikely as this. Supposedly, an Ohio State think tank had discovered a lost brain part that powered the brilliance of Steve Jobs. And Maya Angelou. And Nikola Tesla. And Vincent van Gogh.

Making some casual inquiries, the colonel found to his surprise: The think tank existed. It was housed on the top floor of what had once been the university's administrative headquarters, a rusted structure with a broken heater that ran full strength in summer. There was no locked door guarding the think tank, or even a sign to mark its entrance. It was just a sleepy corridor of nondescript offices. Yet despite the think tank's anonymous appearance, it had a name. An offbeat name, the colonel thought. It was *Project Narrative*.

Project Narrative wasn't listed in any Army database. But it was famous in its own way, renowned in academic circles for its pioneering work with doctors, astronauts, and poets. And when the colonel deftly befriended one of its researchers—fortyish male, black-rimmed glasses, Stanford PhD—he heard that there was truth to the unlikely tale about the think tank's activities. Or so, at least, the researcher asserted.

The researcher introduced himself as Dr. Mike Benveniste, lead analyst at the lab of Professor Angus Fletcher. He spoke in complete paragraphs, dense and technical, like he was spontaneously composing an encyclopedia. He claimed that the Fletcher lab had identified a primordial brainpower that drove intuition, imagination, commonsense, and smart emotion. This brainpower was neglected in modern schools. And impossible for computer AI. Yet it was the key to the mental gifts of Jobs, Angelou, Tesla, van Gogh—and also Marie Curie, Abraham Lincoln, Wayne Gretzky, William Shakespeare . . . The list went on.

The colonel was skeptical. That was also his job: to be skeptical. But his skepticism was more than a professional formality.

He could believe that modern schools were missing something. He could even believe in a science of intuition. But a power beyond artificial intelligence? The idea struck him as far-fetched—and dangerous. The colonel was a seasoned computer expert, proficient with mega-core systems that ran quadrillions of calculations a second. And while he knew that AI had limits—Alan Turing's proof of the Halting problem sprang to mind—he'd learned to never underestimate it.

What, the colonel politely inquired, was this power that lurked in ancient regions of the human head yet was a no-go for space-age computers? The researcher responded by speaking in neuroscience: *synaptic transmission . . . narrative cognition.* Which he then summarized: "We call it Primal Intelligence."

Primal Intelligence was only a theory. It had never been tested outside Project Narrative. It was too new—and too unusual. But after sifting through thick stacks of laboratory documents, the colonel admitted to himself: The theory was unexpectedly compelling. It squared with commonsense. And it matched his own intuition. That didn't prove anything, of course. But the colonel's intuition had kept him alive on hundreds of wartime adventures, high speed and low cover. So after careful deliberation, he made a decision.

He would put Primal to an independent trial. The trial would be a risk, a big one. The colonel didn't want to go down in history alongside Jim Channon, the Army War College officer who in 1982 had authored *The First Earth Battalion,* a New Age manual instructing U.S. soldiers on how to alter time with their dreams. To probe the incredible while avoiding debacle, the Primal trial would need to be run by individuals with big imaginations but no patience for bullshit. Such individuals were uncommon, but the Army did have a pipeline for making them. A pipeline at U.S. Special Operations.

The colonel knew the pipeline well. It had produced him. And it had also produced handheld GPS, quick-clotting medical gauze, and future gear too hush-hush for public knowledge. These ventures had succeeded not just because of the willingness of Special Operations to dare huge but because hard jobs in harder places had instilled Operators with zero tolerance for "magic happy." Magic happy was nice ideas that broke on contact with reality. Magic happy was stoner mysticism and college philosophy. Magic happy was a rearguard luxury and a frontline catastrophe.

Would Special Operations reject Primal as magic happy? The colonel picked up a phone to find out. Moments later, he had an answer: Special Operations would give Primal a shot. Like the Ohio State think tank, they were believers in intuition and commonsense. So if Primal could give them more? Well, they would try anything—once.

At a clandestine site made from bronze rock and gunmetal beams, protected by satellite jammers and radar-guided Vulcan cannons, U.S. Special Operations mastered the Fletcher lab's theory. With the colonel's guidance, they turned it into practical training. Then they ran the training on the Army's most elite units, their names secret, their missions classified.

The training worked. The Operators saw the future faster. They healed quicker from trauma. Faced with life-and-death situations, they chose wiser. In 2023, the Army awarded the Fletcher lab a medal for "groundbreaking research," formally recognizing the existence of Primal.

This book tells the story of the training that Project Narrative and Army Special Ops created. The training is simple, not easy. It is not an optimization hack or a cheat code. It is a different way of using your brain.

It will activate intuition, imagination, emotion, and commonsense, awakening the powers of van Gogh, Tesla, Angelou, Jobs, and all the rest. So that you can use the know-how you forgot you knew. Your lost nature. Your Primal Intelligence.

YOUR LOST NATURE

I n the early 2000s, U.S. Army Special Operations saw trouble coming. Not trouble outside, trouble within: Young Special Operations recruits were underperforming at decision-making, strategic planning, and leadership. The recruits had high—even profoundly gifted—IQ scores. They rated off the charts in ideation, rational analytics, and other advanced metrics. Yet their intelligence turned brittle in dynamic environments. As one observer put it: "They can solve math problems. But not life problems."

This wasn't just an issue for the Army. It was an issue for the recruits. It made them prone to violent anger, dysfunctional relationships, and pill addiction. And what really concerned the Army was that the situation was deteriorating: Recruits were doing worse in 2020 than in 2010 than in 2000. Something was impairing the minds of young Americans and, seeking answers, the Army contacted me in March 2021. They'd heard that I had a different approach to cultivating intelligence. And they asked: What advice did I have for their recruits?

I was startled by the question. I'd never spoken to the Army before. And I wasn't interested in helping it make killers. Combat was already deadly enough, I knew, because I'd met its survivors: Libyan infants orphaned by air strikes; Baghdad teens turned in a roadside flash into quadruple amputees; Afghan women rebuilding peppercorn markets wrecked by the same gunships that had burned up their sons.

Yet as much as I recoiled from war, the Army's worry about young minds resonated with me. In my two decades as a professor, I'd witnessed college students doing better at standardized tests while having greater difficulty with real-world tasks. They displayed more ideological rigidity, more unproductive anxiety, more submissiveness to authority, and more magical thinking. After graduation, the fortunate ones struggled to settle into a career or returned obediently for more schooling. The unfortunate wrote me letters from their bed in a psych ward, or confessed that they survived their office job by spiking their water bottle with MDMA, or jumped to their death on a hike to find peace in the Andes.

The same trap, I could see, was catching younger students. My son and daughter were enrolled at a public elementary school in the American Midwest. Each morning, when I watched them walk together through the school's bright-blue door, I thought of the thirty years of research warning that every day spent in class would be accompanied by a decline in their independence, adaptability, and resilience.

And my desire to reverse those declines wasn't the only reason I answered the Army's knock on my door. I had another, less altruistic motive, one that revealed itself when Special Operations invited me to a training exercise near the forested black-bear wetlands of the Dismal Swamp, on the seaboard of North Carolina.

I arrived at the Swamp with soccer shoes and a stopwatch, like a high school gym teacher, planning to record everything I saw. After being transported at dawn in an armored pickup truck down an unmarked trail guarded with sniper nests, I was met by a cadre of Special Forces instructors who stank of algae muck and cool mint chaw. They led me on a slow hike along a sodden footpath through a sunlit village built of rusty freight containers . . . when an artillery shell detonated with violent unexpectedness.

Immediately, I ran toward the explosion. Alarmed, one of the instructors chased after me. Grabbing my arm, he shouted over the din of munitions and the shake of the earth: "Get down! Head in the dirt and cover your ears!"

After the rattle and blast had subsided, the instructor regarded me with morbid fascination: "Most folk get shook by the blasts. They flinch, or freeze, or back away. You done the opposite. The moment that shell went off, you ran toward it. Boom! Right away, without hesitating, you was into the heat. Where'd you learn to act like that?"

I hadn't learned. It was an instinctive reaction. Pressed by the instructor to explain, I shared the story of Pliny the Elder. Born two decades after Jesus, during the Roman Empire's tilt into madness, Pliny was possessed by a yearning to know everything, everything, everything: the origins of suns, the healing juice of wild rose roots, the muscle pumps of leopard hearts. Devoting his life to amassing all the knowledge in the world, he compiled a vast series of thirty-seven books known as *Natural History*, which he stopped writing only because on a pleasant autumnal afternoon in the year 79, Mount Vesuvius erupted, filling the skies of southwestern Italy with roar and flame. Observing the atmospheric maelstrom from a cozy terrace at his Naples beach house, Pliny didn't flinch or freeze or back away. Instead, overcome with zealous interest—he had never seen a volcano before!—he leaped into a boat and paddled toward the lava. What did he perceive in the inferno light? What secrets of the fire did he learn? We will never know. Overcome by subterranean fumes, he died, lightly buried by a fall of ash.

"He was the kind of dude," the instructor grins, "whose first urge is to feed his curiosity."

Yes. And I am too. That's why I raced toward the blast at the Dismal Swamp—and why I was similarly quick to work with Special Operations. Like every researcher with an unorthodox new theory, I'd spent most of my career isolated and under-funded. And now the U.S. military was offering to do for me what it had done for Grace Hopper, the Vassar College professor who pioneered natural language programming in the 1940s when the Navy handed her a five-ton electromechanical calculator—the Harvard Mark I—with the power to bring her maverick ideas to life. For years, I'd wanted to test my own rogue insights. I'd lain awake on tired nights wondering: *Could I be right?* So I wasn't about to snub a willing research partner just because they thought differently. In fact, their different thinking made them all the more interesting to me.

Sitting down with a quietly enterprising lieutenant colonel named Tom Gaines, I combined my academic research with Special Operations' decades of experience building irregular schools. We developed a new method for training the brain to act intelligently in what the Army called VUCA: volatility, uncertainty, complexity, and ambiguity. And we gave it to a classified Army Special Ops unit, at a schoolhouse so covert that it doesn't exist on any map.

The experiment produced significant benefits, increasing creative planning and strategic initiative under timed duress. Or as the Army put it: Operators got smarter in VUCA and quicker in chaos.

Following that initial success, the Army provided me with direct access to observe Operators as they practiced for missions. After a year of collaborative research, we offered the training to the Green Berets, the Army's specialists in unconventional warfare. It earned accolades from their senior cadre of instructors. So we brought it to the Command and General Staff College, the Army's graduate leadership school in Leavenworth, Kansas, for an independent scientific trial on more than 150 senior officers. According to the Army's metrics, the training improved creative problem-solving scores by almost a full standard deviation, bumping them from normal to high, from high to superior, and from superior to genius.

We then translated the training into the civilian world. We offered it to surgeons, pilots, business execs, astronauts, entrepreneurs, investors, sales teams, social workers, doctors, nurses, teachers, coaches, pro athletes, parents. The training improved decision-making, innovation, communication, and leadership.

Next we took the training into universities. We started with Army ROTC before moving on to college undergraduates, honors cohorts, and professional programs: MBAs, MFAs, MDs, MEds, engineering PhDs. The students improved substantially at overcoming real-world challenges. They coped better with change and uncertainty. They displayed less stress and anger. They anticipated unprecedented opportunities. And they showed the way to others.

Finally, with the help of experienced K–12 educators, we did what I had dreamed from the beginning: We gave the training to public elementary school students. It produced substantial gains in children as young as eight.

What was this training? Why was my theory so different— yet effective?

MY THEORY IS THAT THE modern world has incorrectly defined intelligence.

Intelligence is almost universally defined—including by the U.S. Department of Education, Microsoft and Google, the Nobel Prize in Economics, the Chinese government, and the IQ test—as logic. *Logic* is used in casual conversation to refer to any method of thinking that makes sense to a reasonable person, but logic could not be automated by computers if it did not involve a precisely defined set of mechanical operations. Those operations were identified more than two millennia ago by the Greek polymath Aristotle, and in addition to driving artificial intelligence, they power arithmetic, statistics, design, data analytics, induction, deduction, interpretation, critical thinking, Bayesian inference, optimization, ideation, behavioral economics, organizational psychology, system 2, pattern finding, and just about everything taught and assessed in twenty-first-century classrooms.

Logic pervades these classrooms not only because it is seen as the essence of intelligence but also because it is hard for humans, requiring years of study. Which raises the question: How would our brains think without that study? What's the way we naturally think?

Logic's answer is that the human brain is predisposed toward two nonlogical behaviors: randomness and error. Randomness is the absence of logic. Error is the opposite of logic. Randomness is, in the view of many logicians, a source of creativity, so it is valued within bounds. Error is, however, to be eliminated by targeting its root causes: emotion and cognitive bias.

This logical view of the brain is absurd. It defies basic biology. It seems sensible only because it is repeated endlessly to us from the moment we set foot in school. We are brainwashed to believe it, to our own detriment.

The path back to sanity begins by acknowledging that intelligence is more than logic enriched with generative bursts of randomness. Randomness is capricious and wasteful—while intelligence is purposeful and prudent. This is why the human brain is not random, as you can prove. Try to make a list of random numbers. You will go slowly and your numbers will clump nonrandomly. That doesn't mean, however, that your neurons are running logic. Logic requires data, and in life, data is almost always in short supply. To handle the unstable dark of worldly existence, our brain had to develop mechanisms for acting smart with little, even no, information. Otherwise, intelligence would have been as useful as an empty spreadsheet.

All of which adds up to: The brain has nonlogical intelligence that isn't arbitrary. That intelligence evolved millions of years before AI's data-dependent circuits, investing our primordial ancestors with the ability to succeed in the unknown. At first, this ability was simply accepted as the way of life. But as our ancestors self-reflected, using their intelligence to examine itself, they parsed it into four primal powers: intuition, imagination, emotion, and commonsense.

- Intuition perceives the world's hidden rules.

- Imagination makes the future.

- Emotion knows the path of personal growth.

- Commonsense decides wisely in uncertainty.

These four primal powers are why humans can act smart with little information. Not that we always act smart with little information. But the fact that we *can* act smart is why we're capable of succeeding in situations where AI haywires. AI can make logical deductions and it can spam out chance ideas. But it is mechanically incapable of commonsense or imagination, so it will always underperform human brains when data is thin or fragile, making computer-think a loser in most facets of innovation, leadership, and ordinary life.

That real-world limit of logic reveals why our current educational system is failing. By drilling students to think like computers, it is training them to do what their laptops can do better—while not helping them improve the natural cleverness that AI can't replicate. It is condemning future generations to be second-class algorithms with less practical smarts than primeval humans.

To fix this situation, we don't need to dismantle school; design thinking and statistics can be useful tools. But we do need to enrich classrooms with methods to strengthen the root of Primal Intelligence. That root is not magical. It is not consciousness or some ineffable power. It is a physical operation that runs on mechanical parts of the animal neuron that do not exist in computer logic gates and that cannot be engineered, ever, from electronic transistors.

What is this nonmagical source of worldly ingenuity? What is the ancient brainpower that allows us to be smart in ways that AI never will? Here is where my theory gets so unusual that it was rejected by everyone except for U.S. Army Special Operations. My theory is that intuition, commonsense, and the rest of Primal Intelligence are driven by narrative cognition. Or to put it in regular speak: The human brain is real-life smart because it thinks in story.

Unless your mind is as unconventional as a Special Operator, you're probably skeptical that story is the secret to natural genius. And really, why would you trust a theory of intelligence invented by the kind of dude who runs toward explosions? If that skepticism prompts you to want to dissect my theory—including the specifics of how narrative cognition works in the brain and why it will always be impossible for AI—you can explore the foundational science in part III. But the next ten chapters will jump into what convinced other doubters: training that works.

The training will make you better at innovation, resilience, communication, leadership, and other life skills covered in part II. And it will begin in part I by strengthening Primal Intelligence's four core powers: imagination, emotion, commonsense, and, first of all, intuition.

Awake!
. . . as in ancient time.
—WILLIAM BLAKE

PART I

PRIMAL ACTIVATION

1

INTUITION

Spot the Exception Like Vincent van Gogh and Marie Curie

They sold cars, skin care, refrigerators, insurance, and medical research. They had held their jobs for years, even decades. Yet they all were failing. Their performance was described by their peers as *below suboptimal . . . tragically hopeless . . . like a donkey trying to climb a staircase.* One had sunk so far that if he tripled his commissions, he'd still rank last among his sales force.

They'd been sent to me because their companies viewed them as long past their prime. And certainly, they seemed to have exhausted their powers of growth. They slouched across the classroom and slumped into chairs, staring catatonically at the blank projector screen. When I engaged them in small talk, they became superficially jovial but turned quickly defensive. They did not like to be questioned about their jobs—or really about anything. They preferred to tell me: *Sales is about relationships.*

They repeated this mantra over and over, drawing great comfort from it. When I asked how they cultivated relationships, they replied: *Time. It takes time to cultivate relationships. You can't do it overnight.*

Leaving the projector blank, I got the salespeople onto their feet. Then I led them out of the classroom and into a museum gallery. The gallery was filled with curious paintings, creatively drawn and brightly colored. I invited the salespeople to find a painting that surprised them and to study it for a few minutes. I asked them to imagine what would happen if the scene in the painting were rewound like a movie—and what would happen if it were fast-forwarded. After that, I led the salespeople back into the classroom and ran them through a ten-minute exercise. Then I sent them back to their jobs.

Two months later, I checked on how they were doing. About 40 percent were still failing or had been fired. The other 60 percent had shown improvement—strong improvement. Taken as a group, they had risen in their companies' metrics from poor to average, and several had achieved more considerable gains. One had shot to the very top of his sales team, jumping from dead last to runaway first. "The only way I can figure it," his boss remarked to me, "is that you sawed open his head and transplanted his brain."

These turnarounds prompted their companies to ask: What was the exercise I'd run? What ten-minute training had produced such a dramatic uptick in performance? But that wasn't the right question to ask. The right question was: What was the difference between the 60 percent who improved and the 40 percent who didn't?

I got the answer by asking the salespeople to draw the painting they'd selected in the museum gallery. The 40 percent recalled vague details or no details at all. The 60 percent remembered one unique detail about the painting—and remembered it with specificity. They vividly saw the detail in their imagination. And even now, after months had passed, they could still recall, often with a smile or a jolt of wonder, how strange the detail seemed.

That recall revealed: The salespeople had rediscovered a youthful power of their brain. The power of intuition.

INTUITION MEANS TO KNOW WITHOUT consciously thinking. What intuition knows is a hidden rule of life. That rule enables us to act in ways that no one has previously envisioned. We can solve old problems in fresh ways. We can climb upward on original ladders. We can reinvent ourselves and our world, driving growth—and even revolution.

Intuition arrives as a flash of insight. In fact, it arrives so fast that it can feel supernatural. Medieval theologians saw it as a holy revelation. Nineteenth-century transcendentalists claimed it as a vision of the soul. Modern Jungians (and Myers-Briggs enthusiasts) view it as a mystical perception. Yet intuition has an entirely natural source, as I discover from studying U.S. Army Special Operators.

Operators have a significantly higher rate of intuition than the average Army recruit, and that rate increases over their career. They have *learned* to activate intuition, often with remarkable results. They can see minutes, hours, days ahead, anticipating possibilities that no one else detects.

I log hundreds of these acts of intuition during my research with the Army. Most involve recent events, so they can't be disclosed. But here's a characteristic example from 2003.

In March of that year, half a million U.S. soldiers invaded

Iraq. The invasion went to plan. Indeed, it went so exactly to plan that in just forty-two days, on May 1, the U.S. declared victory against Iraq's deposed ruler, Saddam Hussein. Three weeks earlier, however, a U.S. Special Operator had been walking through a quiet Baghdad suburb, its wooden-latticed mansions gently flanked by palm trees, when . . .

I saw an Iraqi on a bridge. And he spoke better English than I speak. Better *American* English than I speak.

Surprised by this singular fact, the Operator struck up a conversation.

The Iraqi said: "Listen, we could not be more happy that you're here. I am the engineering department head at Mosul University. I lived in Boston for twenty years. I received all of my education at Harvard. We absolutely are glad that you're here. Nobody, nobody liked Saddam Hussein. But if you don't get the power back on, and the hospitals open, and the water flowing, the groceries flowing, trade flowing, fast, then you will never get control of what's coming."

The Operator reported this to his command, warning: "Our plan has failed. We have lost the war." Shortly afterward, the president of the United States stood on an aircraft carrier to announce the opposite: *Mission Accomplished.* The Operator had seen so far into tomorrow that his own government wouldn't catch up for years.

The Operator's intuition can seem divinely inspired—or extremely lucky. But it has the same real-world source as every other intuition that I log. The source is: exceptional information.

Exceptional information is defined by the U.S. Army in the manual *Mission Command*:

> There is information that results from an extraordinary event, an unseen opportunity, or a new threat. This is exceptional information—specific and immediately vital information that directly affects the success of the current operation. . . . Identifying exceptional information requires initiative.

In other words, exceptional information is an exception to a rule. Like a warm-blooded reptile or a rainbow at night, it violates the known laws of its environment, revealing that more can happen than precedent suggests.

This seeing beyond precedent is the opposite of how intuition is logically defined by behavioral economists such as Daniel Kahneman. Following the lead of computer AI pioneer Herbert Simon, Kahneman states in *Thinking, Fast and Slow* that "intuition is nothing more and nothing less than recognition." Recognition is a pattern match, a visual precedent reiterated in the present. As construed by logic, intuition is thus the identification of a nonexception.

Exceptional information demonstrates the contrary: Intuition detects a rupture in a standard narrative, driving a break with the past. To make that break, we need what the Army manual calls *initiative*, which is another way of saying *running ahead of data*. AI can't do this—and while our brain can, it generally doesn't. It has been conditioned by the logic of modern life to feel that it's smarter to function like an algorithm, sticking to patterns and dismissing exceptions as noise. Yet the potential reward for acting on exceptions is enormous. Exceptional information hints at a new rule that can shift the whole world's story. It's a blip—until it changes everything.

In the case of Baghdad 2003, the exceptional information was the Iraqi on the bridge. Previously, the rule of the U.S. invasion had been *We're bringing America to Iraq.* But here was an Iraqi who spoke American better than Americans! Here was an Iraqi who'd used his U.S. education to engineer cancer hospitals and electronic banking! Here was an Iraqi who'd quietly launched his own American invasion—a more forward-thinking one! His example alone, without requiring a single other fact, was enough to alert the Operator: *More possibilities—good and bad—exist in this place than our rule can predict.*

Exceptional information is everywhere in war, because combat shatters existing laws of action. And exceptional information is everywhere else too. No human environment—business, culture, politics—ever stays the same. The better we get at detecting the exceptional, the more our brain can intuit new possibilities for art, science, and technology, as we can see from Vincent van Gogh, Marie Curie, and the Apple computer.

VAN GOGH WAS A VISIONARY painter born in 1853 amid the oak windmills and strawberry fields of the southern Netherlands.

In the centuries prior to van Gogh, painters had discovered that certain colors strengthened each other. Red placed next to green made the green more green and the red more red. In the 1820s, French academics systematized this discovery by using logic to create the red-yellow-blue (or RYB) color wheel. Its logical pattern suggested that in addition to red-green, the most powerful color combinations were yellow-purple and blue-orange.

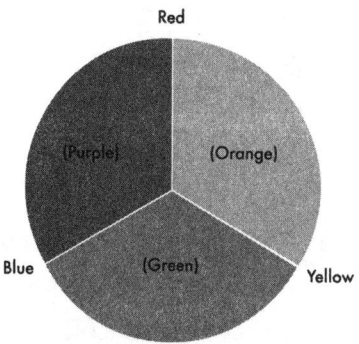

RYB: The Old Rule of Color

During the mid-nineteenth century, these chromatic pairs were employed to great effect by Parisian painter Eugène Delacroix, and in the 1880s, Delacroix's murals at La Chapelle des Saints-Anges caught the attention of van Gogh, exciting his admiration. In those same murals, however, van Gogh noticed an exception to RYB. That exception was green-purple, a contrast that made green more potent than in the red-green combo and purple more potent than in the yellow-purple. Seeing a possibility beyond the old rules of art, van Gogh picked up a brush in May 1889 and painted *Lilac Bush*, which invigorated the eye with its intense clashes between green leaves and purple flowers.

This exception made van Gogh wonder if there were other exceptions to be found. Yes, he discovered. Yellow-blue made yellow more powerful than yellow-purple and blue more powerful than blue-orange. In June 1889, van Gogh used this new rule to paint *The Starry Night*, now revered as one of the most significant paintings in modern art.

Van Gogh had now found strengthening clashes for all of

painting's big colors—except for red. So what was red's opposite? It was, van Gogh discovered, aquamarine, aka cyan. And in what became his last painting of himself, executed in September 1889 at the Saint-Paul asylum, van Gogh colored his beard red and his suit cyan, producing history's most chromatically intense self-portrait, hanging now in the Musée d'Orsay.*

Van Gogh's contemporaries were bemused by his color choices, especially cyan. Cyan was not conventionally regarded as a primary—or even a *secondary*—color. Yet despite cyan's historically trifling place in art, modern science has revealed that cyan produces biology's most eye-buzzing color clash. The source of the buzz isn't the cyan but the red it opposes. Red cones make up almost two thirds of the color receptors in our eyes, giving red twice the biological punch of green and yellow—and nearly thirty times that of purple and blue. That impact factor is why red is powerful on stop signs and ambulances. And red's natural eye pop is heightened by juxtaposing it with cyan, making cyan-red the most vivid color pairing that our visual cortex can process.

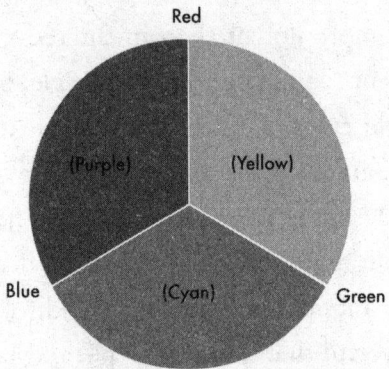

RGB: Van Gogh's Exceptional Discovery

---

* If you can't travel to the Musée, you can see the self-portrait at operationhuman .com/vangogh.

By beating science to this discovery, van Gogh also beat science to an even bigger one: a circle where cyan's ingredients (green and blue) sit across from cyan's opposite (red). This is the red-green-blue color wheel, also known as RGB. RGB now powers every video screen on the planet. But it was unseen prior to van Gogh's intuition.

A decade after van Gogh, the same power of intuition was deployed by Marie Curie. Curie earned two Nobel Prizes, but before she became a legend of science, she was viewed by Paris's male academic community as an oddity—a Polish woman who worked in a leaky shed, stirring iron vats that bubbled with weird light.

Curie's vat-stirring was motivated by what other scientists saw as a trifle: the faint rays emitted by potassium uranyl sulfate, a minor uranium salt. The rays were universally believed to result from a regular chemical occurrence: a change in atomic bonds. The bonds might have been between potassium, sulfur, or uranium atoms, yet regardless, the change wasn't of much interest. All it did was confirm the truth of long-established physical laws such as the conservation of energy.

But then Curie noticed something that was, in her words, "peculiar" and "surprising." What she noticed was: The rays weren't coming from bonds between atoms. They were coming from *inside* a single atom—the uranium atom. Rather than following conventional laws of nature, the rays were a rogue power: radioactivity. As Curie wrote on July 21, 1900, in the research journal *Revue scientifique*: "The phenomenon is profoundly interesting because it appears to be in conflict with science's fundamental laws, laws that have been considered, until now, to be universal."

Uranium was, in short, an exception to the rules. Its inner

energy suggested that the atom contained secrets that physicists were only beginning to discover. And if scientific revolution could hide in microscopic particles, what radical possibilities awaited in the vastness of the universe?

Curie's new physics powered twentieth-century innovations in astronomy, agriculture, medicine, and archaeology. And it also helped birth the globe-changing tech known as electronics, which was itself transformed by intuition on March 5, 1975, when a mainframe engineer entered a garage in Menlo Park, California.

The mainframe engineer was Steve Wozniak, known to friends as Woz. The garage was the site of the Homebrew Computer Club's first meeting. At the meeting, Woz spotted a funny new gadget: the Altair 8800 microcomputer. Other mainframe engineers had dismissed the Altair as too small to be useful: The rule of computing, established in the 1960s by companies like IBM, was that more data was more money, making the microcomputer a leap backward for profitability. But in the Altair's exceptional smallness, Woz glimpsed a new story of the future: a world where compact computers were used to work and play at home. He dashed back to his own house and engineered the Apple I.

The Apple I sparked a personal-electronics revolution and inaugurated Apple Inc., the world's first trillion-dollar company. But Woz didn't create Apple alone. He had help from his cofounder, Steve Jobs. And Jobs had an eye for yet another kind of exceptional information. Where van Gogh, Curie, and Woz saw the exceptional in art, nature, or technology, Jobs saw it in people. As Woz remembered: "He read books that were about the very few of us, like the Shakespeares and the Einsteins, who take the world forward. . . . He always wanted to be one of those special people." Jobs achieved this dream by spotting an exception to the rule of traditional mainframe engineers. That exception was Woz.

Our brains evolved to have the intuition of Jobs, Woz, Curie, and van Gogh. It's how our Stone Age ancestors created the future. But even though it's natural for us to spot exceptions, it's not automatic. The more exceptional the exception, the harder it is for our modern brain to see. Van Gogh glimpsed so far into the future that education is still catching up. When I spoke with the Van Gogh Museum in Amsterdam in 2022, I was informed by a docent that the strongest color clashes are the RYB ones of blue-orange and yellow-purple. The docent assured me, with total conviction, that if I closely inspected *The Starry Night*, I would observe that its stars are orange—except in places where the sky is purple.

This is not correct. Use your eyes and you will observe: The stars in *The Starry Night* are yellow and the sky is blue. Van Gogh's visionary brain spotted the exception to logic's old rules. But as the docent demonstrates, old rules can be hard to unsee, especially in our age of computers. Computers can't process exceptional information. When they hit an exception, they skip over it, back to a preprogrammed routine. To a computer, an exception is what proves the rule. It is a fluke to be regressed to the mean. And the more time we spend with the machines that Woz engineered, the more our brains start to think like them, dismissing the exceptional instead of chasing it.

But we can get back our primal ability to see the special, doing what van Gogh did with color, Curie did with physics, Woz did with tech, and Jobs did with people. To see how, let's return to U.S. Special Operations.

U.S. SPECIAL OPERATIONS HAS A method for activating intuition. I get my first glimpse of it shortly after my initial meeting with the Army. To ensure that I am trustworthy, I'm transported six hours from my Ohio lab to a military installation that looks like a 1950s middle school dropped into a maximum-security penal colony. Then I'm told that it's time to take a lie-detector test.

The test begins when I'm led into a warm, windowless room. There is no polygraph machine, just three Operators in boots and jeans. Kicking back on folding chairs, they roll through a few bland questions about my personal history: *Who are your parents? Are you married? Where did you go to high school?* Their manner is so casual that I relax. I thought this was a big deal. Clearly, it isn't.

Then one of the Operators leans forward. "Your accent"— he smiles—"is fake."

I'm so surprised that I choke. What the Operator has just said is true. I speak with a fake American accent. But no one has ever noticed before. Thousands—tens of thousands—of Americans have accepted it as my natural voice.

I hastily explain: "I was born in England. But I've lived in America most of my life."

The Operators don't buy it. "You're implying that you lost your accent, slowly and naturally, over time. But that's not true. You lost your accent quickly. And intentionally. You *decided* to eliminate your old accent so that you could disguise yourself as an American."

I tense. *How do they know that?* The answer, I will learn later, is that the Operators are spy hunters. And they have detected that my accent is not organic to the American heartland—

or any other U.S. region. It's a Frankenstein, stitched together from television and my imagination.

I try to come clean. "After I came to America, I was mocked at school for my English accent."

"Mocked in what way?"

I have a flashback to a circle of boys jeering at me as a "retard" who lost the Revolutionary War to George Washington. Followed by a memory of a sixth grader with gelled hair boxing me into a corner and screaming, "You dirty limey!" These events upset me powerfully, but they seem mild and almost laughable now. I'm embarrassed to admit to other adults how embattled my younger self felt. So I say to the spy hunters: "I got called names. That sort of thing."

The hunters scrutinize me closely. "And that's when you lost your accent?"

No, I think silently. *No, that is not when I lost my accent.* Instead, the bullying had the opposite effect. I stuck hard with my English accent to show that I wasn't ashamed of where I came from. When I reached my teens, however, my accent started to feel unnatural. I hadn't lived in England for years. I was more American than English. I had less in common with my English cousins than with my American classmates. And the summer after high school, I decided to lose my accent and speak like an American so I could go to college as my authentic self.

That, anyway, was my thinking at the time. But as I reflect on it, in the windowless room, it seems perverse. I created a bogus accent to be more honest about who I am?

The spy hunters see my mind turning. And I realize: *This is bad. I should have answered immediately. Whatever I say now, they won't believe it. They'll think I'm trying to conceal something, like with my sham accent. They won't ever trust me.*

Finally I fumble out that I fake my accent because it feels more authentic. To my surprise, the spy hunters accept this explanation, even though it sounds peculiar. And in fact, it's *because* my explanation sounds peculiar that the hunters are inclined to believe it. They're looking for moments when I confess things that are stranger than fiction. Those confessions are indicators of exceptional information, and if the exceptions fit into a coherent narrative, then I am most likely telling the truth, because the truth is always unexpected yet consistent.

The interview proceeds. The spy hunters probe me with casual agility, digging into forgotten corners of my memory. I find myself speaking about parts of my past that I've kept hidden from my friends, my family, even myself, until at last I complete the gauntlet and Army Special Operations delivers its assessment: I can be trusted to study the brains of U.S. Army Operators.

The spy hunters tell me with a grin that it's now my turn to investigate them. So I start by asking the hunters to share the secret that's fascinated me during the whole interview: "How do I learn to do what you just did? How do I spot exceptional information?"

THE GUIDANCE I GET FROM the spy hunters is: *If you can't see what's exceptional, then treat everything as exceptional.*

"Treat *everything* as exceptional?" I verify.

"That's right. The way you saw the world as a child."

I can't recall how I saw the world as a child. But I know how my children see it. When my daughter was six months old, I took her on a backyard picnic. For myself I packed a sandwich and a lemonade. For her, a jar of carrot puree and a box of plastic spoons.

After twisting open the jar, I handed my daughter a spoonful. She slurped the carrot happily . . . then fumbled the spoon into the grass. "It's okay!" I said brightly, grabbing a clean spoon from the box. "Dad came prepared!"

My daughter peered suspiciously at the new spoon as I dipped it into the carrot jar. And when I offered it to her, she didn't put it in her mouth. She clenched its handle in her chubby fist, carefully inspecting it. Then she burst into tears, howling angrily at me.

I stared at her, perplexed, until slowly I realized: She was upset that I gave her a new spoon. She liked her old spoon. And she thought I pulled a fast one, taking it from her.

To prove my innocence, I held the two spoons, old and new, side by side, demonstrating—*conclusively*—that they were interchangeable. My demonstration failed. To my daughter, the identical utensils were not identical. She continued howling until she got her original spoon.

At the time, I thought my daughter was being silly. But as I come to realize from the Special Operators, I was the one who'd goofed. I'd forgotten a fact about life that my daughter saw: No two things in this world are the same. Every picnic, every person, is unique. Even mass-made plastics have slight variances that might, in some singular circumstance, prove significant.

How did my daughter know this? Was she taught it? Did she articulate it to herself one day while lying in her crib? No. My daughter knew it in her nonconscious brain, deep in her biology. It was tacit knowledge, inherited from nature. It wasn't an intentional decision but a default behavior: *Assume that everything you see is special.*

We lose this default setting over time. As we age, we organize our lives by thinking in patterns and principles, prioritizing discovery less and efficiency more. Until eventually, our brain's default becomes *Assume that you've seen it before.* It becomes, in other words, the opposite of what it was when we were born, replacing slow inquiry with fast judgment.

Our updated default has its advantages. It allows us to stave off distraction and exploit our environment faster. But it deprives us of curiosity, empathy, wonder, and joy. And it also costs us something practical: the ability to detect new threats and opportunities.

To get back that ability, I try to treat everything around me as exceptional. But my adult brain resists. It keeps informing me: *This is a waste of time.* It continues to see patterns and pass verdicts, jumping back to schoolroom habits. Needing help, I return to the spy hunters. "Is there a way to reset my brain so I can go back to seeing everything as exceptional?"

"Sure," they nod. "Immerse your brain in a totally new environment, where everything really *is* exceptional. That'll jumpstart your child way of thinking."

"Can I do that by traveling to another country?"

The hunters frown. "When people travel, they keep reading the usual stuff on their phone. They stay in hotels and eat in restaurants. The only locals they meet are staff and shopkeepers. That's why when they come home, they're still thinking the same. Their body traveled, but their mind didn't."

"Well, can you show me a way to mind travel?"

"Yeah. We can take you to Pineland."

Pineland is a vast Special Forces training site concealed in the central Carolinas. Founded in 1952 on the advice of U.S. Army special agent Colonel Jerry Sage (whose breakouts from German prison camps during World War II inspired the 1963 Hollywood blockbuster *The Great Escape*, and who later taught geography so effectively to high schoolers that in 1979 he was recognized as South Carolina's "Teacher of the Year"), it consists of fifteen thousand square miles of hidden terrain occupied by a fictional foreign army that has invaded America. To organize this "role-play with real bullets," the Army has stocked Pineland with thousands of actors performing unconventional backstories. I meet a middle-aged man with a black-cherry rifle who informs me that his parents were Cuban spies who set up a Soviet enclave in Tennessee's Great Smoky Mountains. I meet a teen girl wearing a carved greenstone necklace who says she's a descendant of the lost tribe of the Apalachee, the shark-eating "people on the other side." I meet a family in a tattered plastic tent who nervously reveal that they are refugees from the United States, a wealthy but forbidding nation to the northeast.

Pineland was created by U.S. Special Operations to help recruits activate their child's eye for exceptional information. And when I visit, I immediately see why it's so effective. Pineland mixes the moondust valleys of Afghanistan and the firefly jungles of the Amazon with the postindustrial rail yards of the Apocalypse. It feels like a never-before world, giving your brain the experience of being born again.

Most of us don't get the chance to enter Pineland, but as I discover from studying its effect on Operators, we can still give ourselves a dose of mind travel. We just need to do like those salespeople who acted like they'd been given new brains. Those salespeople I brought into the museum.

THE MUSEUM WAS FULL OF art. And art brims with the exceptional: van Gogh's colors, Frida Kahlo's surrealism, the *Mona Lisa*'s smile. Those anomalies break the rules of the familiar, helping us reperceive like a child. Sculpture shows the routine contours of the human body from fresh angles. Photography reveals the sky in a thousand unexpected forms. Love is ancient to the heart, but to witness *Hibiscus* by Georgia O'Keeffe is to desire anew. The deeper into museums you go, the more you will feel: *I see something original in what I saw before.*

This reactivation of intuition is what happened to the salespeople when they encountered the exceptional information of the museum's art. Yet the art alone was not enough. The salespeople also had to make a conscious effort to interrupt their adult brain's habits of logic.

Logic doesn't think in the exceptional. It thinks in the opposite: labels. Labels mark what items have in common: *good, bad, weird, normal, black, white.* This facilitates judgment, which assigns things to categories: *smart, dumb, reliable, untrustworthy, valuable, worthless.* Judgment is how bureaucracies function: Corporate managers and government agencies use labels (from demographics, personality tests, and performance evals) to ingest people into organizational flowcharts. Judgment is how computer AI thinks: It uses tags and keywords to label incoming bits of data, allowing for fast sorting, analysis, and retrieval. And judgment is how our brains have been conditioned to operate by modern school and business: To maintain efficiency, we deploy critical thinking to decide (objectively and without bias) whether new pieces of information are *valid, promising, profitable,* or the opposite.

Judgment is fine if you're inside a mathematical simulation filled with generic people and virtual objects. But in the real world, it hampers you from latching onto the uncategorizable, stifling your ability to spot exceptional information. In the case of the salespeople, that stifling was reflected in the speed with which they made snap assessments of each other: *She's a classic soccer mom, He's a bro, They're all a bunch of social climbers.*

To transition the salespeople out of reflexive judgments, I give them a Pineland technique: Shift to Narrative. The technique works by prompting your brain to convert general labels into individual stories. This toggles off logic and energizes intuition with imagination. (Imagination will be covered in depth in chapter 2.)

To run Shift to Narrative, start by noticing when your brain makes a judgment: *prudent, crazy, beautiful, ugly, awesome, uncool.* Focus on the judgment, asking yourself: *Where did the judgment come from?* This question prompts your brain to intuit the judgment's origin story, unearthing a specific behavior, activity, or other event that you have labeled *prudent* or *ugly* or *awesome.* Now forget the label and focus on the event, asking yourself: *What happens next?* This question prompts your brain to translate intuition into original action.

When I ran Shift to Narrative at the museum, one salesperson paused in surprise at a painting of a girl standing alone on a playground, hands clenched, brow furrowed. "Serious," the salesperson said. "That's what I would label the girl."

The salesperson then turned the label into a story. "The girl is serious because she was made to come out to the playground when she was creating something at her desk. If you look at her hands, one is clenched very big, like she's hiding a crayon inside. She was using that crayon to draw a picture she had in her imagination. And she's frowning because she's trying to remember every detail of that picture so she can finish it when she gets back to her desk. And she's hiding the crayon because it's just the right color, and she doesn't want anyone else to take it. She's going to finish her picture and put it in her desk, and every time she looks at it, she'll get so much pleasure, because the color and everything is exactly how she saw it."

You can see why, two months later, the salesperson remembered the exceptional detail of the big clenched fist. Art invites us to intuit these details—and to rewind and then fast-forward them in time, imagining the parts of the story that the artist has left to our mind.*

If you don't have access to a museum, you can run Shift to Narrative on another collection of the exceptional: people. People are constantly labeled by your modern brain: She is *kind*, he is *hardworking*, they are *inventive*. This labeling makes you feel like you're seeing people clearly. But really, it's obstructing intuition. To open your child's eye, search your memory for a specific occasion when the person was kind or hardworking or inventive. Recall every detail of that occasion—then speculate on what that person would do right now. How would they handle a problem or opportunity that you're facing? Tell an original story of their life, starting with what was special about their past behavior and extending it into a new future.

After the salespeople had rediscovered their child's eye in the museum, the next step was to carry intuition into their daily lives. To take that step, we ran the ten-minute exercise that the salespeople's companies were so curious about.

THE EXERCISE BEGAN BY PARTNERING up the salespeople. One was assigned to be the questioner; the other was told to think of their favorite nonwork activity. The questioner was then given five minutes to ask about that activity. The questioner could ask What, When, Who, Where, or How. But they could not ask Why.

So if the activity was hiking, the questioner could ask: When was the first time you went hiking? Where was the last place you hiked? Who would you never take hiking?

Questioners were told: When you hear an answer that sur-

---

* For more examples of artworks activating intuition, go to operationhuman.com /intuition.

prises you, you will want to ask Why. *Why would you never take your boyfriend hiking? Why did you go hiking in a landfill, of all places?* Resist the urge. If you ask Why, you will prompt a judgment, and judgment is the end of curiosity. It's an answer, when you want to drill deeper with more questions.

Instead, recognize that you want to ask Why because surprise is an indicator of exceptional information. To excavate that information, ask more What, When, Who, Where, or How about the detail that surprised you. *Where would you hike with your boyfriend if he asked to go? Who could you bring on that hike that would make it better? When was the first time you hiked on a landfill? What landfills would you not go hiking on?*

As you're asking these questions, you must curb another logical tendency: to identify with the other person. Resist the urge to say: *I think exactly the same!* Or *I know just how you feel!* Or *The identical thing happened to me!* Those apparent epiphanies are actually failures to discover what's unique about the other person. They seem like affirmations but are actually judgments that interrupt curiosity with egocentrism.

Once the five minutes are done, inspect the exceptional information you've surfaced. Use it to hypothesize Why the person does that nonwork activity. If the person agrees with your hypothesis, you get one point. If the person is surprised by your hypothesis, you get one point. Your goal is to get two points, which is to say, your goal is to surprise the other person with your hypothesis—yet have them agree. This occurs when you discover something about them that they did not see themselves. Two points isn't easy to pull off, but effective salespeople accomplish it about 70 percent of the time. Sales is, after all, knowing your customer better than they know themselves. It is intuiting what they want or need but didn't realize.

Long before I ran this exercise with the salespeople, it was used by Army Special Operations. Locked securely in the classified sites where it trains spy hunters, Special Operations has a list of questions that surface exceptional information. More than 95 percent of those questions are Who, What, Where, When, and How. As the Operators explain: "We all want to get to Why, but the fastest way to miss it is to ask it."

This is how the spy hunters in boots and jeans dug up the exceptional details of my life. And you can do the same for other people's lives. By consciously delaying Why, you can detect the unique potential in every person you meet. Like the salespeople at the museum did when they returned to their jobs, perceiving opportunities in clients and customers that their snap judgments had overlooked. Like Steve Jobs when he spotted the exceptional talents of Woz.

And by delaying Why, you can also do like Woz, van Gogh, and Curie: surface engineering, artistic, or scientific opportunities. Focus on surprises that catch your eye in tech, culture, or nature. Then ask What, When, Where—while resisting the urge to judgment. That way, the next time you notice an exception like the Altair 8800, red-cyan, or radioactivity, you won't do the logical thing and skip past it. Instead, you'll open yourself to glimpsing its unique Why, feeding your brain what you need to imagine fresh possibilities like the Apple I, RGB, and modern physics.

Once you've got this process running, you can tune it, making your visions of the future more dynamic and precise. We'll learn how next chapter, where we'll cover Primal's second power: imagination.

2

IMAGINATION

Go Low Data Like Ludwig van Beethoven
and the Special Operators

M orning fog still cloaked the pines when the bomb ex-
ploded.

The blast stunned the Special Operators. They'd been parley-
ing with a guerrilla chieftain. But now their ears rang with the
screams of a child, wounded somewhere in the forest. How badly
was the child hurt? Why had the bomb gone off? Who—or
what—was skulking in the misty trees?

The Operators had no answers for the hundred questions
now buzzing through their minds. But they had to act swiftly—
and precisely. If they hesitated or blundered, the child would die.

What happened next happened many times. And every time,
it happened differently. A rotating cast of Operators entered the
woods to meet the chieftain, who was not a real guerrilla but an
actor playing a role in a U.S. Special Forces training simulation

at a covert site near the black-water tides of Cape Fear, North Carolina. To prepare for the simulation, the Operators had spent seventy-two sleepless hours studying intel reports about the chieftain's sprawling web of illicit business interests: indentured farmers who milked opium pods on highland potash fields; weapons markets stocked with Beretta pistols and night-vision goggles; mule trains for trafficking silver antiques. The Operators believed that the simulation's purpose was to test their prowess at navigating those complex interests. Instead, its purpose was to test how they responded to an unexpected bomb.

That morning, I watched dozens of Operators pass the test. Their fluidness of action seemed eerily paranormal. But the bigger wonder was that no two Operators acted the same. One persuaded the guerrilla chieftain to lead the way into the alien vegetation. Another ventured forth alone, solving the bomb mystery solo. Another convinced the chieftain to do all the work, applauding him when he tamed the wild and rescued the child.

How did the Operators devise—with such alacrity—this range of paths to victory? The short answer is: their training. Lacking that training, most soldiers either freeze when a bomb detonates or charge blindly toward it. The remaining soldiers retreat into the textbook solution: Call for backup. These three standard responses—fright, fight, and dependence—are the same ones most common in business leaders when facing an emergency. And also in elementary school students when asked to solve life problems. So what was special about the training given to the Operators? How had it made them soldiers more than ordinary?

The longer answer is: The training had improved their imagination.

IMAGINATION LITERALLY MEANS "TO SEE things that the eyes don't see." This seeing of the unseen is a normal feature of human life, so normal that we do it constantly. Yet it also seems peculiar, even uncanny: How can we glimpse the invisible? What's the origin of imagination?

Logic has two explanations. The first is hallucination. *Something has misfired in our mental circuitry, veering us into magical thinking.* But this cannot be the explanation. Imagination isn't purely delusional; it can also be accurate. It can see further than our eyes, not just in space but in time, anticipating what happens next. It's how visionaries foresee future technologies, artworks, businesses, and social movements.

That brings us to logic's second explanation: faster processing. *Like a supercomputer, visionaries crunch the facts swifter, beating the rest of us to the destined answer.* Yet this also can't be true. A supercomputer is lots of computers wired together, a conglomerate that can manage big data quicker. But the Operators didn't have big data. They had almost no information. They knew barely anything about the bomb, the child, or the foggy pines. Faster processing wouldn't have made a difference.

To understand how imagination actually works, let's explore its origins. *Imagination* entered the English dictionary in the fourteenth century, when medieval logicians used it to label the part of our mind that produces images. Images are mental pictures compiled from data that comes from sources like our eyes, and like all data products, images are assembled via computation. Computation is data intensive, which is why our visual cortex contains so many circuits—and why the world's fastest computer chips were originally devised for image processing.

Imagination's name denotes this digital process in our mind. Yet this process isn't all there is to imagination. As spectacular as moving mental images are, they're preceded by an even more astonishing act, because before a movie can be made, there needs to be a script. That script tells our cortical circuits what sequence of pictures to display. It's the intention guiding their pixels. And it doesn't come from nowhere. It's invented by our brain. Which means that the visuals tagged by medieval logicians aren't the biological root of imagination. They're an offshoot of a more fundamental act of creation.

What's that more fundamental act? It seems profoundly obscure to us now. You won't find it described in modern psychology books. Yet it's no more mysterious than the source of cinematic images: It's what you think of when you think of movie scripts. And it's ubiquitous in ancient writings about imagination, where it goes by many names: *fable, myth, fiction, tale.* All of which designate the same activity: story.

Story is classified today as a product of imagination. But this is exactly backward. Just as the narratives of screenwriters are the source of movies, story is the source of imagination. It's what powers the default mode network, the part of the brain that envisions alternative worlds and possible tomorrows. It's how children dream the unseen, role-playing adventures that no adult can picture. It's the neural mechanism that Operators use to act smart in mayhem.

Our brain knows this. Yet we have forgotten, because although we're born understanding story, we go to school and are taught it wrong. So to get back in touch with the primal power beneath imagination, let's return to what we once knew. Let's unlearn school, discovering what story evolved to do.

SCHOOL TEACHES US THAT STORY is for communicating.

This myth dates backs to ancient Mediterranean law courts. The courts sat in grand but cramped civic buildings beside the Athenian market (fragrant with roasted lamb and mint perfume) and the Roman Forum (echoing with the jangle of silver coinage and the jingle of cymbal dancers). Amid this hurly-burly, prosecutors and defendants battled for the votes of juries. Both sides came armed with facts to prove their case. But they quickly learned: Facts alone did not sway juries. Juries were motley assemblies of drunken senators and onion farmers, most of whom were quickly bored by details and almost none of whom could remember more than three bits of information without muddling up the particulars.

Faced with this distractible mob, lawyers hit upon an oratorical strategy: connect facts into a story, spinning an easy tale that grabbed jurors' attention and pulled it in a clear direction. The strategy worked. And indeed, it worked so well that it was memorialized by Cicero, Rome's self-proclaimed champion of public speaking, in a suite of rhetorical handbooks—*How to Start an Argument, How to Win an Argument, How to Win Every Argument*—that survived classical civilization's collapse and went on to form the basis for gentlemen's education in the Renaissance and for college writing classes now.

Cicero's handbooks referred to the lawyers' strategy as *narratio*. Which is where we get the word *narrative*. And also where we get the myth that story's purpose is communication.

The myth may not seem a myth. Without needing Cicero (or any classroom instructor), we use story to communicate: We make friends by swapping anecdotes about where we grew up, what we're doing, and where we're headed; we stir hope by sharing tales of success and inspire change by sharing tales of could-have-done-better; we build teams, organizations, and nations by imparting narratives about our common history and our future aspirations.

Yet even so, the myth cannot be true. It cannot be true because story evolved long before language. Long, *long* before language. Millions of years—in fact, hundreds of millions of years—prior to words, gestures, and other forms of oral or visual communication, story was running through our ancestors' brains.

What were those brains using story for? Why would they be creating narratives if they weren't sharing information with each other? This can seem a great puzzle, but really it's not. Those brains were using story to do what brains do: think.

This biological use of story was unearthed at the end of the twentieth century by Anna Craft. Craft trained at Cambridge University and taught at Harvard, but her research is almost unknown because she didn't belong to a high-status field like cognitive psychology, theoretical physics, or computer science. Instead, she worked in preschools, where she observed children imagining themselves as dogs digging holes, doctors healing bones, and dinosaurs trampling homes. And she realized: *Children naturally think in story.*

Craft died at fifty-two from cancer. But later research has extended her observation, revealing that storythinking also occurs in the brains of adults—and of chimpanzees, mice, and even crows. Crows and humans aren't close relatives: Our family trees split apart before the T. rex strode the Earth. So storythinking is biologically very old.

In our logical age, storythinking can seem not just old but outdated. Why think like a crow when we can calculate like a computer? Yet there's a reason that the brains of our ancestors thought in story. There's a reason that those brains survived—and won—the brutal war for life. There's a reason that those brains passed story on to our own brains, which contain billions of elegant machines that cogitate in narrative. The reason is: While logic computes what is probable, story creates what is possible.

The probable is a pattern that has occurred before, allowing its future likelihood to be calculated from past statistics. The possible is an event that has never happened but *could*, because it doesn't contradict the rules of its environment.

The possible has two biological advantages over the probable. First, it can accelerate evolution. Instead of sticking cautiously to what worked yesterday, it can leap into the future, grabbing opportunity. Second, it can act with initiative in uncertainty. It doesn't need lots of reliable data. It can operate with slender information, adapting to hazy environments that glitch computers. While logic is infallible at math problems, story can thus outperform it at life problems. It can drive innovation, resilience, and commonsense decision-making.

Story isn't perfect. If it were, crows would rule utopia. But story can be improved with practice, as we can see by returning to those Operators in the woods.

LIKE ANNA CRAFT'S PRESCHOOLERS, THE Operators think in story. They do so in two main ways, known as causal and counterfactual but referred to by the Operators as past and future:

- When Operators storythink about the past, they reflect on events they've witnessed, asking *why*. Why did that happen the way it did? Why did it happen at all?

- When Operators storythink about the future, they imagine events that could happen, asking *what if*. What if I try this? What if my adversary tries that?

Past and future storythinking are connected in the brain by a feedback loop: The more diverse the *why*s, the more innovative the *what if*s, and the more effective the *what if*s, the more trustworthy the *why*s. In other words: The more creatively that Operators can hypothesize the causes of yesterday, the more dynamically they can invent tomorrow. And the more intentionally they can shape what happens next, the more they can rely on their speculative model of life's hidden rules.

Those linked processes clarify the past while multiplying the future, investing Operators with a mental narrative that looks like:

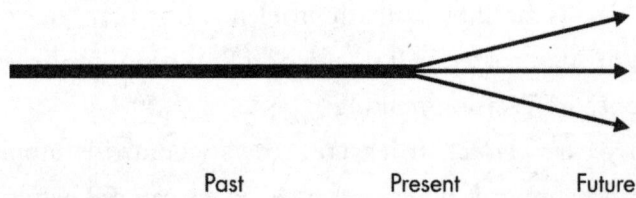

Past   Present   Future

This shape combines an integrated past with a branching future, joining one clear *why* with many creative *what if*s. It is imagination, trained.

Operators aren't the only people with trained imaginations. The same mental narrative can be found in other effective improvisers, from athletes to surgeons to ad-lib comics. All must react to change while remaining on target. The athlete can't rewrite the game's rules as he jukes on the field; he has to reach an established goal. Same goes for the surgeon: Her flexible scalpel has to respect the laws of life. Same goes for the comic: His fluent wit has to land on a punch line.

The adaptability of athletes, surgeons, and comics comes from their story's branching future, which gives them the ability to see fresh possibilities. Meanwhile, the consistency of their purpose over time comes from their story's integrated past. This might seem counterintuitive. Why would the path behind stabilize the route ahead? But in the physical world, the past provides momentum. The more unified our past, the more it propels us in a single direction, so that even as we dodge dangers and seize opportunities, we maintain a greater strategic focus. Like water streaming around a boulder, we bend briefly then return to our overall course.

That's how Operators flow through misty woods with agile purpose. But how did they learn to storythink this way? How did they train their imagination to be both supple and straight?

TO DISCOVER HOW OPERATORS DEVELOP their storythinking, I peer into their heads—with an assist from a cadre of Special Forces instructors. The instructors had, in distant ages past, been Operators themselves, leading A-Teams through lonely deserts and lawless cities on secret jobs: arresting bomb makers, smuggling medicines into internment camps, building underground schools for girls. And they had learned, through long experience, the art of imagination.

"The way to train imagination? Sure, I can tell you," a grizzled instructor nods as we squat in a cinder-block hut thick with body musk and biting flies.

Excited, I take out a research notebook, poised to capture every detail of the training.

"The way to train imagination is: planning, planning, planning, planning."

I hesitate, writing nothing. "What does planning have to do with imagination?"

The instructor flashes me a look of quiet disappointment. "Planning is the main use of imagination," he explains slowly, like he's speaking to someone whose brain is running at half speed.

Needing to go even slower, I repeat back: "The main use of imagination is to plan?"

"Let me break it down, real easy. In school they teach you that imagination is for fantasy and finger painting. But what's the reason that plans fail? The reason is, they didn't consider enough possibilities. They had too narrow a view of what could happen. They were *unimaginative*. Which is another way of saying: Imagination is the source of good planning."

At last, my brain catches up. And as I grasp what the instructor is saying, I also grasp the science beneath it: *Story evolved in the brain to make plans.* Plans are invented sequences of actions, the plotted behaviors that enable Operators to strategize—and crows to build tools from sticks. And plans are made by imagination, which is produced in the brain by story, because a story, like a plan, is an invented sequence of actions. That's why another word for *story* is *plot*, which is another word for *plan*. Even though the modern world teaches us that story is for communication or daydreaming, its primordial biological purpose isn't verbal or wishful. It's cerebral and practical: planning.

"So how," I ask the instructor, "do you get better at planning?"

"A GOOD PLAN HAS TWO features," the instructor explains. "First, a single long-term goal. Second, many possible paths. Or, like I say it: *You can target only one mountaintop. But you can take different routes up.*"

A good plan, that is, looks like the Operators' mental narrative: one *why* joined to many *what if*s. "Makes sense." I nod.

The instructor peels off his sunglasses, revealing his eyes. Calmly raw, they marry the serenity of heaven with the flexibility of chaos. "Sure, it makes sense," the instructor drawls. "But nobody does it. If you do, you're the exception. Or else we trained you."

The instructor is right about the rareness of the Operators' planning method, as I discover from tests on thousands of people, from college students to corporate executives.

First, most people don't have a single long-term goal. The typical order issued by an untrained commander is some version of *Capture that hill and don't get anybody killed.* This order contains two objectives—which are in tension. It invites confusion, friction, and fiasco. Yet it's the way that most leaders think, whether in business, health care, education, or anything else. If you ask for their plans, they will give you a list. One Fortune 50 CEO informs me that he has no fewer than fifteen primary objectives, all essential for success.

Second, most people don't develop many possible paths. They go all in on Plan A. Even when leaders claim to have a Plan B, it's usually vague—or Plan A, lightly tweaked. When Plan A breaks—and Plan A *will* break—the only hope becomes half-Plan B or Plan A with fresh paint.

So it is that most of us waste our lives aspiring to ascend many heights with one climbing technique, falling prey to what Operators call undefined strategy, limited tactics. *Strategy* is your long-term narrative. *Tactics* are the short-term plots you hatch along the way. To consistently reach your goals, your strategy must be precise and your tactics flexible. Which is why Special Operators strive for *defined strategy, unlimited tactics.*

To define strategy, Operators push themselves to prioritize a single objective. They know that the brain cannot plan effectively if it has fifteen primary objectives—or even *two* primary objectives. It's fine to have multiple things that you'd like to accomplish, but don't try to summit two mountains at once. Rank your objectives before you depart, establishing a clear number one. If you don't, then the moment that pressures hit or resources thin, your priorities will come into conflict. The result will be hesitation, second-guessing, disorganization, divided focus, haphazard decisions, and quitting.

To unlimit tactics, Operators practice spotting exceptional information. (See chapter 1.) From the exceptional, they derive possible courses of action, feeding imagination with intuition.

The first part of the training (defining strategy) clarifies *why*, producing the Operators' integrated past. The second part of the training (unlimiting tactics) multiplies the *what if*s, producing the Operators' branching future.

This two-part training is the source of the liquid tenacity that Operators display in response to unexpected detonations. In the case of the Operators stunned by the bomb in the misty woods, they defined their strategy as *Build rapport with the guerrilla chieftain.* (Rapport is a form of trust that makes another person feel part of your team. For more on how it works, see chapter 8.) When the Operators' initial route to this objective was shattered by the blast, they unlimited their tactics by focusing on the exceptional information of the wounded child. One Operator imagined: *What if I personally rescue the child, showing the chieftain that I can be trusted to put others first?* Another Operator imagined: *What if I follow the chieftain as he leads the rescue, dem-*

onstrating that I trust him with my own life? Another Operator imagined: *What if I convince the chieftain to do the rescue solo, proving that I can be trusted to safeguard his camp?* These forking possibilities advanced one core objective—*build rapport*—producing the Operators' fusion of dexterity with direction.

And the training isn't only for Operators. I take it out of the Cape Fear mists to test it in civilian settings, where I observe it working on athletes, paramedics, pilots, firefighters—and on nurses, teachers, parents, and middle school students.

The training succeeds in these disparate populations because it taps into our shared biology. Our brains evolved to flow like Operators up mountains, adapting with fresh plans as bombs explode our path. It's in our nature to activate intuition and train imagination on a single target, engaging life with vehement grace. And so I wonder: How have the Operators kept in touch with nature when most of us have not?

I POSE THE QUESTION TO the Operators when I catch them on a break from training. Backs propped against white pines, they snack on shredded turkey and lemons chewed whole.

As the Operators eat, they inform me that they, too, lost touch with nature. They didn't keep the secrets of imagination alive for thousands of years while the rest of civilization forgot. U.S. Army Special Operations wasn't formed until the 1950s, so it had to do what recruits do now: unlearn school and rediscover *defined strategy, unlimited tactics.*

"How'd you do that?" I want to know.

The Operators shrug nonchalantly. "We went back through history and studied effective planners."

Hearing this, I jot down in my muddied notebook: *Horatio*

Nelson. Nelson was an English admiral who became the most renowned naval planner of the nineteenth century, but no one guessed his future success when he was born in 1758 on Norfolk's chalk coast, the sixth child of a priest. At the age of twelve, frail and slight, he quit the salt marshes of his youth to join the Royal Navy as a deck scrubber, getting violently seasick on his first voyage. After two decades of service in which he displayed an initiative that bordered on insubordination, he was promoted to lead a small squadron of gunships and, hungry to prove his command élan, he attacked a Spanish port in the Canary Islands. The attack was bold but badly planned. Miscarrying, it resulted in Nelson's total defeat, and when Spanish grapeshot shattered his right arm, it also cost him the limb that he used to eat, write, and navigate.

Humbled, Nelson taught himself to work left-handed—and to improve his planning method. His new approach would be to provide his fleet a unified strategy but allow individual ship captains the independence to develop tactics that suited local conditions. He called this "the Nelson touch," and he deployed it in 1805 at the Battle of Trafalgar. Again Nelson faced the Spanish, who now boasted the world's biggest warship, joined by eighteen vessels from Napoléon Bonaparte's armada. Nelson was outnumbered by five hundred cannons and more than ten thousand men. But despite this imbalance in firepower—which left Nelson mortally wounded from a sniper's bullet—his fleet captured two thirds of the enemy with no ships lost of its own, showcasing the power of integrating one global goal with impromptu elasticity.

Spitting out husks of lemon pulp, the Operators agree: Nelson combined defined strategy with unlimited tactics. But actually, they say, they didn't get their planning method from military commanders like Nelson. They got it from artists like Beethoven.

I try and fail to conceal my surprise at the Operators' cultural influences. "Ludwig van Beethoven? The nineteenth-century composer?"

Yes, the Operators explain. Beethoven was rigorously classical in his song structure yet wildly spontaneous with his key shifts and harmonic explorations. That's how he succeeded so irresistibly in an era of political and cultural instability. During the invasion of his homeland, with occupying armies stomping past, Beethoven wrote his Fifth Symphony. Fusing traditional sonata form with pioneering piccolos and contrabassoons, its unified motif and dynamic adaptations are the embodiment of overarching strategy and infinite tactics.

As I stand in the land of foggy pines, watching Operators target a single mountain and scale it variously, I can feel the musicality of their imagination. And I can feel something else too. The velocity. Instants after the bomb explodes, the Operators are focusing on one objective and envisioning multiple paths to get there. Never tensing, never hesitating, they are only energy, adapting at the speed of life.

Beethoven said that when he walked among the oak and copper beech trees of the Vienna Woods, new melodies darted like sunlight through his mind. The Operators have achieved that same inventive pace, their inspiration firing quicker than my eye can process. What's the source of their rapid genius? How are they hatching effective plans so fast?

The answer can be found in the brain's most important narrative: our life story. The story we think to ourselves about ourselves.

YOUR LIFE STORY IS YOUR plan for life. So, like any plan, its most effective shape is:

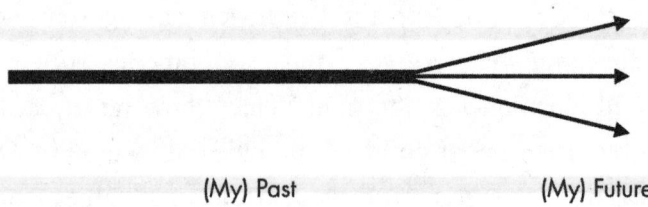

(My) Past   (My) Future

When your past is integrated, it clarifies *why* you live, investing you with long-range direction. When your future is branched, it widens your potential *what if*s, expanding your possible paths to get there.

With this plan for life, you know who you are and what you can do, reducing indecision and accelerating action. If you see a new prospect, you promptly determine if it's right for you. If you're confronted by fresh challenges, you evolve without losing yourself. That clarity of thinking allows you to grab opportunities faster and to waver less in response to setbacks. You make greater progress in your day. You realize more of your life potential.

Your life potential is unique to you. Every human, as we saw in chapter 1, is exceptional. All of us have an individual *why* and original *what if*s. Each of our stories—past and future—is distinct from everyone else's.

Yet even though we've each got our own narrative, our brains come equipped with a common tool for integrating our past and branching our future, making our life plan as flexible, intentional, and fast as a Special Operator. That tool is the third primal power: emotion.

3

EMOTION

Self-Assess Like Antigone and the Singletons

The CEO knew emotion was smart. By trusting himself about whether things felt right or wrong, he'd risen from summer intern to global titan, becoming head of a corporation whose revenue touched half a trillion dollars. But now that he'd reached the top, he didn't know how to spread his emotional intelligence through his team. His managers, his employees, and his C-suite all preferred data and metrics.

Attempting to open their minds, the CEO had spent lavishly on a weeklong course designed to activate their emotional quotient, or EQ. EQ does for emotion what IQ does for intelligence: distills it to logic. Logic runs on identities and equations, so EQ encourages us to identify our emotions in other people, allowing us to equate their feelings with ones we've experienced ourselves: *That man is feeling scared. I can identify, because I've felt scared*

too. Let me guide him through his fear by pinpointing and dis-
pelling the sources of his anxiety, like I would do for myself.

The EQ course had been marketed as a surefire way to make execs better communicators, managers, and decision-makers. But it had disappointed the CEO. It had emphasized the benefits of empathy and the dangers of anger yet had produced no real changes in his team's behavior. That's why the CEO was calling me, hopeful but wary. He'd heard I had a different approach to emotional intelligence, field-tested in elite military units.

This was true. At the request of U.S. Army Special Operations, I'd developed an EQ alternative. Instead of being logical, it was biological, based on the brain connection between emotion and story. That connection is why the narratives of films and novels touch our feelings, prompting joy, sorrow, and other sentiments that we don't get from a spreadsheet. For years, I'd wondered: Why were emotion and story linked like this in our head? Then I'd met a Special Operator—let's call her Lucy Gray—who worked as a "singleton."

A singleton deploys solo, without a team or overwatch, into hostile territory. Because she works alone, a singleton must get very good at self-assessment. She must know when her plan is succeeding and when it needs changing. She cannot be overconfident and she cannot be tentative. She must see herself impartially, with total clarity, gauging her performance accurately every time. Otherwise, her operation will go sideways and she will die.

"How do you do that?" I asked Gray. She was highly organized, so I expected her to have a checklist of everything from her task-completion percentage to her heart rate.

"I do it through feel," she responded immediately.

"Feel?"

"Feel."

Gray's self-assessment came, that is, from emotion. When things felt right, she kept going. When things felt wrong, she adjusted. To her, this seemed semimagical, like emotion was a mystical sixth sense tracking a deeper reality. But as I studied Gray and other singletons, I discovered a biological explanation for their apparently preternatural powers of self-assessment: Their emotions were monitoring their mental life narrative, allowing them to redirect when the narrative departed from its most effective shape.

Our mental life narrative works best, as we saw in chapter 2, when our past is integrated and our future branching:

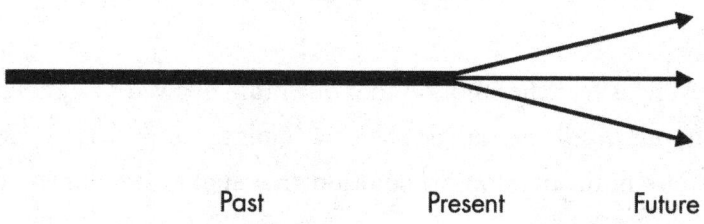

Past   Present   Future

Our emotions help us achieve this narrative by flashing warnings when our past is fracturing or our future is narrowing. To see how it works, let's start with our brain's most ancient emotion: fear.

FEAR IS CORE TO OUR brain's biology. Yet for thousands of years, wise men have warned: *Fear is irrational. Don't listen to it.*

The wise men are wrong. Fear is smart. Very smart. It is sending you critical intel. That intel is: *You have no plan.*

There are different ways to arrive at no plan. Perhaps you had a plan, but it failed. Perhaps you ignored the need to make a plan, sticking your head in the sand. Perhaps you didn't know you needed a plan, and life surprised you. Perhaps you have a plan that looks great on paper but inspires no confidence in your brain.

It's critical to know that you have no plan, because a plan is the key to intelligent success. Without a plan, you have to be lucky. So fear is warning you: *You have passed beyond the edge of your intelligence—and are about to become a captive of events!* Put in the terms of your mental life story, your future has ceased not only to branch but to exist:

Past   Present   Future

Why is fear the emotion that our brain evolved to signal this? Why out of all the signals that our biology could have evolved, did our brain develop an emotion that makes our knees weak and our mind blank?

The answer is: Our brain has evolved a bias to action, because action is how we learn. Unlike a computer, which gets smarter by sitting still, absorbing data, our brain gets smarter by pressing the initiative, gathering feedback and adjusting. This bias to action means that our brain always wants to have a plan, and on those occasions when it doesn't, fear helps it acquire a plan by making us receptive to outside influence. The more scared we get, the more our brain becomes willing to follow others, passively doing what it's told. Fear is thus our brain's ultimate backup plan. It solves the problem of no plan by absorbing a plan from somebody else.

This fear-based way of regaining a sense of purpose is why children are both so bold and so easily scared. Their boldness enables them to grow; their quickness to fear makes them responsive to adult intervention. Yet although there can be survival advantages to being impressionable, this dynamic doesn't always advance our interests. It leaves us vulnerable to con artists who play on our worries. It prompts us to join herds that are stampeding off cliffs. And because our brain's emotion system evolved in ancient eras when death lurked close, our fear is often mistuned for modern life, making us submissive when we're not experiencing an emergency yet.

I discover a smarter response to fear by studying how Gray and other singletons function in combat. Combat stimulates intense fear—so intense that it shortens your depth of vision until you can see only inches in front of your nose. This traps you in a tightening box where there's nowhere to go, prompting your mind to capitulate. To get out of the box, Operators are taught to push their gaze forward, reaching for the horizon. When you do this, your brain sees past the contracting walls of the fear box, glimpsing opportunities in the great space beyond. Those opportunities offer direction, extending your future narrative . . .

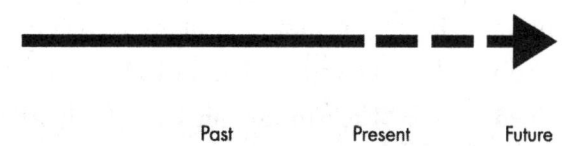

| Past | Present | Future |

. . . enabling you to exit panic and push on.

The noncombat version of this occurs when unexpected problems hit you at work or at home, catching you in a stress box that limits you to coping with the immediate tasks at hand. The result is an increasingly frantic state of disorganization that degenerates into quitting. To extricate yourself from the quit, push your mental gaze toward the long view—your narrative horizon—by remembering your overall strategy, the big life purpose that holds your past together. (See chapter 2.) When you focus on this purpose, it will prompt your brain to invent an initial step forward. Once your brain takes that step, it will get quicker at finding its next one. As one Operator put it to me: "After the first step, your mind starts to clear. Your first step might not be the best, but as you keep moving, your planning gets better and better."

This method of exiting fear is known to Operators as *first-step plan*. A first-step plan can feel a heavy lift when you're awash with stress. But you can lighten the load by preparing yourself prior to your mission. Take a minute to clarify your strategic objective, making it vivid in your mind. The sharper and more specific that objective, the more rapidly you can make a first-step plan, even in disorienting situations. During combat, soldiers who cannot recall their strategic objective—or, just as fatally, have two strategic objectives—will freeze solid, their brains blanked by panic, rescued only when a teammate helps them make a first-step plan. But when those same soldiers are primed prior to battle to visualize a single strategic objective, they can initiate their own first-step plans in seconds. As one Army Operator, who received a Medal of Honor for his initiative, explained to me: "I felt in my gut I would die. But when I remembered my target, I made a hasty move toward it. And success snowballed from there."

The same priming technique works in business execs—and in children as young as eight. All it requires is taking the time, in a nonurgent moment, to identify your most important long-term goal. To assist you in finding that goal, use this singleton tip: Don't target abstract objectives, like "happiness" or "success."

Instead focus on specific objectives, like "writing that novel" or "selling this company." The more tangible the target, the more tangible the first-step plan your brain can make.

If you need help making a first-step plan, you can get it from positive emotion, which we'll cover later in this chapter and in chapter 6. But the critical first step toward making first-step plans is the one we've just covered here: Shift your relationship to fear. If you ignore fear like the wise men or succumb to it like the herd, you weaken your mental story, increasing your fragility. If you take fear as an opportunity to push your eyes toward your primary purpose, you bolster not only your confidence but also your competence, generating a positive loop between courage and ability that will propel you to your destiny.

To keep uncovering the basics of emotional intelligence, let's turn now to fear's ancient partner: anger.

ANGER COMBINES WITH FEAR TO comprise fright-or-fight (also known as fight-or-flight), the brain's primordial mechanism for responding to change and uncertainty.

This mechanism is highly intelligent. To understand why, imagine being dropped suddenly in a room with no doors. How do you feel? You feel trapped, stirring fear in your brain. Next, imagine a door opening in the wall. How do you feel now? You feel less helpless. But you still feel stressed. That door is your only way out. You *have* to get through it. So your brain gets forceful. It transitions toward aggression.

This thought experiment unearths the mental narratives beneath fear and anger. Fear is your brain thinking: *I have no door, no path, no plan.* Anger is your brain thinking: *I have one plan—but only one.* Put in the terms of your mental life story, anger reveals that your future has narrowed to a single branch:

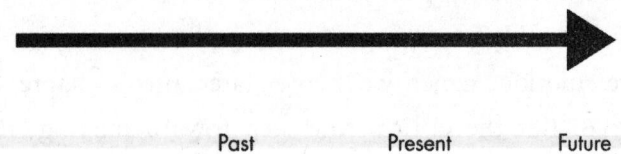

Past   Present   Future

This narrowing is the second characteristic of the fright-or-fight phenomenon known as tunnel vision. The first characteristic—linked with fear—shortens your gaze. The second—linked with anger—constricts it. If you feel anger, you can still see into the future. But you can see only a single path to get there.

Why did anger evolve as the sign that we have only one plan? Why, out of all the signals that our biology could have evolved, did our brain develop an emotion that makes us forceful—even violent?

The answer is: One plan can work. And it's more likely to work when executed assertively. I see this not just with Operators but with firefighters and paramedics. They tell me: "When crises happen, you have to act fast. If your team isn't acting fast enough, you've got to get angry to make them hear." "I use anger to fuel myself in critical situations. It makes me commit my hardest." "Anger is intensity. It focuses the mind and energizes the body to work."

That's why our brain evolved anger. Anger is prompting us toward a plan that can work—if executed with passion and strength. The problem is: Anger gains its benefit at a cost—a very high cost. Even when the plan works, the price is steep. Your anger has inflamed your team with burnout. It has increased the likelihood that you'll get angry next time, shortening your fuse. It has elevated your stress, impacting your health. And the cost is much higher when the plan doesn't work. If you shout orders at people, and the orders don't succeed, then what? You're cooked. You forced your plan and it broke.

Rather than getting aggressive, the smarter approach is to treat anger as a signal to pause and develop operational flexibility. Perhaps you've fallen into the optimization trap, believing that there's one ideal fix for every situation. Or perhaps you're stuck in a one-track mode of communication, such that when people don't understand what you're telling them, you simply repeat yourself more loudly. Or perhaps you're experiencing stress. Stress ranges in intensity, but in all its forms, it stimulates a fright-or-fight response. When that response hits, your brain does a quick gut check: *Do I have a plan that I believe can work?* If the answer is no, your brain enters fear. If the answer is yes, your brain enters anger, executing the plan as forcefully as it can.

You can solve all these problems by making a second plan, which you can do by looking for exceptional information. (See chapter 2 for how exceptional information helps make plans.) The more your brain detects exceptions in the people and environment around you, the more it will see new paths to success. With those paths, you can gain anger's benefits without its downside. March down a path swiftly and authoritatively. If the path doesn't work, back up and quickly try another, joining assertiveness with flexibility.

When you're angry, making second plans can be a challenge. To help yourself, do what singletons do: Remember a time when you made a new plan under pressure. The new plan did not have to be perfect. It could be what singletons refer to as a "hasty plan," aka an improvised response. All that matters is that it was effective. When your brain remembers itself creating that previous plan, it will think: *I have done it before; I can do it again.*

That thought process will calm your aggression, releasing your intuition to explore new paths for action.

Singletons call this intuition releaser *Emotion Reset*. It is highly effective in adults experiencing anger. Anger is, fundamentally, a self-protective mechanism, a last-ditch attempt by your brain to save its health, its goals, its reputation. It is common among people who feel pushed to their limits, whether by their own perceived shortcomings, by the hardness of the situation, or by the apparent intractability of the people around them. I have seen anger in financial traders who can't explain why their investments are bleeding cash; in first responders stunned by an ambulance gear failure; in bosses frustrated that their staff can't do as asked. And I have watched anger evaporate when these individuals performed an Emotion Reset, recalling a time when they'd made a second plan under duress.

For an Emotion Reset to work quickly and reliably, it must be vividly specific. So prepare your Reset in advance—prepare it *now*—by reviewing your past for a time when you shifted your plans, adapting to life before you got trapped.

To complete our survey of how to use emotion to self-assess, let's finish by turning to a pair of feelings so uncomfortable that they're even harder to discuss than fear and anger. Those feelings are grief and shame.

GRIEF AND SHAME SIGNAL DEPARTURES from our primordial story, which exists from birth in narrative brain regions that sit below our conscious awareness, turning the wheels of our behavior without intentional thought. That primordial story is: *I am a good person in a good world.*

Because our primordial story tells us that we are good, it

gives us confidence to trust our instincts, making us brave. And because it tells us that the world is good, it gives us confidence to trust the things we encounter, making us open. The resulting mix of bravery and openness powers growth, which is the long-term strategy of biology, the ultimate goal of existence, the big *Why* of life.

Yet even though growth is our natural origin and destination, it can slow and even stop. The slowing occurs when our bravery and openness carry us into negative experiences:

- First, there are negative experiences that happen to us. We get hurt or see bad things. This causes grief. It makes us think, *The world is bad.* So it splits our primordial story into two stories: *I live in a good world* and *I live in a bad world.* The first story keeps us open, driving growth, so we stick to it when we can. The second makes us closed, protecting us from further grief, so we revert to it whenever we feel unsafe.

- Second, there are negative experiences that we cause ourselves. Maybe we lie or act selfishly. This causes shame. It makes us think, *I am bad.* So it splits our primordial story into two stories: *I am a good person* and *I am a bad person.* The first story keeps us brave, driving growth, so we stick to it when we can. The second makes us self-critical, protecting us from further shame, so we revert to it whenever we feel uncertain.

Grief and shame thus indicate a fracture in the story that our brain is telling itself about its life experiences, revealing that our mental narrative looks not like

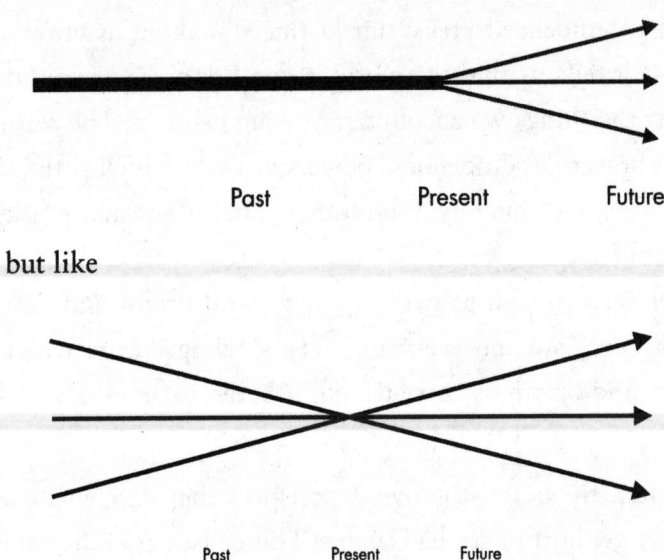

but like

Grief and shame signal the inverse of anger and fear. Anger and fear warn you about a narrowing of your future, while grief and shame warn you about a splintering of your past:

- Grief signals that you have experienced something disturbing, even traumatic or tragic, that you cannot reconcile with the story about life that you tell yourself to get up in the morning. You are therefore living in two worlds.

- Shame signals that you have acted (or are acting) inconsistently, maybe even hypocritically. You are therefore living as two people.

Since your past narrative produces your strategic purpose, grief and shame weaken your forward momentum, dispersing your energy and decreasing your effectiveness at achieving your goals.

When you feel grief and shame, it can be tempting to ignore them. Or to wallow in them. But their purpose in your brain is to guide you to intelligent action:

- For grief, identify the past event that's making you think, *The world is bad.* Then use your overall purpose—the same purpose you use to make a first-step plan—to derive insight from the event, clarifying or altering your worldview.

- For shame, identify the past action that's making you think, *I am bad.* Then decide whether the action was inconsistent with your personal path or a result of people judging you. If the latter, own the event as your true self. If the former, remember your overall purpose and use it to correct the inconsistent behavior.

Both these responses start by focusing on your overall purpose, aka your *why.* But what if you can't see your overall purpose clearly? What if you can't see it at all? A good start is to remember that your biological purpose, now and forever, is growth. A focus on growth—instead of on happiness or success—helps your brain translate setbacks and mistakes into learning.

A focus on growth will, however, get you only so far. Growth is an abstract, generic goal. If you want to regain your full energy and directedness after tragedy or self-disgust, your brain will benefit from a more specific personal purpose. To find that purpose, do what singletons like Lucy Gray do: Draw on maverick gratitude and dumb pride.

PRIDE IS A POSITIVE FEELING toward a past action. Dumb pride is a positive feeling toward a past action that everyone else thinks you should regret.

Regret is our usual emotional response to stupid behavior. It's our brain thinking: *Don't do that again!* But occasionally, we do something dumb that doesn't make us wince ruefully. Instead, it makes us quietly proud. That cheerful lack of regret is our primal brain telling itself: *Good job! You're being smart in a way that no one else sees.* The action registers in our mind as dumb only because it puts us at odds with the rest of the world.

Our brain loves tales about people who go against the rest of the world. This is the most popular storyline of modern books and movies, and it can be found across classic literature too: Romeo and Juliet, Huck Finn, and most classically of all, Antigone. Antigone was an ancient Greek whose uncle condemned her brother's dead body to be eaten by vultures. This horrified Antigone. She knew: If her brother wasn't buried, his spirit would wander for eternity. So Antigone told her uncle that she would provide funeral rites. Furious, her uncle threatened that if she did, she would be interred herself, shut up in a tomb until she suffocated. Antigone was not intimidated. Laying her brother's body in the earth, she sacrificed her life to grant his afterlife, becoming a legend of sisterly love.

As much as we admire Antigone and her fellow freethinkers for fighting the norm, however, our brain has a hard time fighting that fight itself. That's because our brain evolved to be social. It's deeply invested in what other people think. Most of us crave fame and public honors. Almost all of us want to be respected by our friends and families.

To fight your fight, you must buck that desire. You must endure mockery and disrepute. You must survive the disappointment and even judgment of your parents and partners as they watch you dedicate your life to a war that seems to be going nowhere, for a cause they cannot understand. But you can do this. You've done it before. Just search your memory for moments of dumb behavior that don't cause regret. "The dumbest thing I ever did was join the Army," Lucy Gray says to me with a laugh. "But I wouldn't change it for anything." This is her way of saying: *I found my fight.* It caused her pain, making her feel outcast and even ashamed. But if she could go back in time, she'd opt for the same choice, signing up for more hurt.

When you've got a list of dumb actions you'd repeat, submit them to this stress test: *What's the worst outcome that could have occurred? Would I still do it anyway?* In the case of Lucy Gray and other singletons, the answer remains: Yes. Even if they had not triumphed in the end. Even if they'd been defeated, forgotten by history, stripped of their dignity, they'd have done it again. "That's when you know your heart is in it. When you could die and it don't bother you, the mission you're on is the right one."

Most of your stupid behaviors won't pass this test. The reason you don't feel regret is because you got away with them. But when a stupid behavior *does* pass this test, it's primal. It's the rebel self-respect that Antigone felt when she was seized by her uncle and buried alive.

If you're reviewing your past and not surfacing any dumb pride, think back to your childhood, before you developed teenage self-consciousness and adult caution. As children, we fight instinctively for the special in ourselves. One of my earliest memories is from preschool, when I was led onto a bus for a class trip.

After I boarded the bus, I saw that it had no seat belts. This didn't bother the other students. They sat down in their assigned seats. But I felt unsafe. So I did not sit down. I stood in the aisle and requested a seat belt.

I was told by the driver that there were no seat belts, but not to worry, I would be fine. I remained standing. My teacher came over and told me patiently but firmly to take my seat. There was nothing, she said, to be concerned about; the bus was perfectly safe. I did not sit. Finally, the head of the school was summoned. He towered above me, explaining that I was delaying the trip and inconveniencing the other students. He said that if I did not sit, he would be forced to call my parents. And my parents, he was sure, would not be pleased to hear that I was being disruptive.

I continued to stand. Eventually, I was removed from the bus. Only then did I sit, in a corner of the school office, alone, until my mother came to pick me up. I had no hesitation about doing any of this. It did not seem rude or rebellious. It seemed entirely natural. And it *was* natural, for me. I was fighting my fight. I was standing up to an educational institution that was more concerned with staying on schedule than with looking out for the concerns of its students.

There will be a time—likely many times—when your childhood self stood up for something that earned you the scorn of your peers or the scolding of adults, yet looking back now, you admire your antisocial behavior. You are proud that you were that child. Remember that child whenever you get lost, and you will find your *why* again.

THE OTHER EMOTION THAT HELPS singletons spot the exceptional in themselves is maverick gratitude. Maverick gratitude doesn't come from thanking others. It comes from noticing how you respond when you get thanked.

You'll get thanked for a lot of things in your life. And those thanks can be extraordinarily magnificent, poignant, and sincere. You can receive big annual bonuses, the tearful gratitude of people telling you that you've changed their life, or the intimate appreciation of the ones you love.

Yet you will notice: Some thanks matter more. And the thanks that matter most are the thanks that surprise you, stirring a reciprocal appreciation. They make you want to thank the thanker back for how they've done the unconventional and recognized the unconventional in you. You had resigned yourself to the fact that you were doing a thankless task, one for which you'd be at best ignored and at worst abused. When you instead receive gratitude for that lonely mission, it validates your core sense of purpose. Unlike regular thanks, which the world dispenses because you are doing what it values, you have been thanked for disregarding the world and fighting your fight.

Even a small dose of this unexpected gratitude can be immensely potent. Singletons have been awarded fistfuls of medals, but they don't place much stock in those formal displays of military thanks. "Let me tell you what a medal is," one singleton scoffs to me. "It's how the Army takes credit for what you did." That's why their medals aren't displayed proudly in their homes and offices but are instead stuffed in drawers and chucked carelessly in boxes. However, if you thank a singleton for her mission, her personal fight, she will become emotional. She will treat you like kin, braving any danger with you.

Your brain contains the same gratitude-analysis mechanism. If big thanks don't touch you deeply, then you're probably being thanked for advancing someone else's purpose. But if little thanks feel big, you're advancing your own mission. Let those little-big thanks be your guide, and you will never lose sight of why *you* fight.

WE'LL COVER OTHER POSITIVE EMOTIONS—INCLUDING hope, wonder, and optimism—in later chapters. But you've now got the basics of why emotion is smart. It's not smart because it allows you to identify the feelings of other hearts. To really learn about those hearts, you have to focus on what's exceptional about them, valuing how they defy your expectations. (See chapter 1.) Instead, emotion is smart because it sees inward. It's a tool for diagnosing when your own life plan is faltering.

If you feel irritable, aggressive, or angry, that's your brain warning: *Your plan is breaking.* If you feel fear, that's your brain warning: *Your plan is broken.* If you feel regret or sadness, that's your brain warning: *You do not have a plan, because you do not know exactly who you are—or what world you're living in.*

And emotion doesn't only tell you when things are going wrong. It also points you to a fix. The fix comes from dumb pride and maverick gratitude, which reveal your overall life purpose. That purpose gets you moving when you are paralyzed with panic or worry. It expands your options when you are stressed or angry. It guides you to find growth in grief and shame.

You don't need to wait for negative signals like anger and shame to benefit from emotion. You can engage its help proactively. Before singletons launch a mission, they envision every future step, checking for moments that stir stress or anxiety—and planning work-arounds.

And just as crucially, before singletons launch a mission, they review their personal history, walking step by step from childhood to the present. They remember *every detail of their past*, scanning for moments that prompt sadness or regret. Singletons do this because they know: Those moments will surface in a crisis. In a crisis, your old demons return to scream: *You are failing again! You will lose, just like before!* Or to put it more clinically: When you encounter failures or setbacks, the shame and grief of the present will be amplified by the shame and grief of your past. That present-past combo will make you feel that you are a perpetual loser. The smart thing, you will be certain, is to give up now. Why prolong the misery when the issue has long been decided?

To prevent the quit, don't mindfully dissociate or stoically compartmentalize. Those cages cannot hold your past for long. Instead, slay your demons in advance. You will have to face them eventually, so why not before your next adventure? Deal with them one by one, on your terms, not in a mob that ambushes you in a vulnerable moment. (For more on how to do this, see chapter 6.)

Emotion drives Primal Intelligence in partnership with intuition and imagination. (See chapters 1 and 2.) Emotion reveals what has worked and what's not working now; intuition and imagination reveal what could work in the future. Or, put in terms of your life story, emotion uncovers your *why* and signals when you need to develop more *what ifs*; intuition and imagination help you generate those *what ifs*.

But after you've generated those *what ifs*, how do you know which one to pursue? How do you know when it's better to execute your current plan with assertiveness and when it's better to switch course? You can't decide purely on the basis of your inner narrative. You must also account for your external environment, which is gauged by the fourth and final primal power: commonsense.

4

COMMONSENSE

Meet the Moment Like Ben Franklin and the Stock Picker

He began picking stocks in college. And he got good—extremely good. He beat the market decade after decade, earning billions in assets and a sandalwood mansion overlooking the Caribbean.

He was still young, his hair barely flecked with gray. Yet he was ready for retirement. He just needed someone to manage his cash while he sunned on endless sands of white. But who could he trust? Most investors were too stiff in their thinking; they religiously followed past data, acting like algorithms instead of accessing their intuitions. The remainder were more dexterous—to a fault. They got seduced by imaginative speculation, leaving solid ground to flirt gratuitously with risk.

To feel safe in retirement, the stock picker wanted a financial planner who possessed his own savvy. But he didn't know where to look. What, exactly, was the mental skill that had made him rich? It was a kind of reasonableness, he was certain, yet it wasn't logic. Logic was too robotic, too stuck in past trends to anticipate fresh opportunities. What he was looking for was something else, a brainpower that accelerated plans when they were working—and pivoted swiftly when better prospects materialized. But what could that brainpower be?

I had an answer, derived from studying Operators who dominated in smooth times and choppy, outperforming both chance and data. The answer was: commonsense.

COMMONSENSE IS FAMOUSLY THE ABILITY that distinguishes humans from AI, which can ace complex calculations yet fumble a decision obvious to children.

How can children behave more sensibly than computers? Have they absorbed more situational context? Are they better at drawing inferences? (That is: Do the brains of four-year-olds contain environmental datasets that digital machines haven't learned to download? Are their neurons running algorithms unknown to the world's top software engineers?)

No. Children act smarter than AI because they can perform a simple mental operation: They can know when they don't know. You will see this when a child enters an unfamiliar house or encounters an unfamiliar person. The child will hesitate, realizing: *I don't know this place. I don't know that face.*

As elementary as this operation is for children, it's impossible for logic. Logic exists in the mathematical present, an eternal state of equation that prompts AI to think that its current knowledge is what it has always known—and all there ever is to know. This feature of computer cognition is why large language models like ChatGPT lie. They're not trying to deceive. Quite the opposite: They aim to tell the truth. But when queried about something they don't know, they don't know that they don't know. So they fabricate guilelessly, filling the gap in their knowledge by extrapolating from past trends.

Unlike AI, our brain is able to detect when those trends end. It does so via the same mental mechanism that lies at the root of intuition, imagination, and emotion. (See chapters 1, 2, and 3.) That mechanism is story. Story doesn't occur as timeless math. It inhabits the temporal past-future of *why* and *what if*. And *why* and *what if* can operate as tools for gauging environmental novelty: When our brain finds itself unable to grab onto a firm *why* for what it sees, or when it imagines two *what if*s that conflict, it realizes that it has hit the perimeter of its understanding. While computers can be programmed to recognize known unknowns, story thus gives our brain the power to detect *unknown* unknowns.

That power is the basis of commonsense, which, as our childhood hesitation reveals, works by tracking environmental novelty, aka volatility. The greater the volatility, the greater the possibility of exceptions to our current rules of action. This possibility registers in our conscious mind as the warning: *There is relevant info you don't know.* When the warning is gentle, it prompts us to start imagining new plans. When the warning is strong, it primes us to switch plans, fast.

Commonsense thus has a purely negative function: to make us doubt our current plan. But this function can be repurposed positively by our brain. When commonsense isn't sounding the alarm, our brain knows that volatility is low, allowing us to power forward on our current path. Our brain's confidence in a particular strategy thus results not from spreadsheets of evidence that it will work but from the absence of one strong indicator that it can't. Human decision-making is low information, all the way down.

Practically, this means that our brain works best when it inverts the behavior of a computer. A computer seeks verification from data; our brain seeks falsification from the unexpected. That difference is why humans and AI can be effective partners, with AI running the show in routine situations and humans taking over in changing times. But it's also why so many human brains now suffer from unproductive anxiety, chronic hesitation, and analysis paralysis. They've been trained in school and business to imitate computers, amassing facts and acting only when certain that they're right. By doing so, they're acting against their nature, which is to have a bias toward action that is interrupted only if the brain realizes that its current conduct won't work.

When we're children, our action bias leads to much errant behavior. Our limited life experience makes the fanciful seem feasible, dashing us in directions that cannot succeed. But as we grow, becoming experts in different areas, commonsense allows us to be both accurate and agile. The accuracy comes from assertively trusting current rules when life is stable, downplaying imaginative possibilities to seize on solid realities. The agility comes from quickly prioritizing exceptions when our commonsense detects a shift in conditions.

This answers the stock picker's question. What enabled him to invest prudently in stable markets while capitalizing fast on financial flux? It was his commonsense, aka his primal power to detect the density of unknown unknowns. That power helped the stock picker separate superficial economic blips from fundamental changes, revealing when to keep it rote—and when to get creative.

Commonsense can do more than warn us to change plans. It can select the new plan that best fits our situation. We'll see how in chapter 7. But first, the basics: How do you acquire common-sense if you don't have it?

"DID YOU ALWAYS HAVE COMMONSENSE?" I ask the stock picker.

He smiles. "No. When I was a teen, I was very adrift from reality."

"What changed?"

"It wasn't a single moment."

"You started investing in college. Was your commonsense sharpened by a class? Or a professor?"

He smiles wider. "Not at the college I attended." Then he pauses, reflecting. "Although I guess, in a way, I did have a teacher." He pulls out an old paperback, its pages thumbed and yellow. It is Carl Van Doren's Pulitzer Prize–winning biography of Benjamin Franklin.

The fifteenth child of a candlemaker, Franklin was born in 1706 near the heart of the colonial American city of Boston, at a boxy wooden house on Milk Street. Over his long life, he became renowned for switching smartly between traditional wisdom (dispensed in his *Poor Richard's Almanack*) and groundbreaking science (like his 1752 lightning-kite experiment).

This ability to stick to reliable precedent yet adapt to fresh intel was nurtured by Franklin's irregular education. Too poor to finish school, he learned from newspapers, and as he turned their oversize pages, he noticed they had two distinct goals: pleasing their readership and educating it. To do the former, journalists wrote comfortable stories that upheld conventional morality and mainstream sentiment. To do the latter, journalists broke news that surprised expectations and overturned opinions. The two modes of reportage were logically opposite, yet successful newspapers swiveled deftly between them, guided by editorial commonsense.

The same editorial commonsense was developed by Franklin when he apprenticed at *The New-England Courant* and later enabled him to grow wealthy from his own newspaper, *The Pennsylvania Gazette*. In fact, it enabled him to grow so wealthy that he retired from daily print work in his early forties, devoting himself to building hospitals, traveling Europe, and reforming the U.S. postal system. He was awarded honorary degrees from Yale, Harvard, and Oxford. He created the Franklin stove. He stewarded the American Revolution.

To share the secret of his success, Franklin penned dozens of commonsense aphorisms, like

1. Be slow in choosing a friend, slower in changing.

2. Read much but not too many books.

3. Write injuries in dust, benefits in marble.

4. He who gives promptly gives twice as much.

5. You may delay, but time will not.

6. The way to be safe is never to be secure.

The first three aphorisms remind us to go slow, carefully investing in things that possess a long track record of success. The last three urge us to go fast, reacting speedily to change. Logically, these two sets of suggestions contradict each other. But they're connected by our commonsense, which, by knowing when we don't know, helps us hold on to the tried-and-true in certain times while leaping quick when novel prospects appear.

I am fascinated by Franklin's aphorisms. And my fascination deepens when the stock picker points me to another Benjamin, Benjamin Graham. Born in 1894 to a London porcelain salesman who immigrated to New York City, Graham spent his adolescence in poverty but lifted himself to astonishing prosperity. He wrote Broadway plays. He invented pocket calculators. He developed a financial theory—value investing—that earned its acolytes billions. And he credited all this success—in literature, in tech, in business—to the commonsense he gained from Franklin: "[He is] the character after whom I have consciously modeled my life."

Wondering if I can achieve similar returns, I immerse myself in Franklin's aphorisms. Studying them for an hour each morning, I repeat their homespun phrasing as I go about my day. But my worldly wisdom doesn't improve. My diction is changed; my behavior not so much. Graham got something from Franklin that I haven't.

Curious to find what I'm missing, I contact U.S. Special Operations. They introduced me to the power of commonsense. Perhaps they can explain how to cultivate it.

LIKE THE STOCK PICKER, THE Operators admire Ben Franklin. They respect that he was self-taught through reading and life experience. They appreciate how he got multiple degrees—without going to college. And they share his belief that it's possible to teach commonsense.

To do that teaching, they've devised a training course that switchbacks between routine and novelty, tuning the brain's ability to recognize: *There's something here that I don't know.* The course sits on a mudstone flat populated with butcher birds and encircled by a forest of thin pine trees whose uniform tallness suggests that they were all planted at precisely the same instant a century ago. Hidden in the trees is an asphalt complex of vintage airfields, digital junkyards, and barbecue pits. Nothing about it seems commonsensical, I remark. This prompts the Operators to grin mysteriously.

Intrigued, I ask to tour the course. The Operators oblige, giving me a private run-through. It does not go well. I fail. In fact, I get a zero. I have absolutely no commonsense.

The Operators are impressed. It takes a lot, they tell me, to completely delete the brain's power to detect its limits. They hypothesize—correctly—that I dwell entirely in classrooms or in front of a computer. But they assure me that I can reactivate my commonsense. All I need to do is—to use their term—*recycle* through the course, with a little remedial training.

Here's that training, summarized on a three-by-five card:

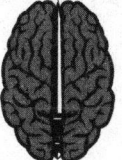

TUNE YOUR ANXIETY

Past: NONE   Future: NEAR

Light enough to grip existing fundamentals.

Strong enough to spot emerging fundamentals.

true anxiety detects your environment's true volatility.

Let's run through how it works.

THE CARD'S TOP INSIGHT IS explained by an Operator with a Hawaiian suntan and a Wild West mustache. "Anxiety," he assures me, "is good."

This is the opposite of what I'm used to hearing, but it reminds me of when my son and daughter were sent home from elementary school with "fidget toys." The toys, I was informed by an accompanying sheet of paper, were to calm anxiety.

"What do you have worries about?" I asked my children.

"Tests," they replied. "Tests at school."

Unsure what to make of this, I took my children to a psychiatrist. She studied them carefully, then returned with a diagnosis. "Your son and daughter are worried because they don't know what's on the school tests—so when they try to imagine, their heads fill with *what if*s. Each of the *what if*s runs toward a different future, like horses hauling the brain in different directions. That inner tug-of-war creates mental tension—or, as we call it, anxiety."

When the psychiatrist said this, I thought of the branching tomorrows made by imagination:

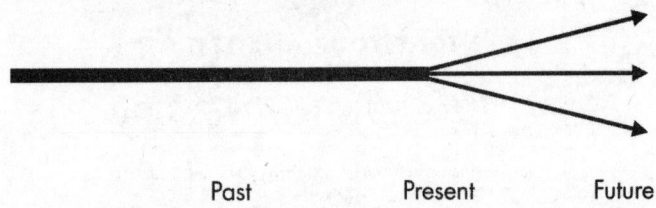

Past   Present   Future

In the woods with the Operators, I'd seen the Future arrows as good, but in the psychiatrist's office, I became concerned that the arrows were wild animals pulling the Present apart.

"How do I get rid of my children's anxiety?" I asked the psychiatrist.

"You don't want to do that. It wouldn't be good for them."

"It wouldn't?"

"No. Anxiety is healthy. It keeps us alive, by alerting us not to roam too far beyond our zone of competence. And it helps us grow, by pushing us to develop our skills and to improve our plans so that we can pass the real test: life."

The Operators smile when I relay this story. They agree with the psychiatrist: Worry is an intelligent tool. The more *what ifs* our brain can imagine, the stronger our anxiety, alerting us: *There are unknown unknowns ahead.* This narrative mechanism is how our brain measures potential volatility. Like our other emotions (see chapter 3), anxiety is thus a diagnostic signal that reveals the shape of our mental narrative. The higher our anxiety, the more our future narrative is branching, so the more our commonsense is warning: *You're entering uncertain times; prepare to abandon familiar plans.*

"You gotta be anxious to act sensibly," the Operators counsel. "Folks who breeze ahead are out of touch with reality." As proof, they catalog the recruits who arrive at the commonsense course and fail. There are the positive thinkers who are certain that faith conquers all. There are the Zen lords who dedicate themselves to being mondo chill. There are the analytics gurus who spin data into confident predictions. There are the mindfulness proponents who dissipate stress by meditating. There are the psychics who trust their extrasensory inklings. There are the gamblers who carelessly push their luck. There are the suburbanites who expect that—come war, plague, or Armageddon—there will be hot water from the shower faucet.

The list reminds me of my own initial response to Special Operations training, when I entered the Dismal Swamp—and sprinted toward an explosion. My lack of nerves, I realize, was a sign that I had zero commonsense. On an actual battlefield, I'd have been dead in seconds.

My first step into commonsense was to get anxious about the future. And for all of us, this is the first biological step, one we take when our ten-month-old brain grows concerned at our parents' absence. This step is necessary—and healthy—because it's impossible to know what will happen next. Whatever your speculator's hunch, your statistical paradigm, or your clairvoyant eye might tell you, the future is uncertain. It's the definition of something we don't know. And since commonsense is knowing when we don't know, the sure sign that your commonsense is switched off is having no worries about the coming minutes.

"Does this mean that the more tense you are about the future, the more commonsense you have?" I ask the Operators.

They shake their heads. "Absolutely not. Anxiety keeps you appropriately vigilant, looking for potential problems, preparing possible solutions. But if anxiety is too strong, it sabotages commonsense, abandoning solid plans because you get spooked by ghosts."

This answer scrambles me. I understand, in theory, that it's good to be anxious but not too anxious. Yet in practice, where's the line between appropriate watchfulness and self-destructive worry? How do I imagine enough *what if*s to gauge volatility but not so many that it tears my head apart? What's the second step into commonsense?

THE SECOND STEP IS: TUNE your anxiety by ridding the future of the past.

"It works like this," the Operators explain. "When you feel

an anxiety about the future, ask: *Is it really about the future? Or is it about the past?*"

Most of our anxieties about the future are actually anxieties about the past. They flash us back to problems that have already occurred—and that we're worried will occur again. They signal that our brain is imagining how life could have gone differently— *What if I'd done that instead?*—splitting our past narrative into alternative histories:

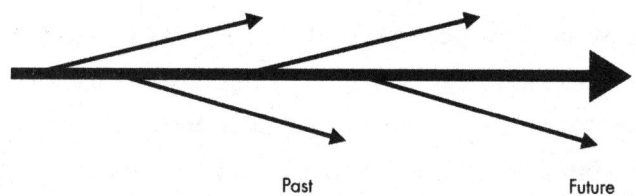

Past   Future

Those alternative histories will never happen. Yesterday is unchangeable. Your brain knows that. But it's reliving the past because it wants you to remember what went wrong—and fix it.

So fix it. You can do this by updating your standard operating procedures, or SOPs. *SOPs* is Operator-speak for plans that have performed reliably over time. You have those plans, even if you've never been anywhere near the U.S. Army. They're your regular routine, your usual approach, your daily habits. To update them, incorporate the *what if* from your alternative history so that next time, you do what you wish you'd done last time. Like pilots do after a crash and safety engineers do after an accident.

Because SOPs have a lengthy track record, they must be updated carefully. Any change should add more wisdom than it subtracts. If you can't imagine a change that accomplishes this, don't sacrifice the weight of experience to a single worry. Instead, chalk up the past problem to bad luck. Then let go of the anxiety and hang on to your SOPs, accepting that no plan is perfect.

Really? Just act like the crash didn't occur? Yes, I'm assured by Special Operations pilots. Unless you can find a new SOP that protects more lives than the old SOP, trust the old. (If that feels irresponsible, know: There's usually a way to update an SOP. For help on how, see chapter 5.)

By processing old fears, you help your brain hold on to durable rules (aka the fundamentals of your environment). But commonsense is more than sticking to classic procedures. It's also seizing on new threats and opportunities—seizing, that is, on exceptions to rules. That seizing takes active vigilance, which comes from anxiety. But not past anxiety. *Future* anxiety.

Future anxiety is worries about events that haven't happened before. These worries are the other half of commonsense. The more of them you feel, the higher the volatility ahead:

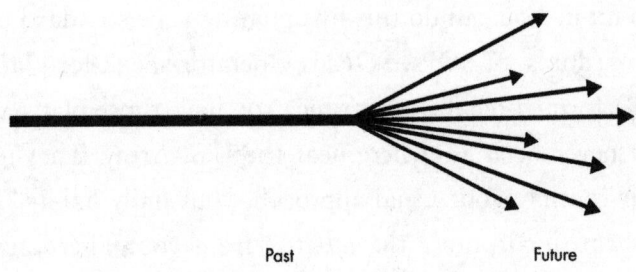

Past   Future

Does this mean that the more concerns you have about tomorrow, the more sensibly you'll respond to new dangers and prospects? No. If you have too many worries, your brain will get overwhelmed, reacting slowly—or even locking up entirely. To maximize commonsense, you need to dial down your future anxieties, concentrating your attention on the most valuable.

You can do this by taking the third and final step: Finish tuning anxiety by focusing on your upcoming objective—*without peering any further down the road.*

Don't, in other words, look too far into the future. The future is the embodiment of an unknown unknown, so the more of it you gaze at, the more *what ifs* will proliferate—and the higher your anxiety will climb. This is counterproductive. The events of the distant future will be changed by the events of the intermediate future, which will in turn be changed by the events of the near future. Far-off challenges that seem probable now will vanish in the tide, while others will arise. So focus your anxiety where it belongs: on the part of your mission that happens next. That will allow your brain to gauge the density of unknown unknowns that lie in your path.

Operators call this *Now + 1.* It's fixing your gaze one action ahead, to the *what ifs* that you can most effectively detect—and most powerfully affect.

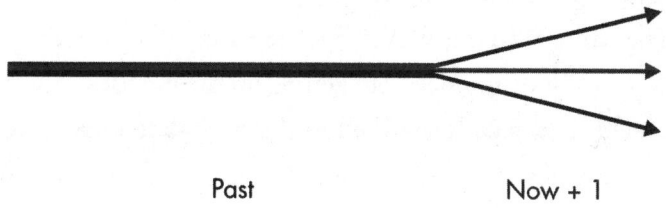

Past   Now + 1

When you spot potential problems in the Now + 1, imagine potential response plans. *But don't implement those plans just yet.* Instead, push forward, waiting to see what happens. If the problem strikes, you'll be prepared. If it doesn't, you'll remain in touch with reality.

THAT THREE-STEP METHOD IS HOW Operators tune anxiety. They address past problems they know are real, then focus on near-future problems that could be real—or not. This resolves known unknowns and lets the brain concentrate on unknown unknowns, maximizing commonsense.

"So, learn from the past and don't second-guess the future," I sum it up. "Pretty sensible."

"Sure, it's sensible." The Operators frown at my glibness. "That's why it's called commonsense. But most folks act the opposite. They stress about things that have happened already. And act to prevent things that never have."

These are the insights summarized on the three-by-five card that the Operators waterproof and distribute to recruits, who arrive in increasing numbers with zero commonsense, their natural intelligence depleted by years of classrooms and computers. By processing past worries, the recruits help their brains develop SOPs that work reliably in stable settings. And by focusing on Now + 1, the recruits keep their brains primed to seize emerging opportunities when the world turns.

The same training works outside of combat, even in math-heavy fields like finance, budgeting, and analytics. Success in these fields is typically credited to dispassionate logic. But it actually comes from learning how to worry correctly, as I see by returning to the stock picker.

THE STOCK PICKER IS GOOD at math, yet many other investors are better. His edge, he says, comes from his *market sensitivity*. It's a skill I hear referenced by other stock pickers, along with related ones like *price alertness* and *active vigilance*.

Where do these skills come from? How do they work? I get only vague answers. Yet when I study the stock pickers in action, I find that they employ a two-part mental mechanism: Before trading, they process old jitters; when trading, they focus on the market's next instant. The stock pickers, in short, do like the Operators. They tune their anxiety.

Because of this tuning, the stock pickers don't get skittish from flashbacks to bad trades. And they don't react to phantoms. They use intuition and imagination to plot potential pivots they could execute if needed. But they don't jump the gun, chasing conditions that aren't real yet.

"That's the recipe for commonsense," I observe to the stock pickers.

They nod agreeably.

"Did you all get it from Ben Franklin's aphorisms?" I ask.

No, the stock pickers smile. They recognize Franklin's face from hundred-dollar bills, but that, they say, is as far as it goes. By digging into the stock pickers' backgrounds, however, I discover there's more to the story. Even though the stock pickers haven't studied Franklin, they've cribbed from his heirs: commonsense investors who used the same two techniques as Special Operators—*Past Anxiety: NONE* and *Future Anxiety: NEAR*—to tune their anxiety to be light enough to trust durable currents yet strong enough to spot fresh market forces.

As a case study in *Past Anxiety: NONE*, there's Warren Buffett, the twentieth century's most successful long-term investor. Rejected in 1950 from Harvard Business School for acting more farmer than banker, Buffett trained instead with Ben Franklin disciple Benjamin Graham. Graham had made a small fortune in the 1940s by rejecting the method of Wall Street speculators. That method was algorithmic. Using data to forecast stocks, it treated past and future as subsets of an eternal mathematical present, encouraging speculators to believe that they could calculate tomorrow's revenues from yesterday's spreadsheets.

Graham had learned the folly of this speculative method from Franklin. Sure, in stable markets, you could rely on historical averages and other statistical instruments. But because markets were contested spaces, it was in their nature to get choppy, busting prior analytics. Guided by this commonsense insight, Graham dispensed with computational prognostication and coined his own investment rule: *Rather than trying to predict what a stock will be worth tomorrow, focus on getting the cheapest price today.* This rule didn't ensure that you would turn a profit. But it did guarantee the best value now, maximizing potential gains and minimizing potential losses.

Buffett relentlessly applied Graham's rule for two years on Wall Street, haggling and scrounging for cut-rate deals, before heading west to the meatpacking yards of Omaha, Nebraska, to launch his own fund. In 1964, he leveraged that fund to acquire the failing textile company Berkshire Hathaway. And over the next five decades, he increased Berkshire Hathaway's worth ten-thousandfold, generating hundred-billion-dollar payouts that vastly exceeded Graham's career earnings.

This improbable triumph led Buffett to be feted—in sitcoms, rap songs, soap operas—as the Oracle of Omaha. But he denied any psychic wizardry. His rare earnings had come, he said, from enlarging Graham's rule with his own commonsense insights. And of those insights, none had been more valuable, Buffett reckoned, than his discovery of the power of processing past anxiety. As proof, he shared a personal story.

Once upon a time in a District of Columbia classroom, a teacher told young Buffett to stand at his desk and address his fellow students. It went badly. So badly that whenever Buffett thought about public speaking, he gagged up stomach bile.

Throughout high school, throughout college, he could not contemplate giving a speech without getting physically sick.

To cope, Buffett avoided even the most minor oratorical moments. He cornered his professors and demanded to know whether he'd ever be asked to talk in class. If the professors said yes, he dropped the course.

Buffett was doing the opposite of a Special Operator. He was abandoning plans because of a past anxiety. Yet rather than spending the rest of his life running from stage fright, he decided after working for Graham to take a public-speaking course offered by another Ben Franklin disciple: Dale Carnegie. The course was peppered with Franklin's standard operating procedures, supplemented by Carnegie's own: *Anxiety before public speaking is normal. Calm your nerves by developing a prespeaking routine.*

These SOPs worked for Buffett. Eliminating his fears about public speaking, they made him an effective communicator, prompting him to realize that there was a smarter way to handle worries that sprang from a failed task: Instead of taking those worries as a cue to avoid the task at any cost, use them to develop an SOP for handling it next time.

Buffett valued this lesson so highly that he placed his Carnegie diploma—and not any of his university degrees—on the wall of his Berkshire Hathaway office. Every time he looked at that diploma, he recalled the commonsense technique: *Convert past anxiety into standard operating procedures.* And it guided him to a trillion-dollar SOP.

The SOP was: *Be greedy when the market is scared.* It extended Graham's investing rule—*focus on getting the cheapest price today*—with Buffett's discovery of the role that anxiety played in pricing. Pricing was the value ascribed to stocks by investors. Like Buffett, those investors had struggled with emotionally-jarring failures, yet unlike Buffett, most of them hadn't learned the commonsense technique of converting setbacks into standard operating procedures. When a temporary sell-off shook the economy, they suffered flashbacks to unprocessed angst about big financial crashes, triggering the same nausea that young Buffett had felt at public speaking. And so, in the grip of past anxiety, the market stampeded to unload stocks that the Oracle could gobble at cheap prices, turning worry into money.

AS A CASE STUDY IN *Future Anxiety: NEAR*, there's James Simons, the math PhD who ran history's most lucrative hedge fund.

In 1964, when Buffett was launching his takeover of Berkshire Hathaway, Simons was assisting the U.S. Army at the Institute for Defense Analysis. The institute had been born in April 1956 and baptized on October 4, 1957. That chill clear day, the Soviet Union catapulted Sputnik, the world's first satellite, into orbit. And as the bleeping metal capsule zipped over America—once, twice, ten times, a hundred—it caused the citizens below to panic.

The panic startled the U.S. government, which had grown certain of America's global supremacy. America had invented the atom bomb! America did half the world's manufacturing! And so in the years prior to Sputnik, the U.S. government had violated the first rule of commonsense: *Be anxious about the future.* Convinced that its mass-made nukes would deter foreign aggression, it had slashed investment in the Army's missile program— allowing the Soviets to win the race to space.

When the U.S. government's failure to worry was exposed by

Sputnik's abrupt appearance in the sky, the American public responded by overcorrecting. Staring deep into tomorrow, they imagined endless death weapons the Soviets might one day engineer. The resulting howl of consternation whipped the U.S. military-industrial complex into a frenzy. Congress proposed the development of one, no, two, no, five, no, *ten* new kinds of rockets. It called for the creation of nuclear-powered fighter jets. It funded a fleet of mechanical elephants to fight communism in Asian rainforests. It demanded the formation of a space program—and a plan to colonize Mars with robots. To prevent more Sputniks, anything and everything had to be done.

The problem was: The United States could not do anything and everything. Despite the nation's great wealth, it lacked the factories or the scientists to develop atomic airships while also conquering the solar system. Decisions had to be made. Should the U.S. government prioritize the elephants or the rockets? And if the rockets, should it opt for single-stage missiles to drop warheads on Moscow or multistage boosters to carry humans to the stars?

Those decisions fell to the Institute of Defense Analysis, which was tasked with picking the wisest national security investments. The institute could not lapse back into pre-Sputnik serenity—or peer too far into the years ahead, paralyzing itself with possibilities. It had to focus on the near future, the Now + 1, maximizing commonsense to react fast to the Cold War's emergent unknowns. And react fast the institute did. When the Soviet Union devised an intercontinental missile, the U.S. devised the Minuteman: an intercontinental missile that fired quicker. When the Soviet Union made a recon satellite, the U.S. made Transit: a recon satellite system that could map the planet. When the Soviet Union launched the first vehicle that landed on the lunar surface, the U.S. launched the first vehicle that landed—and took off again.

Simons spent three years at the institute's cryptology branch, where he absorbed its commonsense emphasis on near-future concerns—and applied it to financial speculation. In a shuttered brick room tucked behind Princeton University's engineering quad, Simons pondered: *How could Now +1 be leveraged into a method of investing?* And with three of his colleagues, he authored a classified brief, "Probabilistic Models for and Prediction of Stock Market Behavior," that related short-term stock performance to market volatility.

After Simons was fired from the institute for criticizing the Vietnam War, he chaired Stony Brook University's math department and then, in 1978, gave up tenure to try his investment method in action. At a Long Island strip mall, flanked by a blouse shop and a pizza parlor, he started a fund that became known as Renaissance Technologies.

Renaissance did well, and following the 1987 Wall Street crash, it did better than well, achieving a breakthrough. As chronicled by Gregory Zuckerman in *The Man Who Solved the Market*, the breakthrough was driven by James Ax, a Stony Brook professor who devised a correlational algorithm that uncannily forecast commodities prices, generating cash so fast that Simons stuffed it with every dollar he could muster.

In 1989, however, the algorithm began to falter. It leaked money, then bled, until it was down 30 percent. Simons got nervous. But the plunge didn't faze Ax. He was certain: His math was perfect. It had calculated the market's root logic, isolating timeless fundamentals. He told Simons: Keep pumping in currency; profits are guaranteed.

Simons didn't believe in perfect math—or in blindly trusting computers. Computers could be programmed to execute human insights, accelerating trades in stable conditions, but computers weren't capable of commonsense. They stuck to logic while the world turned, burning capital. So instead of embracing Ax's calm, Simons heeded his own anxiety. He unplugged the infallible algorithm, handing control to Berkeley professor Elwyn Berlekamp.

Berlekamp built a new computer model based on the short-term trading method that Simons had developed at the institute. This Now + 1 approach clarified the amount of near-future volatility in the market, allowing the model to exploit anomalies (i.e., exceptional information) spotted by Berlekamp. The results were extraordinary. In 1990, the model's first full year of operation, it generated gains of more than 50 percent.

Simons had made the right call in replacing Ax with Berlekamp. And thanks to his anxiety, Simons kept adapting intelligently. During the early 1990s, the anomalies spotted by Berlekamp were detected by rival investors, ironing out Renaissance's edge. Simons got nervous again, recruiting Henry Laufer and other mathematicians with fresh intuitions that propelled Renaissance to 60 percent annual returns, while Berlekamp, now at a competing fund, barely kept pace with the market.

What made Simons a wise investor was not logic; Berlekamp was the more gifted mathematician. Nor was it financial intuition; Berlekamp was better at detecting anomalies. It was that Simons had learned to train his gaze relentlessly on the Now + 1. This tuned his anxiety to detect volatility spikes—and react fast. As Simons expressed it to a dithering Berlekamp: "When you smell smoke, you get the *hell* out!"

Where Warren Buffett had mastered the rule summed up on the Operators' three-by-five card as *Past Anxiety: NONE*, Simons had mastered *Future Anxiety: NEAR*. The former helped Buffett grab existing fundamentals, making him the champion of long-term growth. The latter helped Simons spot emergent fundamentals, allowing him to surf the high-risk waters of opportunity.

To get the most from your own commonsense, rediscover what your ancestors knew: Anxiety is not a sign of something wrong with you. Tune it, and it can do for you what it did for Ben Franklin and the stock pickers: let you know when you don't know. That way, you don't get creative when dull and boring is smarter. You save intuition and imagination for the volatile times when you need them.

IN THIS CHAPTER AND THE three previous, we've covered four interconnected ways of thinking in story:

1. Intuition. This fuels story, like data does for logic.

2. Imagination. This is how story invents flexible tactics and long-term strategies.

3. Emotion. This creates a feedback loop between story and personal growth.

4. Commonsense. This indicates which story is best for what situation.

Each process has its own mental action. Intuition latches onto exceptional information, uncovering hidden rules that stimulate new *why*s and *what if*s. Imagination sharpens and extends those *why*s and *what if*s, enabling our brain to overcome problems and capitalize on opportunities. Emotion assesses our performance, signaling when we're struggling to process hard events—and identifying personal goals that give us direction. Commonsense assesses our environment, allowing us to accelerate confidently in familiar situations and adapt quickly to emergent threats and opportunities.

Put in terms of your story . . .

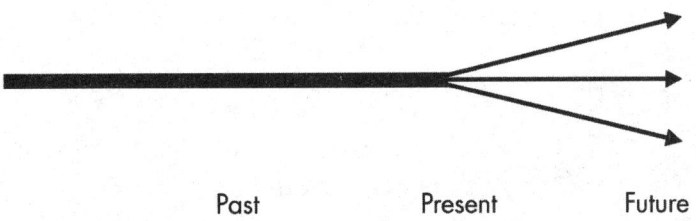

         Past   Present   Future

- Intuition initiates your story by revealing what's exceptional about you and the world. (See chapter 1.)

- Imagination grows your story by developing your exceptionalism into an integrated past and by developing the world's exceptions into a branching future. (See chapter 2.)

- Emotion maintains your story by revealing when your past is fragmenting or your future is narrowing. (See chapter 3.)

- Commonsense directs your story by revealing when you need to change course—and by helping you choose which future branch is best for your current situation. (For more on how to choose, see chapter 7.)

Your story generates your life plan, which generates all your other plans. Although those plans can seem to pop to mind like magic, they're thus made by intuition, imagination, emotion, and commonsense. As I put it in a report to U.S. Special Operations Command:

- Intuition sparks plans.

- Imagination shapes plans.

- Emotion sustains plans.

- Commonsense selects plans.

These four powers are our Primal Intelligence.

Why primal? Because this intelligence is neglected in modern schools but is part of our ancient nature. Because it requires biological hardware that computers lack, making it impossible for artificial intelligence. Because it helps us thrive in life's primordial murk and flux, allowing our brain to act smart in uncertain and changing times when data thins and logic breaks.

Most of us are good at one or two primal powers, but few of us are good at all four. Maybe we have quick intuitions but aren't so solid at commonsense. Maybe we understand our emotions but aren't effective at imagining strategies for transforming our future. Or perhaps it's the reverse. Perhaps we have sound commonsense but our intuition is less than visionary. Or perhaps we're a creative who struggles with shame, anxiety, or anger. (To determine your specific Primal strengths and areas for improvement, use the diagnostic quiz at the back of the book.)

Whatever our mental profile, the temptation is to dwell in the parts of Primal we know, skipping the parts we don't. That's why imaginative people go to museums and befriend musicians, while commonsense people diversify risk and value traditions. But life provides us the opportunity to do different. Primal's four powers are stronger together: Imagination makes commonsense nimble; commonsense makes emotion effective; emotion makes intuition purposeful; intuition makes imagination perceptive. That combined strength lives inside all of us, waiting to be awakened.

Once you go full Primal, you can incorporate your whole intelligence into everything you do. To get you started, part II will translate imagination, intuition, emotion, and commonsense into six practical applications: leadership, resilience, communication, coaching, decision-making, and first of all, innovation.

To be a doer, a builder, a leader,
against a sea of troubles.

—HENRY REED, AS TOLD BY MAYA ANGELOU

PART II

PRIMAL APPLICATION

5

INNOVATION

Welcome the Stranger Like Albert Einstein and Steve Jobs

Her job is to make tomorrow. For ten years, she plotted the arc of a Silicon Valley moonshot factory. Now she's building her own creative launchpad: a research startup that funds bold new plans to end poverty, disease, and violence. Yet it's hard, she says, to find such plans. She has combed New York, Cambridge, Tokyo—and even Mars. Everywhere, people claim to have big, fresh ideas. But those people are mostly just hackers or grinders.

Grinders live by the motto *Work harder*. Hackers prefer *Work smarter*. Grinders trust in the old-school ethic of grit and effort. Hackers swear by new-school productivity tricks like the 80/20 rule. Grinders believe there are no shortcuts. Hackers are sure that there's an angle, an edge, a faster way to get ahead. Grinders keep the system going. Hackers grift off it.

Tired of grinders and hackers, the tomorrow maker has

contacted me at my lab because she wants to bring back change's real source: innovation. *Innovation* is now a hackneyed buzzword, but when it entered the English language five hundred years ago, it was a synonym for sin. God had made the world perfect. To introduce the new was to do what Eve had done to paradise: ruin it.

In the sixteenth century, innovation's reputation was rehabilitated by original thinkers—Michelangelo, Andreas Vesalius, Francis Bacon—who created wonderworks. Those novel doings were rationalized at first as the rebirth of a golden classical age, but during the seventeenth and eighteenth centuries, people accepted: The new really *was* new. It toppled medieval philosophy with the experiments of the Scientific Revolution. It disrupted feudal economies with merchant entrepreneurs. It scrapped royal oligarchies, minting democracies.

This astonishing creativity was continued in the nineteenth century by the Industrial Revolution and in the twentieth century by the computer revolution. Yet as the years rolled on, innovation took on the less imaginative features of these two latter-day revolutions. It became—like automated factories and artificial intelligence—increasingly rote and shallow. Mass-produced gadgets and "disruptive" apps were celebrated as innovations, even when they were just incremental tweaks or ways of stealing other people's business.

This loss of imagination can be seen in how innovation is taught today at business schools. The teaching is based in ideation, a process for generating new ideas via random association. It's described in Adam Grant's *Originals* as "kiss more frogs to find your prince." It's what happened to Pixar and Apple after Steve Jobs. And it's the mechanism of generative AI.

Generative AI speeds up ideation by programming computers to do divergent thinking, brute forcing brainstorming. The upshot is prolific pseudocreativity: In seconds, AI can spam out more "art" than all the painters of the sixteenth century. Yet because ideation works by arbitrarily combining old stuff, the result is the opposite of innovation. Innovation isn't random; it's purposeful. Which is why it's transformative, remaking life.

In our age of robots kissing frogs, such purposeful transformation can seem a lost cause. But we can recover it through intuition. (See chapter 1.) Intuition can't be programmed into computers, yet it can be consciously engaged by our brain, allowing us to do like Vincent van Gogh, Marie Curie, and Steve Wozniak: spot exceptions that drive original art, science, and technology.

When I explain intuition to the tomorrow maker, she's intrigued. But she wants to go further. She asks: Can we amplify the potential of exceptional information? Can we turn it into breakthroughs—smarter, quicker, bigger?

Yes. We can. Special Operators have trained their brains to do just that. In combat, no plan survives contact with the enemy, forcing Operators to innovate at the pace of life and death. They do so via three methods:

1. Turn an exception into a new rule.

2. Leverage conflict.

3. Eat your enemy.

These methods use imagination to accelerate intuition. And they don't just work for Special Operators. They can fast-track revolutions in science, business, art, tech, and education. Let's run through how.

THE FIRST METHOD FOR ACCELERATING intuition into innovation is *Turn an exception into a new rule*. To accomplish this, Operators imagine *what if* an anomaly became the norm.

An anomaly becoming the norm isn't probable. But it's possible. It can happen—and it *has* happened, countless times. An example from economics is paper money. An example from agriculture is Mesoamerican corn. An example from music is the Moog electronic synthesizer. An example from science is relativity.

Relativity was developed during the first two decades of the twentieth century by Albert Einstein. Einstein is widely credited with having ushered in a computational approach to science, but Einstein himself denied this, insisting in his 1925 Argentina lectures on relativity that physics "was not a system in which individual laws can be derived via logical deduction." Instead, he said that "to go from empirical facts to a fundamental law of physics, it requires a free creative act."

To explain what he meant by a free creative act, Einstein listed six examples in his 1933 speech at London's Royal Albert Hall:

1. Joseph Lister, who innovated medicine with new laws of sterilization.

2. Louis Pasteur, who innovated biology with new laws of immunology.

3. Michael Faraday, who innovated chemistry with new laws of electromagnetism.

4. Isaac Newton, who innovated physics with new laws of motion.

5. Johann Wolfgang von Goethe, the eighteenth-century German scientist and playwright.

6. Shakespeare.

The last name—Shakespeare—is the same creative whom Steve Jobs listed, alongside Einstein, as one of his two major inspirations. (See chapter 1.) But what do scientific and technological innovators like Einstein and Steve Jobs have to do with Shakespeare?

You can find the answer in Shakespeare's *Hamlet*, which opens with a scholar seeing a ghost and declaring: "This is wondrous strange!" To which Hamlet responds: "Therefore as a stranger give it welcome." Which is to say: *If something is weird, embrace it.* Or in other words: When you see an exception, double down, turning the anomaly into a new rule.

This is what Einstein did. In school, he was taught that an object's speed was linked to its point of origin: If a bullet was shot south at five hundred miles per hour from a plane flying north at five hundred miles per hour, the bullet's speed would be zero. But Einstein saw: There was an exception to this rule. The exception was light. Light always flew at a constant velocity, regardless of its point of origin. Whether it was emitted from a stationary lamp, a plane flying north, or a star blazing at five hundred million miles per hour, the light moved at the same speed.

Einstein wasn't the first to notice this exception, but he was the first to double down. He began his double down by noting that what was exceptional about light was that it ran on local time. Local time is what it sounds like: In local time, clocks do not all go at the same speed, governed by a universal time standard, but proceed at different tempos, determined by regional conditions. This explains why a clock traveling past on a light wave will ticktock slower to our eyes than a clock sitting beside us: The clock on the light wave is inside its own time zone.

Local time had previously been invoked by physicists to calculate "true" time, but no one had ever proposed that *all* time was local. Einstein did. In 1905, he took the exception of light and turned it into a new rule: *Everything, everywhere, runs on local time.* This new rule became the law of relativity, transforming the world. Previously, gravity acted instantly at a distance. Now gravity bends space-time. Previously, the universe sat still. Now it is expanding. Previously, time had always existed. Now it has a creator: the Big Bang.

The same method employed by Einstein can be used to innovate any field. For an example from business, let's dig deeper into the method of Steve Jobs.

JOBS LED A CONTINUAL REVOLUTION in personal electronics for thirty-five years, from 1976 until his death in 2011. Seeing the potential of the computer mouse, digital animation, and the smartphone, he helped launch the Apple Macintosh, Pixar's *Toy Story*, and the iPhone, inspiring millions to follow his vision for the future: *Think Different.*

How did Jobs innovate, not once but continually? To find out, I schedule a visit to engineering teams at Apple. I arrive at their sunny offices in Cupertino, California, almost exactly a decade after Jobs's death. I ask the teams if they can share Jobs's secret to innovation. In response, they laugh. They tell me that Apple has lost the secret. If I want to find it, I should go read a biography of Jobs. The most useful one, they tell me, is by Walter Isaacson.

Leaving Cupertino, I immerse myself in Isaacson's biography. It's rich with extraordinary anecdotes. But its central thesis is the opposite of what I expect. According to Isaacson, Jobs was not himself exceptional. He was a tweaker who made minor mods to other people's great ideas. There was nothing profoundly inventive about him.

I return to Apple, perplexed. Is it true that Jobs wasn't an innovator?

The engineers shake their heads. No, Jobs really *was* an innovator. His uniqueness is evident across the stories that Isaacson collected. But somehow, Isaacson failed to spot the exception in the pages that he himself was writing.

What went wrong? What did Isaacson miss that Jobs saw?

The solution to the mystery is the same thinker who anchors Einstein's list of innovators: Shakespeare. Shakespeare pops up early in Isaacson's biography, during one of its remarkable stories. The story begins when Isaacson asks Jobs to explain how he transformed from a conventional suburban kid to a driver of change. Jobs responds by crediting his teenage encounter with Shakespeare's *King Lear*. Isaacson, naturally, is curious: "I asked [Jobs] why he related to King Lear . . . but he didn't respond to the connection I was making, so I let it drop."

Let's not let it drop. Let's pick it up, returning to *King Lear* and exploring why Jobs connected differently to Shakespeare than Isaacson did.

By asking Jobs why he "related" to King Lear, Isaacson reveals that he himself reads Shakespeare as a source of relatable characters, people with whom we have something in common. This way of reading Shakespeare isn't unusual. It's how we're taught to read literature in school. School approaches literature through logic, and logic has a specific tool for analyzing literature: interpretation.

Interpretation treats literature as a set of symbols, or in other words, representations. This is because logic thinks in equations, which is another way of saying identities; and also because logic thinks in abstractions, which is another way of saying commonalities. If you put identities and commonalities together, you get universal characters: the hero, the villain, the joker, the helper, the innovator. That's why Isaacson labels King Lear as an archetype of the willful striver—then asks Jobs how he relates to that archetype.

When we encounter *King Lear* outside the classroom, we read it differently. Instead of analyzing it for conventional personality types, we're struck by its wild originality. As another of Jobs's heroes, Vincent van Gogh, put it: "My God, the beauty of Shakespeare! But of course, reading Shakespeare can make you shocking to others, and without wishing harm, offend society with your unconventionality."

Unconventionality is the way of Lear. He is not like any king—or any anyone—we've seen before. The same goes for the play's other characters: They're individual, surprising, unprecedented. And as the play proceeds, those characters commit, ever more intensely, to their peculiarities. Until they crack the world around them, bending reality and revealing the innovative power of the exceptional.

This is logic's opposite. It is leaning into singularity instead of leaning into commonality. It is doubling down on what is unique, not reverting to what is universal.

Like van Gogh, Jobs encountered Shakespeare outside the classroom. He read him not for a high school test but out of personal curiosity, so rather than identifying with Lear, he had his child's eye opened. When Jobs saw with that eye, the result was what his Apple colleagues referred to as a "reality-distortion field." In the field, the old rules of life were suspended while Jobs pushed forward an exception—until it became the new rule.

There are dozens of stories about how Jobs did this. Here's one I hear from the Cupertino engineers. In 2005, Jobs partnered with Motorola on the ROKR, a candy-bar phone that could download one hundred iTunes songs. The ROKR was a disaster. Barely any sold, and the few that did delivered underwhelming performance: An outdated handset that played a tiny music catalog through a tinny earpiece. The sales data said: Abandon the project. Jobs did the opposite: He doubled down on what was original about the ROKR. While his competitors smirked at the notion of a jukebox mobile, Jobs drove Apple to create the iPhone.

What Isaacson saw as Jobs being a "tweaker" was really Jobs identifying the exceptional potential of specific gadgets. In them, he perceived the same singularity that he had seen in *King Lear*. And just as Shakespeare relentlessly intensified Lear's individuality, so did Jobs make each gadget more itself, eschewing generic compromise to magnify exceptionality.

THE SECOND METHOD THAT OPERATORS use to accelerate innovation is *Leverage conflict.*

Conflict instantly emerges in your brain when your intuition latches onto an exception, because an exception is by nature in conflict with a rule. Such conflict has no place in logic. Logic is harmony, synchronicity, and unity, making conflict a sign of error and dysfunction. A bug has glitched the algorithm, or bad data has corrupted a computation. One side of the argument is ignorant or acting in bad faith.

Logic's predominance in our modern schools and businesses has left us emotionally uncomfortable with conflict and has not equipped us with a method for benefiting from it. Most of us therefore respond to conflict by attempting to eliminate it as quickly as possible. When we hit an exception, we try to choose between it and the rule. Or we seek a rational compromise that gives us a bit of both.

Those rapid resolutions deprive our brain of opportunities for growth. So instead of seeking a quick path out of mental tension, do like an Operator: Embrace the tension, pushing your imagination to make a new rule that maintains the old rule's underlying rationale while including the possibility opened by the exception. In other words: Try to invent a new rule that joins the old rule's *why* with the exception's *what if*.

This method taps into imagination's core mechanism: story. Story is powered by conflicts between characters and their world, which is to say, between exceptions and rules, which is to say, between individual *what if*s and global *why*s. By leaning into the tension between a rule and an exception, you engage your brain's powers of storythinking, accelerating the development of new rules of action.

Here's an example. In the early 1900s, a young woman (let's call her Delilah) was living in a small Midwestern farming community. That community encouraged its young men and women to get married at the age of eighteen. But Delilah did not want to get married. She preferred to be on her own, in the fields with the animals. She felt keenly that she was the exception to the community rule. And she saw that she had two logical options. One: She could run away, making her community unhappy. Two: She could submit to the rule, making herself unhappy.

Delilah didn't want to choose. Or compromise. So instead, she leaned into the tension. As she did, she had an epiphany: The community had created the rule to transition teenagers into caring for other people. The community understood that teens needed time to focus on their personal needs and wants, developing independence, but the community did not want teens to become shallowly self-absorbed. After giving teens five years to explore their individual inclinations, the community therefore imposed marriage at the age of eighteen. Marriage led to parenting, which led to the next phase of growth: developing the capacity to put the needs and wants of other people first.

Understanding that this was the *why* beneath the rule of marriage, Delilah went to her parents and proposed an original way of satisfying the community's desire for her to put others first. She would journey to the city of Ames, in central Iowa, where she would study veterinary science. She would then return to her farming community and become its veterinarian. That would satisfy the rule's *why* (putting the community first) and also her exceptional *what if* (living on her own, in the fields with the animals).

By simultaneously fulfilling both the old rule and the exception, Delilah led the way to a new rule: When young people turned eighteen, they would make a plan for how to give back to their community. That plan could be marriage—but it could also be college or anything else that put others first.

Delilah was the great-grandmother of a soldier I met in U.S. Special Operations. Special Operations is full of stories about how to generate innovation from the conflict between the *why* of a conventional rule and the *what if* of an exception. Here's another example.

Back at the beginning of Army Special Operations, it established a training curriculum with a final test: an obstacle course of logs and ropes. At the end of the course was a bell. The instructions to the recruits were simple: *Ring the bell before time expires, and you pass.*

One day, a recruit arrived at the course—and realized that he wasn't going to beat the clock. He simply wasn't fast enough. Logically, he had two options: He could quit or he could run the course and fail. He didn't like either choice. So as he stepped toward the starting line, he leaned into the tension in his mind, pushing the course's *why* against his own *what if.* And suddenly, he saw a new path. When the clock started, he ran *around* the obstacle course. Skipping its barricades, he rang the bell in record time.

The initial response from Army Special Operations was shocked incredulity. But the recruit reminded the Army that the goal of the course was to ring the bell before time expired. He'd figured out how to do that. He should pass.

At any other military school, the recruit would have been disciplined for insubordination. But not at this school. The Army passed the recruit. And as the Army monitored his career after graduation, it saw that he outperformed many of his classmates in field missions. His ability to *avoid* obstacles made him a better Operator. His success was the exception to the old rule that the best way to prepare recruits for real operations was with obstacle courses. So now Army Special Operations faced a conflict of its own. Should it go with the exception and eliminate obstacle courses? Or should it forget the exception and stick with the existing curriculum?

You can guess what the Army did: It rejected both options, refusing to choose or compromise. Instead, it leaned into the tension between the old rule and the exception, coining a new rule. Can you imagine the Army's innovation? Can you invent a new rule that satisfies both the obstacle course's *why* and the exceptional recruit's *what if*?

Here's what the Army did. It realized that the rationale behind the obstacle course was to determine whether recruits could navigate challenges to reach an objective. And it realized that the exceptional recruit had shown that, in the real world, there's more than one path to a goal. So the Army came up with a new test: Recruits were handed a map with a target destination marked in red. The recruits could get to the destination however they chose, so long as they arrived in time. Some recruits went straight, over every obstacle, running at full speed, day and night. Some recruits built rafts and let rivers carry them. Some recruits trekked in the opposite direction to small towns, where they traded in their rations for vehicle rentals.

The Army's new test satisfied both the old rule's *why* and the exception's *what if*. By doing so, it innovated military training, inspiring the creation of a curriculum where recruits prepared for real operations by figuring out their own way around obstacles.

With this technique, you can do like Delilah and the Operators did, innovating your community or your organization. You can even innovate the entire world, like Charles Darwin.

CHARLES DARWIN'S INNOVATION CAME IN 1859 when he proposed the theory of evolution by natural selection. The theory's modest origin was a bird-watching excursion on a small island chain. Its massive effect was to transform science, economics, and philosophy. The theory challenged the view that progress was powered by logical design, unveiling a world where evolution instead came from biological conflict. Raising questions about old rules of morality, power, and meaning, it sparked the invention of new art, new politics, new paths to purpose.

Darwin's innovation has become so core to modern science that it has the feel of unavoidable reality. It was, we're taught in high school textbooks, based upon rigorous scientific data—which is why natural selection was simultaneously discovered by Alfred Russel Wallace, a naturalist who examined one hundred thousand insect specimens in Malaysia during the 1850s.

But Darwin's innovation was not inevitable. Its supporting evidence was so quirkily eccentric that Darwin hesitated for decades to make it public, fearing pushback. His concern turned out to be well-founded; after he finally did publish, his theory was "disproven" in the 1870s by the eminent mathematician Lord Kelvin, and by the late nineteenth century, it was viewed as untenable by most scientists. Although Darwin went to his grave believing in natural selection, he was forsaken by even Alfred Russel Wallace, who declared in his 1889 book *Darwinism*: "Man's body may have been developed from that of a lower animal form under the law of natural selection; but . . . we possess intellectual and moral faculties which could not have been so developed, but must have had another origin."

What prompted Darwin to imagine differently? It started with the same story source that inspired Einstein and Jobs: Shakespeare. Darwin recalled that when he was a schoolboy, he "used to sit for hours reading the historical plays of Shakespeare, generally in an old window in the thick walls of the school." So it was that Darwin came to value his ability to do like Hamlet and spot exceptional information: "I think that I am superior to the common run of men in noticing things which easily escape attention, and in observing them carefully."

This ability led Darwin to observe many exceptions, one of which was Thomas Malthus. Malthus was an eighteenth-century priest and amateur economist. In 1798, he demonstrated that biological populations inevitably over-reproduce, exceeding their food sources. Or to put it bluntly: Parents have too many children, dooming some to starve.

Malthus's demonstration conflicted sharply with the accepted rule of eighteenth-century science. The rule was that nature was logically harmonious, making it inconceivable that life would impose suffering on innocent children. Guided by this rule, most of Darwin's contemporaries (from Anglicans like the archbishop of Canterbury to communists like Karl Marx) rejected Malthus, discarding the exception that he had surfaced.

Darwin did different. He didn't choose between the rule and the exception. Instead, he placed the rule and the exception in tension—a tension that produced a new rule.

It happened like this. From December 1831 to October 1836, Darwin sailed around the world on the HMS *Beagle*. On the trip, Darwin brought his Shakespeare. And as he voyaged past South America, he was struck by the incredible variety of a group of island birds, the Galápagos finches. Those finches came in many species, each with a unique beak that was exquisitely suited to its environment. The finches that lived in nut-rich trees had wide, blunt beaks for cracking nuts. The finches that lived in grub-rich trees had long, sharp beaks for spearing grubs. This neatly confirmed the rule that nature was harmoniously ordered.

But two years later, in 1838, Darwin encountered Malthus. And he realized that Malthus had correctly observed an exception to the rule. The exception was: *Nature wasn't harmoniously ordered in its production of children.* Galápagos finches (like all earthly species) had too many children. There was not enough food—whether nuts or grubs—to support every egg they laid.

How could this be? How could the finches have beaks that were so harmoniously suited to their environment yet have breeding behaviors that doomed their offspring to fight cruelly, desperately, and inharmoniously over who got enough food to survive?

Having raised this conflict between an exception and a rule, Darwin leaned into the tension between *why* and *what if.* Darwin reminded himself of *why* the old rule of natural harmony existed: The beaks of Galápagos finches were perfectly suited for their specific environments. Then he asked himself: *What if* nature drives the Galápagos finches to blindly generate children? Until finally, Darwin struck upon a new rule.

The rule was: *Every child differs from its siblings.* Which is to say: *We are all born with our own unique characteristics.* In the case of the Galápagos finches, some hatchlings have longer beaks and some have blunter. The former do better in grub-rich trees, while the latter do better in nut-rich trees. Over time, young finches with these characteristics outcompete their siblings in the battle for food, surviving to become parents themselves. What seems like nature's cruelty is thus the reason that life is so harmoniously adapted to Earth's varied niches, joining the old *why* of natural order with the new *what if* of too many children.

Darwin named his rule the "Divergence of Character." It's hard to think of a rule that's more Shakespearean. Just as the history plays that Darwin read on the HMS *Beagle* dismantled the old archetypes of theater, replacing a universal *king* with individuals such as Richard II and Henry V, so did Darwin's natural history dismantle the old theory of timeless biological characters. Each of us had a unique role to play upon the world's evolving stage. Each of us lived our own story. (See chapter 2.)

Although Darwin's rule was doubted for decades, it gained traction when twentieth-century discoveries in genetics yielded the modern evolutionary synthesis. According to that synthesis, evolution is driven by mutant individuals that double down on their exceptional genes until they become a breakthrough species. Innovating life.

THE THIRD METHOD THAT OPERATORS use to accelerate innovation is *Eat your enemy*.

"Eating your enemy is an ancient war ritual," an Operator explains as she escorts me through an open-air workout shed where ponytailed women are dragging half-ton sleds. "My Celtic ancestors did it in the age of Stonehenge. They believed that by consuming their enemy's body, they absorbed his spirit, gaining his power for themselves."

At the back of the shed is a primitive kitchen stocked with jars of white powder. I peer apprehensively at the jars, wondering which of the Operator's enemies they contain.

"We do it metaphorically now, of course," the Operator continues, dumping a scoop of powder into a steel shaker, followed by a splash of iced beetroot juice. "We consume the best aspects of our enemy's thinking—his plans, his methods, his worldview—making them part of our own behavior."

As an example, she tells me about her middle-school enemy: a sweet-faced bully who led a pack of mean girls. "She'd pounce on me to take my lunch. Not to eat it, just to smash it in the dirt. One day, she tore off a necklace my grandma gave me and threw it down a storm drain. I tried everything to avoid her. But she always found me. Until one day, I figured it out: Without her pack of girls, she was no stronger than me. Her power was recruiting others to her cause.

"So I took her power and made it part of my life. I rounded up a bunch of loners, kids like me who generally kept to themselves, doing their own thing. We walked the halls together, in a pack. The bully never touched me again."

The Operator swallows her beetroot concoction. "We call it *eating* because you incorporate your enemy's power into you, like you digest food into your body, so you grow your own strength instead of turning into what you hate. I didn't become a mean girl. I stayed weird. And in fact, I became more myself, because with my pack, I could be as weird as I liked without being scared."

To do like the Operator and eat your enemy, you must exit computer-think. Computer-think teaches that your enemy is your opposite, but this hides your enemy's true nature. Your enemy isn't you in reverse. Your enemy is an individual, because we're *all* individuals. Opposites exist only in the abstract realm of logic. In the real world, everything is asymmetrically distinct. Night is not the contrary of day. It's a unique world, with its own idiosyncratic species, like sonar-eared bats and big-pupiled bush rats.

So forget black-and-white and employ your eye for the exceptional to identify what's *special* about your enemy. Be curious, not judgmental. Focus on how your enemy surprises you, not how he reminds you of other rivals. Ask What—delaying Why. (See chapter 1.)

Once you've identified your adversary's exceptional character, put it in tension with what's exceptional about your own organization. Then hold those two exceptions close together in your mind. Remember *why* your organization works the way it does while imagining *what if* it ran like your competitor. Push on the tension to generate new strategies, products, or services that you can use to outcompete your adversary.

A classic example of *Eat your enemy* is Japanese industry after its defeat by America in World War II:

1. Japanese industry identified America's exceptional feature as a democratic individualism that nurtured innovation. And it identified its own exceptional feature as a neo-Bushido culture of rectitude, politeness, and honor.

2. Japanese industry wondered *what if* it could get more individual initiative out of its workers, powering innovation. And it remembered *why* it had its Bushido culture: to produce high-quality products with a low defect rate.

3. Combining this *what if* and *why*, Japanese industry built factory assembly lines that fused flexible decentralization (encouraging individual initiative) with rigorous integrity (promoting high quality), producing the innovative but reliable vehicles that stormed the U.S. market in the 1970s.

An even more classic example of *Eat your enemy* is the Lord Chamberlain's Men, a London theater group founded in 1594. One of the group's members was a young playwright named William Shakespeare who had achieved minor popularity in the early 1590s for writing *The Comedy of Errors*, *Titus Andronicus*, and *Henry VI*. Meanwhile, the group's main enemy was a crosstown theater company, the Admiral's Men, which was achieving outrageous success thanks to the equally young playwright Christopher Marlowe.

1. The Lord Chamberlain's Men identified the exceptional feature of Marlowe's rival plays as larger-than-life antiheroes—Tamburlaine, Doctor Faustus, and the Jew of Malta—who dominated the action, overshadowing every scene. And the Lord Chamberlain's Men identified the exceptional feature of their own Shakespearean plays as sprawling troupes of quirky characters.

2. The Lord Chamberlain's Men wondered *what if* they gave audiences a magnetically charismatic but deeply flawed character who ruled the stage like Marlowe's antiheroes. And they remembered *why* audiences liked Shakespeare's ensemble approach: Its riotously diverse psychologies generated a sensation of spontaneous life.

3. Combining this *what if* and *why*, the Lord Chamberlain's Men produced Shakespeare's *Richard III*, a play that pitted a beguiling tyrant against a variegated crowd. The audience response was so enthusiastic that the Lord Chamberlain's Men asked Shakespeare to write more plays that placed domineering personalities in tension with vibrant casts, leading to breakthrough scripts like *Henry V* and *Hamlet*.

The more you consume the intelligence of your rivals, the more you accelerate your own innovation. And even if you have no rivals—whether because you've eaten them all or because you prefer collaboration to competition—you can still employ this method. Just add a twist: Do it internally, within your team, like Carl von Clausewitz.

CLAUSEWITZ IS BROUGHT TO MY attention by a Special Ops officer who works at a classified site adjacent to the Pentagon, on the tidal waters of the Potomac. The officer has just ushered me through a digital lock into a gloomy technology vault filled with experimental gadgets for covert missions. The gadgets fascinate me. But most fascinating is the computer.

The computer is a military artificial intelligence. It has memorized the strategies of the world's greatest generals, living and dead. It can make a billion decisions a second. It has the optimal solution for World War III.

"It's superintelligent, no question." The officer nods. "But our teams beat it."

I'm impressed. "Your teams have beaten the computer?"

The officer clarifies. "Our teams always beat it. They beat it every time."

I'm now astonished. The AI gets beaten—*every time*—by human teams?

"The more they war-game against it," the officer continues, "the bigger their victories. We thought the AI would improve by playing humans. But the reverse happened. The humans keep evolving, while the computer gets more predictable."

"Do you have a theory about what the computer is doing wrong?"

The officer smiles. "The computer's not doing anything wrong. Our teams are just doing something it can't."

"What's that?"

"Taking the initiative. The computer can only recycle old

plans. It creates the illusion of newness by randomly blending past tactics. But it's all derivative. There's no deep innovation, no real surprises. The more you play it, the better you get at anticipating it."

"And the human war-gamers come up with genuinely new strategies that can't be anticipated?"

"Yes. But that's not the really interesting thing. The really interesting thing is that the computer can beat individual humans, but it can *never* beat our human teams."

I don't get why this is so interesting. "Wouldn't you expect teams to be smarter than individuals?"

"No," the officer says. "In war games, individuals usually outcompete teams. Teams are inefficient and divided. They squabble and disagree while the enemy is acting rapidly and purposefully. That's why military organizations are hierarchies run top down by single commanders. If you've got two leaders issuing orders, you're not just fighting the enemy. You're fighting yourself."

"But your teams are different?"

"That's right. Our teams can think individually, together. They can combine their unique perspectives into one coordinated intelligence that allows them to invent original rules of strategy. Those rules fundamentally shift what you can do on the battlefield, outdating history."

This is why the Special Ops teams always beat the computer at war-gaming. The computer can master the rules, but the teams can pool their intelligence to rewrite the rule book. While the computer is optimizing combat, the teams are innovating it.

"How?" I want to know. "How do your teams make new rules that change the game? What's the secret to how they innovate?"

"The secret is: Our teams read Clausewitz."

CLAUSEWITZ WAS A PRUSSIAN ARMY officer born in 1780 amid the fieldstone towers of central Prussia. He is beloved by Special Operators, who urge me to study "his big book." But I resist. I find Clausewitz disquieting. He fought for a militocracy that wore the skull-and-crossbones *Totenkopf* made infamous by Adolf Hitler's paramilitary Schutzstaffel, aka the Nazi SS.

But finally I sit down to read Clausewitz's big book. When I do, I find to my surprise that it preaches the power of individual creativity. And even more to my surprise, I discover: Like Einstein, Steve Jobs, and Darwin, Clausewitz read Shakespeare.

Shakespeare came to Clausewitz through the German Romantics Johann Wolfgang von Goethe and Alexander von Humboldt. Those Romantics prompted Clausewitz to read their own deep influence: *Hamlet*. The play was available to Clausewitz in a popular German translation, but he wanted to imbibe the original, so he purchased an English copy of Shakespeare's *Dramatic Works*, printed in 1824 in London, which he kept in his personal library. Inspired by Shakespeare and his Romantic acolytes, Clausewitz then arrived at a new theory of war.

The old theory was that battles were won by mathematics, data-driven decisions, and other logical operations. This had been established by the potent arguments of eighteenth-century Enlightenment philosophy—and also by a less theoretical proof: Napoléon Bonaparte. Born in 1769, Napoléon was a French artillery officer with a Corsican accent, a provincial haircut, and an astonishing aptitude for military strategy. In combat after combat, he out-calculated his opponents, until he gained the reputation for having reduced war to a science of infallible laws.

Napoléon's science of war was directly impressed upon

Clausewitz on October 14, 1806. The occasion was the Battle of Jena-Auerstedt, where Napoléon seized control of Prussia and took twenty-five thousand prisoners, among them twenty-six-year-old Clausewitz. Clausewitz spent the next ten months as a captive in France, after which he returned to Prussia to rebuild its armed forces—and strike back against Napoléon. Initially, this seemed a futile gesture. Yet at last the tide turned, and in 1815, Napoléon was defeated by the Prussians and their allies at Waterloo.

These events led Enlightenment military theorists to infer that the Prussians had beaten Napoléon at his universal science, outreasoning the master. Clausewitz disagreed. Following Shakespeare and the Romantics, he had come to value individual psychologies. Those psychologies had been ironed out of Napoleonic armies, which relentlessly drilled soldiers to follow orders. Yet no matter how automated armies got, they retained one independent thinker: the commander. The commander was responsible for the Army's plan, and no two commanders planned identically. They perceived different opportunities in the same battlefield. They glimpsed alternative paths to victory.

To logic, this suggested that one—or both—of the commanders must be wrong. But Clausewitz perceived otherwise. He saw that the best plans were not logical, because logical plans were predictable. Instead, the best plans were original. They seized the initiative, generating surprise.

During the 1820s, as Clausewitz sat with his copy of *Hamlet*, recording his views about original plans in leatherbound notebooks, he experienced a flash of inspiration: *What if I could do more than argue on paper for the practical value of original planning? What if I could test my hypothesis by creating an organization that actually invented more original plans?*

To run this test, Clausewitz plotted an experiment at the

Prussian War Academy. The academy was a logic-based institution that trained military staffs to act as bureaucracies that executed commanders' rational decisions. Clausewitz changed that, installing a curriculum that encouraged staff officers to use each other's exceptional characteristics to drive innovation. Here's a sample exercise:

1. Split into two teams. Have each team independently make a plan for the future.

2. Bring the teams together to share their plans. Don't rank the plans or choose between them. Instead, *trade* them. Have each team identify what is exceptional about the other's plan—and double down on it, producing innovation.

3. Bring the teams back together again. Again, don't choose between them. Instead take their two innovations and place them in tension—until the tension produces a final plan that combines the advantages of both.

In short, have each team swallow the other. Then have the organization swallow both.

This pioneering approach to military thinking concerned traditionalists who venerated Napoléon, but its effectiveness was put to a real-world test by Clausewitz's student Helmuth von Moltke. Moltke studied for three years under Clausewitz, from 1823 to 1826. After Clausewitz's untimely death from cholera in 1830, Moltke ascended to become chief of staff of the Prussian army. Using Clausewitz's method, he constructed his staff as a team of many minds who ate each other's plans, improving their collective imagination.

This hive mind was unleashed in 1866 against the rival Austrian Empire and then in 1870 against the intrusions of Napoléon III. Moltke's staff won both wars with astonishing speed. So total were these victories—and so mythical was Moltke's ensuing reputation—that for the next two decades, no European nation dared to provoke Moltke's hive mind. When Moltke retired from running the army at the age of eighty-eight, he had presided over seventeen years of peace. Clausewitz's rogue experiment had worked.

After Clausewitz's death, his notebooks were edited by his widow, Marie von Brühl, to produce his big book, known now as *On War*. For most of the nineteenth and early twentieth centuries, *On War* was regarded as an obscure if interesting curiosity. But over the past seventy-five years it has become, I am told, "the bible" of U.S. Special Operations.

The bible of U.S. Special Operations? This strikes me as highly irregular: Clausewitz's students didn't just fight Napoléon III. They also ascended to lead the Imperial German Army. And during the twentieth century, that army battled in two cataclysmic world wars—against the U.S. military. Clausewitz's book trained the fighting force that killed thousands of American soldiers.

"Clausewitz is our enemy," agree the Operators. "So we ate him."

"You ate Clausewitz?"

"Yeah. That ain't hacking. And it ain't grinding. It's going outside our system to incorporate violently different thinking."

Which is why it makes the future smarter, quicker, bigger.

6

RESILIENCE

Build Antifragility Like the Clinic Patient and the Third Grader

The patient was a medical miracle.

A few months earlier, he'd checked into a lakeside clinic in the southern United States. Joining him were a dozen other patients, all suffering the same symptom: a lost sense of purpose. They felt no direction in life, no inner compass, no reason to get up in the morning. One said: "My life is like a boring dream. None of it feels true—or much of interest. I used to pray for change. But now, I don't really care."

Before coming to the clinic, the patients had tried mindfulness, meditation, and positive thinking, all to no avail. Now the patients were here to attempt something else: journaling. Grabbing ballpoint pens and spiral-bound notebooks, they sat at pinewood tables from early morning to late afternoon. They wrote down their thoughts. They wrote down their memories. They wrote down anything that sprang to mind.

The patients were skeptical that the journaling would work. And it didn't. The patients remained numbly apathetic. Except that one patient. In his journal, he wrote a story. And the story produced a major change, reigniting the patient's sense of purpose. He made a plan to start a business. He rediscovered his love for his girlfriend. He felt joy at the sight of his children.

The clinic staff were thrilled. Sensing a larger breakthrough, they distributed the patient's story to other patients. And . . . it had no effect. So the staff studied the story closely. And saw nothing special about it. Which is when they called me, hoping that I could crack the mystery.

THE PATIENT'S STORY INSTANTLY INTRIGUES me. And I get even more intrigued when I find that it's connected to another mystery: antifragility.

Antifragility first crosses my radar when a Special Operator tells me: "I don't have any post-traumatic stress." He says this like it's normal. But it's highly atypical. Most Operators experience post-traumatic stress (PTS), many powerfully. There's the Operator who listens compulsively to an audio recording of his teammates burning alive on a mission gone bad. And the Operator who has a psychotic break in a maternity ward, later explaining: "The Army needs to tell soldiers before they come home that your newborn baby smells the same as the inside of a human body." And the Operator who walks into his office, kisses a picture of his four daughters, draws his pistol, and stands at attention before the flag while executing himself.

The Operator without PTS has undergone abnormally high levels of combat stress. He has spent more than a decade at war.

He has been ambushed by suicide bombers and blanketed with live grenades. He has walked into machine guns at point-blank range. He has seen friends die. Yet he experiences no flashbacks. He doesn't get anxious when he's stuck in traffic or on a busy city block, imagining where snipers might be hiding. He doesn't wake up, drenched in sweat, from nightmares. He doesn't drink hard or medicate with ketamine, psychedelics, or antidepressants. "People act like I'm a miracle. Or missing part of my brain. But the docs tell me the important stuff's all there."

He's relaxed and even jovial when talking about his war experiences. He has no anger toward his enemy, only respect. He doesn't get tight at the thought of going back to combat. He's as mentally healthy as when he first deployed. In fact, he's *healthier*. He has gained perspective, grown in confidence, and deepened his sense of life purpose.

This is antifragility. It is the power of hearts that get tougher from heartbreak, loving harder with experience. It is the power of minds that get wiser from wrong turns, fortifying themselves with lessons learned. And above all, it is the power of children, who spend their days running and falling yet spring back, each morning, to run on again.

Antifragility can seem impossible. Yet we all have it within. The only reason antifragility appears unreal is that most of us lose touch with it over time. As we age, our resilience brittles. We stop being hungry for hard things. We suffer impacts from which we don't recover.

Could it go differently? Could we all be like this Operator? Could we retain the mental elasticity we had at birth? Could we fight and fight and fight, never winning but never growing despairing or bitter? Could we strive on, ever young?

I want to believe so. Yet the Operator perplexes me. I can't figure out his secret. Until, with the help of that clinic patient's story, I realize: The Operator's secret is *two* secrets, each relating to a different part of his mental life story.

The Operator's mental story has an integrated past and a branching future:

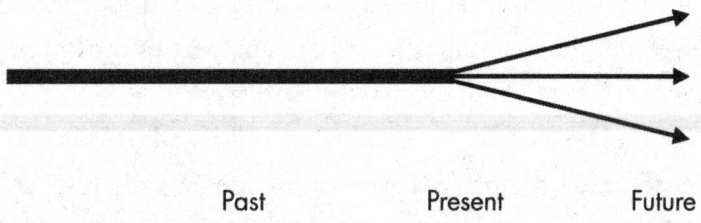

Past   Present   Future

This shape, as we saw in chapter 2, combines long-term direction with short-term flexibility. But it is placed under intense duress by war, which narrows the future with fright-or-fight and splinters the past with grief and shame:

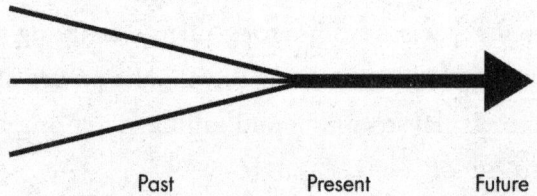

Past   Present   Future

That's the shape of combat PTS. It hinders soldiers from creating long-term plans while making them inflexible and prone to anger in the present.

To achieve antifragility, the Operator had learned to flip the second narrative into the first, leveraging battlefield trauma into purpose and adaptability. He achieved this via two Primal methods, the first of which is revealed by that clinic patient's mysterious story.

———

THE STORY WAS THE LAST entry in the patient's journal. But the journal's earlier pages were full of other tales. Many described tragic events: the death of the patient's younger brother by suicide; the infidelity of his high school sweetheart; the patient's own history of alcohol abuse. Yet despite their painful content, the stories were all told matter-of-factly, displaying no emotion. They read like scientific reports or case logs authored by a robot.

This, I learned from the clinic staff, was because the patient was suffering from dissociation. Dissociation literally means disconnection or separation. It happens when our mind detaches from the world—or from itself. Dissociation occurs naturally when we experience a negative surprise. The surprise can be a traumatic event, like the tragic episodes recorded by the patient in his journal. But it can also be an everyday jolt: an unplanned monetary expense, an uncomfortable interaction with a friend, a public mistake.

Negative surprises are harbingers of psychological pain: disappointment, nausea, horror, guilt, anguish. But before the pain hits, our mind feels shock. Suddenly, life feels unreal. Instead of being immersed in a flow of activity, we become aware of events drifting by at a remove, as if on a television screen. This frozen detachment is dissociation. It happens because the negative surprise has prompted our brain to think: *The rules of life must be different than I thought.*

Dissociation is a normal response to crisis and failure. It helps us grow by separating our brain from its old worldview, providing space to develop new rules of life. But dissociation can turn unhealthy if our brain finds itself unable to develop those new rules. Perhaps the new rules it imagines are too dark, too grim, too nihilistic: *The world is an evil place. Life is pointless. I am irredeemable.* Or perhaps it cannot imagine any new rules at all. Either way, our brain can't figure out how to turn the negative surprise into a source of learning or adaptation. So rather than spending its time in unending grief or shame, it decides to exist at a remove from life, observing events but not emotionally experiencing them.

This mental numbness is not enjoyable. In fact, it's marked by an absence of joy. Joy requires attachment to life. But even though mental numbness is a kind of zombie state, our brain prefers it to living in pain, which is why unresolved grief and shame can trigger self-medication. Sick of feeling hurt, our brain resorts to alcohol and other drugs to dissociate further.

The longer dissociation persists, the more it starts to feel normal. But it is not; our brain was born for life's thrills and spills. The patient at the clinic recognized this, leading him to seek treatment for his alcohol use. But when he got sober, he didn't feel substantially better. He still had no motivation to work or socialize. He woke up early every morning, made breakfast for his kids, and drove to his office, because he knew, intellectually, that he should. But he was just going through the motions. He took no pleasure in any of it. He felt, he said, like a ghost.

That was when he tried positive thinking and mindfulness. He meditated, daily, for three months. All to no effect. Unable to feel better, he gradually abandoned hope of a purposeful life. He sat alone for hours, staring out the window. He smiled at parties while his inner dialogue ran: *This is dumb. Why are we here? It's all fake. Nobody cares.* He increasingly referred to himself as "broken."

The patient wasn't broken. He was stuck in dissociation. By

kicking his alcohol use, he'd eliminated a barrier to reconnecting with life. He hadn't, however, made the reconnection. And while he'd been told that mindfulness, meditation, and positive thinking could make him feel more present, there was a good reason that they hadn't helped. Mindfulness and meditation are meta-cognitive techniques for interrupting negative thoughts and judgments. They work, in other words, by prompting dissociation. Rather than alleviating the patient's root condition, they were reinforcing it. The same went for positive thinking: By encouraging the patient to shift attention away from negative things he'd witnessed, it was detaching him from his lived experience.

It was in this chronic state of disconnection that the patient arrived at the clinic, where he penned the eerily numb tales on his journal's opening pages. What, then, was different about the final story? How did it inspire sudden purpose?

THE FINAL STORY IN THE patient's journal contained a narrative ingredient absent from his earlier stories—and absent also from the stories in the other patients' journals. The ingredient was a fortunate plot twist. Something good had happened to the patient when his life was going badly.

This mattered because plot twists have a specific brain effect: wonder. Wonder is a positive surprise, the opposite of the negative surprises that trigger dissociation. It's the emotion of a religious conversion or other spiritual experience. It's the sensation of being born again.

When we derive wonder from a plot twist in a novel or a movie, it can provide a temporary uplift. But when we derive wonder from our own life story, it can be transformative. By proving to our brain, from its own experience, that the positive can come from the negative, it turns the bad into a source of good. The grief and shame that had fueled dissociation become sources of awe, integrating our past. And an integrated past, as we saw in chapter 2, provides the brain with long-term momentum. It gives us our *why*, investing the day with personal purpose.

This is what the patient's plot twist did. And because a twist isn't just positive but also a surprise, it works differently from positive thinking. Positive thinking is a conscious attempt to convince your brain of something it doesn't already believe, so positive thinking often feels inorganic to—and even in conflict with—your brain's lived experiences. And while your brain might prefer to forget some of those experiences, it knows that to deny them is to deny its own truth, engaging in a contrived happiness that lacks real joy.

A positive surprise works differently. A surprise is an unconscious response that prompts the brain to acknowledge that its current beliefs are inadequate. After all, if they were adequate, the brain wouldn't have experienced surprise. To account for the plot twist, the brain must open itself to new beliefs, and since the surprise was positive, those beliefs will be positive too. In the patient's case, his new belief was that life could be more than tragic, pointless, or mechanical. It could be beautiful.

What was the plot twist that did this? What was the journal story that reversed the patient's dissociation, restoring his life purpose? Well, it wouldn't do any good for you to know. Remember how the patient's story didn't help the clinic's other patients? Hearing about other people's positive surprises doesn't change your story about yourself. That's why motivational speakers, inspirational self-help biographies, and feel-good movies don't have a lasting effect on your own sense of purpose. In fact, they can often fuel dissociation, making your brain feel like it has to escape from its difficulties by pretending to be somebody else.

What does have a lasting effect is to do like the patient and review your own history for times when life positively surprised you—or when you positively surprised yourself. Sometimes those moments are big dramatic events, but mostly they're the sorts of experiences you had daily as a child, like making a new friend or learning how to do something you didn't think you could.

When you remember one of those moments, *the key is to focus on the surprise.* The surprise reveals that the memory is creating wonder in your brain. The longer and more intense the wonder, the more it integrates the fractures of your past, strengthening the long-term purpose you develop from difficult things that you've experienced.

After I explain this method to the clinic staff, I share it with Special Operators experiencing severe post-traumatic stress. The Operators respond warily, wanting to know: *Why would my brain work this way? If the good surprises exist inside my brain, why would I have to consciously remember them? If the positive plot twist is already part of my personal history, why would I have to work to make it part of my mental life story?*

The answer lies in our emotions.

EMOTIONS ARE STRONGER WHEN THEY'RE negative. Negative emotions evolved for self-protection, and our brain values safety more than anything, more even than purpose. That's why many Operators struggle with suicidal thoughts when they return home. Their negative emotions kept them alive in combat, but they've lost touch with their positive emotions, so now they cycle between two states: false positivity and true negativity.

In false positivity, Operators go dutifully through the motions of happiness, performing the role of good parent and spouse but feeling empty. In true negativity, they are overcome by shame and grief. They are certain that they are worthless. They are certain that the world is doomed.

When Operators seek help for true negativity, they're typically prescribed cognitive behavioral therapy, or CBT. CBT was developed in the 1950s by University of Pennsylvania psychologist Aaron Beck after he noticed that psychological depression was alleviated when patients consciously interrupted their negative thoughts. CBT has since become the dominant psychotherapy reimbursed by insurance companies, and it is the main nonpharmaceutical treatment authorized for soldiers, active duty and veteran.

CBT does exactly what Beck discovered. But as Operators point out, it has two limitations. First, it neglects the fact that Operators trust their negative thoughts. Those thoughts kept the Operators and their teams alive in combat by promoting vigilance and commonsense. (See chapter 4.) Interrupting negative thoughts therefore seems dumb, indeed dangerous, to Operators. They feel safer in negativity.

The second limitation of CBT is that interrupting negative thoughts doesn't produce love, joy, or other positive emotions. In pursuit of those emotions, Operators diligently reframe negative events, looking on the bright side: *That hurt, but I learned something about myself. Or at least I got a good story out of it.* They fill their homes with upbeat quotes: *If you want a rainbow, you need to live through rain. If you are thinking positively during negative times, you have already won.* And they schedule hours of family fun: Little League, board games, dinners together. But most Operators end up stuck in false positivity. They create a bubble of happiness that bursts when they remember who they are and what they've seen. Or they find themselves faking the good life, acting happy while they feel sad, apprehensive, or empty. As one Operator informs me: "Positivity is lying to yourself, to make the suck easier until you sleep forever."

Trapped between true negativity and false positivity, Operators cycle between pessimism and minute-to-minute coping. So they're caught off guard when the same technique that worked for the clinic patient works for them. By reviewing their lives for positive twists, then focusing on the feeling of surprise, Operators experience more genuine wonder, love, joy, and gratitude, recovering a greater life purpose.

That purpose doesn't depend on ignoring, discounting, or otherwise interrupting the negative. In fact, the brain's sense of life purpose can be *increased* by the negative. The greater the negative, the more surprising a positive twist. And the more surprising a twist, the greater the wonder it generates, making true negativity a source of true positivity. This allows Operators to embrace the whole truth of their experience, finding the strength that comes from life integrity. And it is a recipe for antifragility, which leverages heartbreak into uplift.

To benefit like the Operators, you don't need to be suffering from extreme dissociation or suicidal thoughts. You can be experiencing everyday grief or shame—or burnout. Burnout is a common reason for diminished life purpose. It can be a symptom of emotional exhaustion, in which case the remedy is to take a break. Not just a day. At least two weeks. If the break doesn't help, the source of your burnout is probably depersonalization.

Depersonalization occurs when your brain stops seeing other people like they're really people, treating them instead like bots, phantoms, or pixels on a screen. Depersonalization is caused by modern workplaces, hospitals, schools, and other human ecosystems that are constantly interfering with your own human needs and desires. To save you from constant hurt and anger, your brain mentally separates from the people around you, causing the numb indifference of burnout.

You can recover purpose from burnout, grief, and shame. Just follow the clinic patient's path and review your past for positive surprises. If you feel grief, search for a time when life positively surprised you, maybe through nature's glory or a serendipitous day. If shame, a time when you positively surprised yourself, maybe by taking a brave chance or succeeding at something hard. If burnout, a time when someone else positively surprised you, maybe by getting you an unexpected gift or by apologizing when you thought they never would.

Once you find the surprise, recall every detail you can, seeing the story vividly in your mind. (To help capture all the details, you can write the story down, like the patient did at the clinic.) And don't focus only on the story's good parts, ignoring the bad. That's positive thinking. That's going back down the road to dissociation. Instead, remember what the Operators discovered: The more bad there is, the bigger the surprise that comes from the good; and the bigger that surprise, the greater its power to generate purpose.

Purpose you will know when you feel optimism.

OPTIMISM IS WIDELY UNDERSTOOD AS the belief *This will succeed*. But that's not optimism. It's wishful thinking.

Wishful thinking is an age-old delusion glamorized in modern times by a method known as *visualizing success*. Visualizing success has been promoted by self-help gurus like Tony Robbins (in his 1991 bestseller, *Awaken the Giant Within*) and Rhonda Byrne (in her 2006 blockbuster *The Secret*, thirty million copies sold in fifty languages). It traces its origins to New Thought, a nineteenth-century occult movement that spawned the advice of Napoleon Hill's 1937 *Think and Grow Rich*:

- "When visualizing the money you intend to accumulate, (with closed eyes), *see yourself rendering the service, or delivering the merchandise you intend to give in return for this money. This is important!*"

- "To get satisfactory results, you must follow ALL instructions in a spirit of FAITH."

In other words: Trust your future to a wishing well. If your wishes don't come true, it's not a problem with the wishing well. It's a problem with you. You didn't visualize your wish strongly enough. You didn't believe, completely, in the magic of the wishing well.

This is nonsense, as you learned back when you were a child. When you were a child, you believed completely in magic. You were pure of heart and had no doubt that wishes came to pass. Then you found out: No matter how fully you believed, no matter how pristine your faith or detailed your dreams, wishes did *not* always pan out.

Happily, however, you can still live in optimism. Because optimism isn't *This will succeed.* Optimism is much, much stronger. Optimism is *This can succeed.* Why is *can* stronger than *will*? Well, if you tell yourself that you *will* win and you don't, your confidence will crack. But if you tell yourself that you *can* win, then you'll retain the faith, no matter how many times you lose, as long as you win once. That one time is all you need to keep possibility alive, which is why *can* lives on long after *will* has shattered.

This is the solution to the mystery of the clinic patient. By discovering one positive surprise in his past, the patient realized: *Life can turn around. Good can happen improbably, illogically, when everything seems bad.* Out of this discovery came optimism, durable and purposeful.

Optimism is the first secret to antifragility. It's how the Operator without PTS leveraged grief and shame to strengthen life purpose, increasing grit and persistence. So let's turn now to the second secret: how the Operator used fright-or-fight to branch his future, boosting adaptability. Like the first secret, I came to it through a mystery.

THE MYSTERY DREW ME IN when I was appointed "faculty master" of a university dorm in California. I lived in a house across from a rose garden. I hosted trips to museums. It was idyllic. Except for one thing: I was constantly on the phone with students' parents. The parents were enormously proud—yet enormously concerned. They'd tell me that their children needed to learn to relax—then, seconds later, that their children needed to learn to succeed at a real job.

Initially, I dismissed these remarks as helicopter parenting. But as I lived alongside the students, I saw them struggling in exactly the ways their parents had noticed. They were excessively stressed about their grades, robbing them of the fun of learning.

Meanwhile, they underperformed outside the classroom; the most common feedback they received on internships was *Obedient and pleasant but lacks initiative. Needs to be more self-directed.*

How could students need to unwind—yet need to go harder? How could they be working too hard but not hard enough? It seemed an enigma, but it had a simple explanation, as I discovered at an event I hosted for dorm alums.

The alums were doctors, television stars, fashion moguls, musicians, and tech entrepreneurs who'd donated money to the dorm. Over dinner—served on plastic cafeteria plates—I launched into a speech expressing my gratitude for their financial assistance. An alum swiftly cut me off. She was the grateful one, she said. I was giving her the chance to support students, and nothing gave her more pleasure than helping others succeed as she had.

The other alums nodded in agreement. They were thankful to me. I was giving them life's most precious gift: the opportunity to make a positive impact.

An awkward silence followed as I said nothing. Not just because my prepared speech had been interrupted but also because I was a fraud. I wasn't helping students succeed. I was watching them struggle. Finally, I confessed this. I described the enigma of the students' behavior, and I asked the alums for help. They knew—more than I did—the path to transitioning out of college into life. Why were my students having such a hard time?

Another awkward silence followed. Until eventually, a surgeon in a sensible sport coat spoke up. "The problem," he said, "is school."

"School?"

"To succeed, I had to forget what I learned at school, and I had to teach myself what school should have taught me. School should have taught me to think for myself. Instead, it taught me to think like school."

The other alums nodded in vigorous agreement. And for the next two hours, over canned-fruit desserts and canteen coffee, they regaled me with tales of how school had prepared them to succeed at school, wrong-footing them for everything else.

I resisted this explanation for my students' difficulties. I didn't want to think that I was the problem. Like most professors, I believed that I was teaching students to think for themselves. But like most professors, I wasn't.

The bulk of university coursework is designed to measure whether students produce the correct answer, follow the right rubric, or apply an approved theoretical method. And the same goes for the rest of modern education. High school is filled with standardized tests, and so are middle and elementary school. As tests have proliferated, students have learned: There are right answers and the system has them. When students are given a problem they can't answer, they feel that their unfitness has been exposed by an all-knowing machine, triggering the threat response of fright-or-fight: freeze in shame, get belligerent, or passively submit to adult guidance. Instead of learning to trust their intuitions, students are conditioned to feel foolish, disruptive, or helpless.

This school dynamic explained my students' paradoxical behavior. The students were unable to relax because they were inhabiting a surveillance apparatus, and since that apparatus was evaluating the students on their performance on academic tests, it wasn't building their real-world competence at figuring out what to do when their relationships hit the rocks, their boss was clueless, or their best-laid plans collapsed. Was it therefore any surprise that the students were overdriven at school and tentative everywhere else? When they were in class, they felt relentlessly judged, and when they ventured outside, they felt dangerously unprepared.

I now had the explanation to the enigma. I didn't, however, have the solution. The struggles of the dorm students increased, year after year. And as they increased, I became convinced that the problem wasn't just my school—it was school itself. School inevitably trained students to think like it: artificial, abstract, unreal. Education in a classroom was miseducation for life.

I was wrong, as I discovered several years later when I found USAJFKSWCS.

USAJFKSWCS IS A CLANDESTINE ARMY Special Operations school. Protected by razor wire and blast deflectors, it sits on the At-lantic coastal plain in a sandhill forest thick with the chatter of woodpeckers. Even by the standard of military acronyms, USAJFKSWCS is unpronounceable, perhaps because the Army never wants the school's name uttered aloud. The school's instruc-tors, however, have a work-around: They refer to USAJFKSWCS as "Swick."

Swick specializes in cultivating self-efficacy and adaptability through independent problem-solving. To foster that problem-solving, Swick aggressively deprograms the belief in right answers instilled by the standardized assessments of modern educational institutions. As a Swick instructor growls at me: "The more a kid believes there's a right answer, the less she trusts herself to invent an original answer."

Swick training has three core components. They're simple to

grasp. So simple that they can be adapted for students as young as eight, the age at which modern school starts to negatively impact self-efficacy and adaptability.

The first component of Swick training is *perspective shifting*. In perspective shifting, you imagine how someone else would solve a problem, freeing your brain to see that there can be different paths to effective answers.

For young students, this can be done via exercises such as Creative Friend:

Creative Friend

Get a three-by-five card. Think of a person who acts differently from you. On the front of the card, draw something unique about that person. On the back, write three one-sentence stories:

- If my Creative Friend had $100 to spend, they would . . .
- If my Creative Friend were sad, they would . . .
- If my Creative Friend could change one thing about the world, they would . . .

When you encounter a challenge you can't solve, imagine what your Creative Friend might do.

The second component of Swick training is *old problem, new answer*. It pushes you to imagine a fresh way of solving a problem that other people have already tackled.

For young students, this can be done via exercises such as Make-Your-Own Multiple Choice:

Make-Your-Own Multiple Choice

Select a real-life problem. Ask a teacher for an answer and write that down as option A. Ask a parent for an answer and write that down as option B. Ask a friend for an answer and write that down as option C. Then invent your own answer and write that down as option D.

The third component of Swick training is *work-around*. It helps you find an alternative plan that satisfies your primary plan's main objective.

For young students, this can be done via exercises such as Backward Forward:

Backward Forward

Imagine a character who wants to do something—but is blocked by an obstacle. Storythink backward, speculating on *why* the character wants to do the something. Then storythink forward, imagining alternative *what if* paths that could satisfy the character's underlying motives.

After I visit Swick, an eight-year-old arrives at my lab upset that her parents won't send her to astronaut school.

"*Is* there an astronaut school?" I ask her parents, curious.

"Not that we know. But anyway, we cannot afford it."

After doing the three Swick exercises, the student reconsiders her problem. She explains to me that she wants to be an astronaut so that she can float in space. But she's realized that there's another place that things float: "Water. Fish float in water."

"You're not a fish," I point out. This is part of the training: When a student's imagination gets going, teachers gently provide real-world resistance, shifting students out of magical thinking into practical innovation.

"People can float in water, too," the student replies. "Like scuba divers. Scuba divers look a lot like astronauts. They have helmets and breathing tanks."

"I don't know of any scuba-diving schools around here."

"There's a pool near my house. I can teach myself to scuba dive there."

"Do you know how to swim?"

"My father does."

When her father picks her up, the student asks if he can help her learn to swim. He's delighted.

"I still want to be an astronaut," she informs him as they leave.

"Step by step," he replies. "Little feet up the mountain."

THIS SWICK TRAINING IS THE second secret of the Operator without PTS. It's how the Operator learned to grow from obstacles and setbacks, instead of getting disheartened or angry.

In the Army, the second secret is known as *Planner Not the Plan*, a reference to a quote from five-star general Dwight Eisenhower. The quote runs:

Plans are worthless, but planning is everything. . . . The very definition of "emergency" is that it is unexpected, therefore it is not going to happen the way you are planning. So, the first thing you do is to take all the plans off the top shelf and throw them out the window and start once more. But if you haven't been planning you can't start to work, intelligently at least.

In other words: Don't plan in order to make plans. Plan in order to get better at planning, so that when something unexpected happens, you can create the plan the situation requires.

To do Planner Not the Plan, you must let go of logic. Logic develops the plan. The perfect plan. The plan that anticipates every contingency. And then, just in case, logic develops Plan B, aka the backup plan. So that if the unforeseen occurs, it's already been foreseen.

Life overturns this logical method. To life, Plan B is just more Plan A. If Plan A breaks, so will Plan B. Both are based on the same outdated methods and assumptions. Instead of developing the plan, you must therefore develop the planner. You must plan not to have a plan but to train your brain at planning, so that when Plans A, B, and Z all shatter, you can keep moving forward, maintaining initiative and leading through chaos.

Now you know the two secrets of the Operator without PTS. The first secret, optimism, comes from discovering positive twists in the past, yielding direction in the long term. The second, Planner Not the Plan, creates positive twists in the future, providing flexibility in the short term. The first secret integrates the brain's personal history, producing grit and perseverance; the second branches the brain's tomorrow, promoting self-efficacy and adaptability.

When combined, the Operator's two secrets can make you stronger from setback and smarter from failure, nurturing anti-fragility. Antifragility contradicts logic. How can victory come from its opposite? But history abounds with tales of people turning loss into growth and disappointment into inspiration. Like a clinic patient who recovers purpose from years of numbness. Like an elementary student who makes a new plan when her first one crashes. And like the story of you.

7

DECISION-MAKING

Into the Ambush Like George Washington and the Astronauts

The astronauts had a problem.

They were huddled in blue jumpsuits outside their mission simulator, the virtual-reality cockpit where they practiced flying to the stars. The simulator was meant to prepare them for every contingency: electrical fires, blown engines, crew deaths. But the astronauts had noticed: The better they performed at simulated tasks, the more prone they were to catastrophic failure in real life. Practice, practice, practice made perfect—until it killed them.

This mystified the astronauts. How was their training upgrading their performance—yet introducing massive vulnerabilities? It made them wonder: Did they need to reprogram the simulator? Should they cut back on training? Was there even a case to be made for doing no training at all?

No. That wasn't the answer, I knew. I'd seen this paradox before. Not in people but in computers.

In computers, the paradox works like so: The more data you give an AI, the better it performs. But also the more likely it is to haywire unpredictably. It makes decisions quicker and with greater accuracy, until suddenly, it dumps commodities at fire-sale prices, diagnoses healthy newborns with brain tumors, and pilots cargo planes into mountainsides.

This paradox is *the optimization trap*. It happens to logical systems in biological environments. The logical system acquires more and more data, refining its algorithms and going faster and faster. Then abruptly, the environment changes. The change out-dates the data in the system. And indeed, it does worse than outdate the data. It makes the data a liability. To follow the data is to march robotically to doom.

This poses a challenge for human bureaucracies that find themselves in shifting times. But it's more than a challenge for AI. It's a disaster. Because AI is following the data at electric speed, it isn't marching to doom. It's *racing* to doom, spitting out bad decisions at calamitous velocity.

Optimization is thus the best state of affairs and also the worst, producing bursts of total dominance that abruptly shat-ter. Biology learned this long ago: Hyperspecialized organisms flourish briefly then go extinct, while generalist species trot stol-idly along. That's why maximum adequacy is the prime charac-teristic of life's long-term winners—like the human hand. The hand is not ideal at any task. It could be perfected in a million ways. But the hand is acceptable at countless tasks, so for every challenge that it loses to an optimized rival, it wins many more.

The human brain works the same. It isn't brilliant at one

mental task; it's satisfactory at lots, explaining how AI can be so much smarter than the brain yet so much dumber. AI takes one feature of intelligence—logic—and accelerates it. As long as life calls for math, AI crushes humans. It's the king of big-data choices. The moment, though, that life requires commonsense or imagination, AI tumbles off its throne.

This is how you know that AI is never going to run the world—or anything. But we humans can't lounge around, secure in our dynasty. Instead, we must face the same problem as the astronauts: How do we get the benefits of disciplined regularity without the downside of the optimization trap? How do we train our brain to be its best at our current task yet also adequate enough to survive an unexpected shift in conditions?

Years ago, Army Special Operators discovered the answer: commonsense. By detecting unknown unknowns (see chapter 4), commonsense lets us know when we don't know, driving two kinds of intelligent decision-making: (1) deciding when it's time to switch plans and (2) deciding which new plan to select.

We learned about the first kind of decision-making in chapter 4, which laid out a method (tuning anxiety) for determining if volatility is rising, outdating our old plans. We'll explore the second kind of decision-making in this chapter, which will extend commonsense into a rule for always selecting the smart plan, whether you're in a digital simulator or a real mission gone sideways. With that rule, you can optimize standard operating procedures in stable environments—and improvise good-enough plans when conditions veer.

The rule is: *Match the newness of your plan to the newness of your environment.* Here's the story of its discovery—and how to use it.

———

THE INSIGHT CAME WHILE SPECIAL Operators were training recruits to respond to an ambush.

An ambush is the most shocking event that soldiers can experience. It transitions you, in a flash of terror, from hunter to target. When new recruits are ambushed, they typically run away. Bad move. That exposes your back to the enemy's unchecked gunfire. When new recruits are given time to think about how to best respond to ambushes, they typically say: *Drop and take cover.* Worse move. That leaves you prone in a curated murder zone.

So what's the smarter move? It is, I am confidently told by the Army's most experienced Operators, to attack into the ambush.

Attack *into* the ambush? This seems suicidal to me. But the Operators patiently explain that when you attack into the ambush, you achieve two wins at once. First, you regain your initiative, pushing events instead of being pushed. Second, you put your enemy on the defensive, disrupting his planning. With a single maneuver, you thus double shift the odds, pressing your opponent to make bad decisions as you increase your likelihood of acting smart.

This method is so simple and effective that it seems a surefire way to turn any brain into a Special Operator. But as the Army discovered, there's a complication. When recruits are taught to attack into an ambush, they succeed in training—then fail catastrophically in combat. Like the astronauts in their simulator, they ace the test only to explode on contact.

This happens because recruits who memorize a lesson treat it as a prescribed instruction, aka a program, and programs work only in familiar situations. When the environment shifts—when the ambush is irregular or innovative—the recruits' mental computer can't pattern-match it. Instead of charging forward, recruits freeze in place, run away, or dive for cover. And in the killing field, they die.

This made the Army realize: To really learn to attack into an ambush, recruits had to discover the lesson for themselves, acquiring it not as a program but as commonsense. To set the conditions for recruits to do this, Special Ops breaks the lesson into three steps, each based upon a legend of commonsense decision-making.

THE FIRST COMMONSENSE LEGEND IS George Marshall. His step is: *When the fundamentals change, junk your most successful plans.*

Marshall was appointed leader of the U.S. Army on September 1, 1939. Hours earlier, Hitler had invaded Poland, initiating World War II. Marshall was on the verge of his fifty-ninth birthday, yet prior to his promotion, he was far from the Army's senior officer. He was, in fact, outranked by thirty other generals.

Marshall possessed one quality, however, that set him apart: He was willing to fire top commanders, including ones with chests full of medals. To prepare the U.S. Army for war against Hitler, he force-retired hundreds of officers for being out-of-date. The officers were outraged. Had they not proved themselves in past wars? Were they not the best of the best, according to the military's established metrics?

Yes, Marshall agreed. These officers had mastered the rules—the *old* rules. But war was different today from yesterday. What was optimized for Monday was doom on Tuesday. So the Mondays had to go.

Marshall maintained this method with unflinching determination. During the war, he fired more than a dozen active-duty generals. Not because they were bad generals but because their decision-making was based on past data. Their expertise guaranteed victory in the previous fight and ruin in the next one.

What Marshall did with his generals, effective decision-makers do with their plans: discard them, immediately, when the fundamentals of the environment shift. To do this rapidly and accurately, flip your relationship to expertise. Don't trust your expertise when it tells you that a plan will work. That makes you prone to expert bias, leaving you vulnerable to the delusion that your past experience matches current events. Instead, trust your expertise when it tells you: *I have never seen a situation like this one before.* When expertise tells you this, it has hit its limit, requiring you to innovate.

This flipped use of expertise is why Army Special Operations pairs every young lieutenant with a seasoned sergeant. The sergeant might not always come up with the freshest strategies. But the sergeant can instantly see when a situation is unprecedented, warning the lieutenant: *Change the plan!* Every organization benefits in the same way from old-timers. Old-timers have seen it all—or at least they've seen all that's happened up to now. When they're surprised, that's a good indicator: The world is changing.

This flipped use of expertise is also the value of studying history. And of encouraging democracy. Not because history contains all the answers or because democracies always vote for smart courses of action. But because if an incident startles a historian, you know: The old norms are gone. And if an event rattles a democracy (like Sputnik did in chapter 4), it lies outside collective experience. No matter how clever the current plan, it's time to replace it.

So, what if it's time for a replacement? How do you find the new plan that the situation requires? You take the next common-sense step, illustrated by the second legend.

THE SECOND COMMONSENSE LEGEND IS Thomas Paine. His step is: *New plans require boldness.*

Paine wrote the book on commonsense. Literally. Paine was friends with Ben Franklin, the guru of joining orthodoxy to enterprise (see chapter 4), and in January 1776, while working as a magazine writer in Philadelphia, Paine penned a forty-seven-page pamphlet titled: *Common Sense.* It became a phenomenon, selling more copies than there were residents of Philadelphia (and indeed, more copies than there were also residents of Charleston, Boston, and New York).

Common Sense declared that everything "right and natural" urged America's thirteen colonies to renounce the British king and form their own government. Why, then, had the colonists ignored both "the design of Heaven" and "the weeping voice of nature"? Why were they paused, indecisively, on the threshold of revolution? "It is because," Paine said, "no plan is yet laid down. Men do not see their way out—Wherefore, as an opening into that business, I offer the following hints."

In other words: We hesitate when we have no plan. Which is bad for two reasons. First, it makes us reluctant to tear up our existing plans, so instead of following Marshall's lesson (see above), we cling to a course that life has already outdated. Second, when we do finally accept that our plan is busted, we don't act rapidly to make another. Instead, we freeze in uncertainty. Not knowing which way to go, we go nowhere, allowing events to engulf us.

To stave off both fates, *Common Sense* reminds us that new plans do not spring, mature, from the womb. They emerge as "hints." Every innovation, no matter how brilliantly revolutionary, thus initially appears half formed. This can make the innovation seem *de*formed, prompting us to throw it away—or equally imprudently, to throw away the abnormal half. When we do this, we lop off what is really new, falling into the clutches of expert bias. Even as we think that we're improving the innovation, we're actually destroying it.

Instead, remember: Peculiarity is the sign of the exceptional. Rather than deleting the parts of new plans that seem odd, treasure them. Accelerate the innovation by concentrating its original qualities. Cut away the tried-and-true and double down on the eccentric, until you make a breakthrough.

To do this requires courage, which is another word for boldness. Boldness is hard when chaos is making you fearful, pushing you to retreat into the emotional haven of the familiar. But that retreat is the comfortable walk to death. When life bucks, your only hope is to match its rhythm. So do like the revolutionaries who took inspiration from Paine. Quit the well-lit path to seize the hint in the dark.

This is the second step. But it requires one more. Because as you are dashing into danger, you will want to know: How much risk is good? How much boldness is too far?

THE THIRD AND FINAL COMMONSENSE legend is George Washington. His step is: *Be as bold as the situation is uncertain.*

Washington guided Paine's thirteen colonies to victory, establishing the democracy that Marshall would later lead against

Hitler. This achievement made Washington so famous as to be forgotten, his character obscured by myths. But in the eyes of Special Operators, there is one absolute fact about Washington: He was the master of commonsense. He always knew when he didn't know, enabling him to gamble if the situation was chancy and to hold on to the dice if it wasn't.

When Washington had the British trapped at Yorktown, he selected the least imaginative plan in his arsenal: a classic siege, executed on mathematical principles. But when the Continental Army was collapsing in the winter of 1776—its soldiers deserting from poor morale—Washington responded to precarity by green-lighting an extraordinarily hazardous plan: a surprise attack at night across the iceberg waters of the Delaware. For routine logistical operations, Washington picked boring quartermasters. But for treacherous missions, like transporting the Fort Ticonderoga cannons or waging guerrilla war, he opted for wild-minded commanders like Henry Knox and Francis "Swamp Fox" Marion.

To win your own revolution, act like Washington. Accelerate risk-taking as volatility and uncertainty increase. Do this, and you will meet the moment rather than lagging behind or overshooting. Commonsense acts commonly in common circumstances and uniquely when life gets unprecedented, mirroring the nature of the times.

WHEN YOU COMBINE THE THREE steps of Marshall, Paine, and Washington, you get: *Match the newness of your plans to the newness of your situation.* So if the situation is familiar, use a familiar plan. If it's novel, use a novel plan. And if it's *really* novel, use a *really* novel plan. When looking at your life story . . .

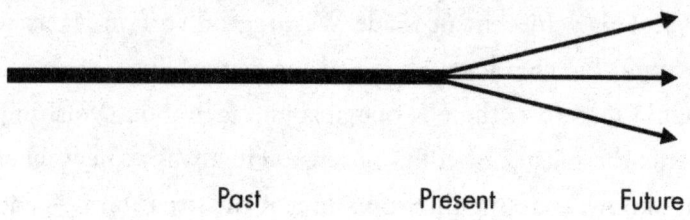

Past   Present   Future

. . . that's how you decide which future branch to take.

This may sound obvious, even blindingly so. Yet it's not the way that most people act. Most people take their biggest risks when they feel secure and are at their most tentative when life gets volatile. That's because commonsense has been depleted by the modern world. The modern world offers greater short-term stability than a state of nature, making us bored—and prone to unnecessary gambles. We fritter away golden hours on idle fancies when dull but disciplined industry would rocket us forward. Meanwhile, when unexpected events disrupt our routine, our minds are emotionally unprepared to adapt. Unlike our primeval ancestors, who wrestled constantly with bracing challenges, we lack fresh memories of occasions when we have overcome hard shocks. Instead of rapidly remembering our big priority and fashioning a first-step plan (see chapter 3), we turtle, hoping that somebody, anybody, will arrive to save us.

To recover your natural powers of intelligent choice, practice being proactive about situational change. You can do this by focusing on a simple commonsense indicator: a loss of effectiveness. Effectiveness flows from plans that work and ceases when plans stop functioning. Between these two states, the plan will continue to operate but not as well: Your battle strategy is still taking ground but incurring greater casualties; your product line is still selling but not as strongly as last quarter; your weekly meetings are still motivating employees, but burnout rates are climbing.

That loss of effectiveness reveals that the environment is changing. Commonsense is therefore warning: *Your current plan will work a little longer, but engage your powers of innovation to start developing new plans.* If you heed the alert, you can exercise your powers of adaptive planning in lower-pressure settings, before the stakes get so high that stress swamps initiative.

This account of commonsense resonates with the astronauts. But they have one lingering concern: How *fast* is commonsense?

Fast is crucial in the astronauts' line of work, where a millisecond can spell success—or death. No matter how good a decision is in theory, it's worthless if it's an instant too late.

I assure the astronauts: Commonsense is plenty fast. As proof, I point to Neil Armstrong.

BORN IN WESTERN OHIO TEN months after the stock market crash that inaugurated the Great Depression, Armstrong is famous as the first human to walk on the moon. But before he walked, he had to land. And what landed Armstrong on the lunar surface was his commonsense decision-making.

That decision-making was rooted in Armstrong's dual background: test pilot and engineer. The engineer in him respected standard operating procedures. (See chapter 4.) Unlike pilots who went cowboy on routine missions, Armstrong stuck to protocol, flying as unimaginatively as an instruction manual. But because Armstrong had test piloted hundreds of aircraft models, many of which malfunctioned mid-flight, he was willing to scrap SOPs at a moment's notice, improvising solutions whose novelty matched the novelty of the situation.

This willingness saved Armstrong's life in March 1966 when he was command pilot of *Gemini 8*. The mission was the first to dock two spacecraft in Earth orbit, and Armstrong flew it by the book, leading to a linkup he called "a real smoothie." Then, out of nowhere, things got rough. Malfunctioning mysteriously, the *Gemini* module began rolling. Observing in horror from a hundred miles below, mission controllers at NASA's Houston Manned Spacecraft Center could not explain the module's aberrant behavior. All they knew was that the module was rotating faster and faster, like an aircraft in a supersonic spin. The stars outside its silica windows whipped past once every five seconds . . . then once every three seconds . . . then once every second. In another half instant, Armstrong and his copilot would black out—and tumble to death.

But that didn't happen. Instead, Armstrong exited his SOPs, disabling the module's orbital system. Then, in a move no astronaut had ever performed, he engaged *Gemini*'s reentry thrusters. Those thrusters weren't meant for maneuvering in space. They were intended for entering Earth's atmosphere. But Armstrong's radically unprecedented action was just the thing for his radically unprecedented situation. He stopped the roll and safely piloted *Gemini* home.

Armstrong carried that fast decision-making with him while training for the moon landing. The training took place in a low-gravity simulator: the Lunar Landing Research Vehicle, or LLRV. The LLRV looked like a prehistoric insect made from stainless-steel tubing. And unlike a computer simulation, it really flew. Instead of hewing to mathematical rules, it embodied the dynamic instability of flight, allowing Armstrong to practice unscripted emergencies. As he coolly remarked: "It was a contrary machine, and a risky machine, but a very useful one."

The machine's risk and its utility converged on May 6, 1968. For five minutes, during a practice session at Houston's Ellington

Air Force Base, the LLRV flew normally, just as it had on twenty-one previous outings. Then without warning, it drifted up in a half backflip. Armstrong checked his instrument panel: The gauges indicated that nothing was wrong, guiding him to stick with the plan, just as he'd done on flight after flight after flight. But the truth was that the LLRV had suffered a fatal glitch. Its helium system had lost pressure, depriving the engines of fuel and dooming the bug-shaped simulator to smash into the ground, vaporizing in scarlet flame. Moments after Armstrong consulted the gauges, that's exactly what occurred. Armstrong should have died in shock and fire. But a split second before the LLRV spiraled, his commonsense overruled his dashboard and he ejected to safety.

This harrowing episode prepared Armstrong for the actual moon landing a year later, on July 20, 1969. The landing began with Armstrong allowing his onboard guidance computer to autopilot the lunar lander. The computer flew smoothly—so smoothly that the astronauts observed that it was "better than the simulator." Space, it seemed, was as timelessly predictable as a math equation.

Happy with the programmed descent, Armstrong kept his hands off the throttle. Then suddenly, he noticed an unexpected boulder field. Immediately taking control, he redirected the lander, inventing a flight plan that was as novel as the unfolding moon landscape.

A minute later, Armstrong settled gently on the lunar surface. His rapid commonsense had made the incredible possible. Toggling fast between automated instructions and creative intuition, humanity had touched down in the heavens.

A FEW MONTHS AFTER I meet with the astronauts, one of them contacts me privately. He understands that new plans always involve risk, but he wants to make sure that his risk-taking is intelligent. He doesn't want to compound a crisis by flailing indiscriminately.

This is a prudent concern. Good decisions meet the situation's volatility without adding to it. Which is hard, because when life gets choppy, our brain can get overanxious and trend toward panic, exaggerating the problem and making it worse. To prevent that self-inflicted damage, here's one final commonsense decision-making technique from Special Operations: Call in an expert—not to tell you what to do but to tell you what *not* to do.

The technique works like this. When you hit uncharted turbulence, present your response plan to an expert. Ask him one— and only one—question: "Can you prove that my plan will fail?" If the expert can prove that your plan will fail, your plan will fail. You need to invent a different one. But ignore the expert's other advice. If the expert tells you that he has a plan that will work better, it will work better—yesterday. If the expert cautions you that there's no evidence that your plan will work, it can work—now.

Special Operators call this *Go Where Experts Can't Say No.* It protects you from acting dumb while also allowing you to take appropriate risk. It's a straightforward way to maximize commonsense decision-making in uncertain environments. And if you're an expert, you can run it solo: When you hit an unfamiliar situation, venture plans that make your expertise wary—but that it can't shoot down.

Train your brain in this way of thinking, and you'll escape the optimization trap. When conditions change, you'll switch off simulator brain. And you will ambush back.

8

COMMUNICATION

Answer Why Like Maya Angelou and Abraham Lincoln

A billion dollars. That was the company's annual marketing budget, splashed on internet ads, TV, and social media.

Yet revenue was stagnant. The company was seeing no return on its gigantic advertising investment. Something was clearly misfiring—but what? Hunting for an answer, the company's execs toured the world's top business schools. They talked to senior professors with deep experience. They talked to young faculty with brave new ideas. Then they talked to me.

The meeting began with the execs laying out their research. They'd analyzed thousands of ads. Most—more than 99 percent—had evaporated without impact. A tiny fraction had, however, produced sizable revenue spurts. That tiny fraction was further divisible into two categories. The first category was the largest. Its ads generated fast profits yet proved short-lived. The second category contained barely a dozen ads. Those ads made less instant impact but sustained, even grew, their influence over months and years.

The company wanted to know: What was the secret to the sustained influence of that second category of ads?

Curious, I studied the ads. They included the "1984" commercial that helped turn Apple into history's biggest tech upstart. But that ad wasn't the second category's top performer. The honor went to a TV spot made three years later. It was produced for a company that claimed to be leading "a revolution in footwear" yet was rapidly losing market share. During the previous twelve months, earnings had plunged 40 percent.

The ad was "Just Do It." The company was Nike.

The Nike ad featured Walt Stack, an eighty-year-old jogger with a peacock tattoo on his sun-bronzed chest. His motto was "Start slow . . . and taper off." The ad presented him on that gradual taper, inching cheerfully across San Francisco's Golden Gate Bridge.

The ad was quicker than Walt, finishing its run in a brisk thirty seconds. When it was done, the execs asked if I needed a replay. I didn't. The difference between the Nike ad and the ads that sparked quick, short sales was obvious.

Those other ads worked by inciting fear. They made viewers feel that they had to buy—or else. The Nike ad worked by sparking imagination. It invited viewers to join it in creating a story of personal accomplishment.

When I explained this to the execs, they blinked, surprised. It wasn't what other scholars had said. What, they asked, was the basis for my conclusion? What data was I drawing on?

I didn't have any data about the Nike ad. But I'd worked with Army Special Operators who specialized in marketing, or as they called it, psychological operations. So I knew three relevant things about how ads worked in the brain.

First, when the brain gets scared, it becomes susceptible to other people's narratives. (See chapter 3.) That's why the citizens of violently repressive regimes are more likely to assent to government propaganda.

Second, this fear-based communication is fragile. The moment a regime (or a corporation) stops being able to manufacture terror, it loses its power to program our brain. We regain our agency, developing our own free narrative (or, less happily, we fall into the clutches of the next fear-merchant).

Third and finally, stories that spark our imagination become integral to our personal narrative. If I imagine myself in a world that your ad creates, then my story merges with yours to form a bigger tale that lives on after the ad has disappeared from memory.

That, I said, is why people buy Nike. Not because they're brainwashed by the ad but because the ad prompts them to imagine their own Just Do It future. That future becomes part of their biography, enduring when the fears roused by other ads have faded away.

The execs nodded, accepting my analysis. But they still had questions: How was the Nike ad firing imagination? What specific techniques was it using to engage the brain? Could I provide a blueprint for doing the same?

Sure, I said. I could provide a blueprint. It contained three main techniques. They were easy to see because Nike had lifted them from a famous source: the grandmaster of imaginative communication, William Shakespeare.

THE FIRST TECHNIQUE IS TO start in the middle.

This contradicts logic. According to logic, effective ads start at the beginning. They provide the first data point, then the second, then the third, and so on, until the picture is complete.

Sounds smart, but story did not evolve for linear information transfer. In fact, as we saw back in chapter 2, it did not evolve to communicate at all. Its powers of communication are built upon a more fundamental capacity: the power to help the brain react intelligently to the unexpected. The intelligent reaction occurs—as logic predicts—via three operations: *beginning, middle, end.* However, the operations don't run in that logical order inside the brain. What makes them smart is that they run *middle* → *beginning* → *end.*

Here's how. Story whirs into action when your brain encounters an unexpected event. Maybe it's a crisis at work. Maybe it's a surprise in the financial markets. Maybe it's someone behaving in a flabbergasting way. This, your brain realizes, is the story's *middle.* It's a problem or an opportunity (aka a piece of exceptional information) that traces its origins to earlier happenings. The crisis at work didn't come from nowhere; the market didn't shift arbitrarily; the person didn't snap at random. These events had prior causes.

To locate those causes, your brain jumps back in time, speculating on the story's unseen beginning. Your brain might conjecture, for example, that the work crisis was triggered by a concealed rift between two coworkers; that the market shift was driven by an accidental commodity glut; that the person's behavior stems from a hidden feature of their psychology.

This backward jump is causal thinking. It's what children do when they wonder, *Why?* It's what scientists do when they hypothesize new laws of nature.

Once your brain has settled on a plausible cause, it shifts direction and leaps into the future, surmising the cause's possible effects. It imagines the consequences of the concealed rift, the commodity glut, the hidden feature of psychology. In short, it anticipates the story's end, speculating *what if?* By doing so, it helps you figure out how to respond intelligently to the unexpected event, regaining the initiative and acting with purpose.

This forward jump is creative planning. It's what leaders and inventors do when they craft original strategies and technologies. It's what scientists do when they hatch novel experiments. It's what science fiction writers do when they draft new tomorrows.

By tapping into this storythinking mechanism of *middle → beginning → end*, you can engage your audience to cocreate the future with you. Start with an unexpected middle that stirs curiosity, prompting your audience to jump backward to hypothesize a beginning, and their imagination will leap ahead to invent an end, completing the story without your telling it.

This technique of starting with the middle was discovered by ancient storytellers. Three thousand years ago, Homer's *Odyssey* started in the middle of a hero's journey back from war, prompting audiences to imagine *why* the hero had gone to war—and *what if* he made it home.

Centuries later, the same technique—dubbed *in medias res* by the Roman poet Horace—was deployed relentlessly by Shakespeare. *Othello* begins in the middle of an argument in the middle of the night. *Much Ado About Nothing* begins in the middle of a love story: When the curtain rises, the romantic leads, Beatrice and Benedick, have already broken up. *The Tempest* begins in the middle of a storm that is sinking a ship in the middle of the ocean—and it also begins in the middle of a decade-long battle between two Milanese princes, one of whom is on the sinking ship and the other of whom has spent years mastering magic on a nearby island.

Shakespeare's middles prompted Renaissance audiences to ask *why*—then *what if*, flashing forward to imagine the future. And this technique remains how we imagine the future today. We do the imagining via science fiction, which was popularized in 1818 by Mary Shelley, a teenager with Shakespeare's *Tempest* on her nightstand. Inspired by the play's middle-beginning story of a scientist who conjures monsters, Shelley crafted *Frankenstein*, which begins mid-voyage to an icy realm where a scientist is in mid-pursuit of a conjured monster, prompting our brain to rewind time to imagine the pursuit's origins—then fast-forward to *what if*s ahead.

This sci-fi technique was picked up in the 1860s by Jules Verne, another Shakespeare reader. And in the 1890s by H. G. Wells, a third Shakespeare reader, who used it to craft the visionary sci-fi *The Time Machine*, which jumps into the middle of a future civilization before leaping back to the beginnings of life on Earth, then forward to the end of time.

To inspire similar visions in your audience, depart from logic. Don't begin by laying out first principles. Start halfway through a story, so that instead of passively absorbing information, your listeners' imaginations whir into motion, dreaming what could happen next.

THE SECOND TECHNIQUE IS TO focus on exceptions to rules.

This also contradicts logic, which encourages us to use story archetypes. Archetypes are universal story characters and structures, like heroes, good versus evil, and fairy-tale endings. To logic, there's nothing more powerful than the universal. But to your storythinking brain, *universal* is another term for generic. It is familiar, clichéd, uninteresting.

What catches your brain's attention, stimulating it to imagine *why* and *what if*, is the opposite of the universal: an anomaly. An anomaly is a character or event that breaks the rules. It is, in other words, a piece of exceptional information. (See chapter 1.)

Shakespeare had an eye for anomalies, which is why his characters aren't archetypes. They're exceptions. Hamlet is a deep-thinking action hero. Cleopatra is a hardy intriguer with a vulnerable heart. Falstaff is an old man who behaves like an adolescent.

Then there is Shylock, star of Shakespeare's *The Merchant of Venice*. A Jew in a Christian city, he is abused in the streets for his strangeness. But while his judges view themselves as heroes of a binary moral parable, Shylock reminds them that life is not so starkly mathematical. In their Christian souls lies an unholy lust for revenge, and in his flinty psyche, innocent laughter.

Because Shakespeare's characters are exceptions, they catch our fascination, launching our imagination. We speculate on where they came from: What unusual parents or cultures lie at the origin of their odd behaviors? And our imagination continues to work after Shakespeare's characters have left the stage. Mentally joining them on future adventures, we mingle their lives with ours, experiencing communication's word-root: *communion.*

After Shakespeare, this technique was continued in 1930s Saint Louis by a young girl who memorized *The Merchant of Venice.* The young girl was Maya Angelou, and she would grow up to write an extraordinary memoir, *I Know Why the Caged Bird Sings*, that starts by revealing her as an exception to the world's rule of beauty:

The age-faded color made my skin look dirty like mud, and everyone in church was looking at my skinny legs.

Wouldn't they be surprised when one day I woke out of my black ugly dream, and my real hair, which was long and blond, would take the place of the kinky mass that Momma wouldn't let me straighten? My light-blue eyes were going to hypnotize them.

Here, Angelou dreams of waking up to find that she looks "like one of the sweet little white girls who were everybody's dream of what was right with the world." But like Shylock, Angelou catches our imagination not because she is the archetype but because she breaks it.

THE THIRD TECHNIQUE IS TO write in riddle.

A riddle connects two things that contradict. (*What gets wetter the more that it dries?* Or *What has a bed but never sleeps?* Or *What do the rich need but the poor have?*) This logic breaker stimulates curiosity and then suspense, making us want to get the answer faster. (If you don't know the riddles posed above, you'll be feeling that suspense, pushing you to skip ahead to the solutions at the end of this paragraph.) So it is that riddles build forward-looking engagement, stretching the *what if* power of your audience's imagination to join you at a future destination. (You've made it. The answers are: *a towel*; *a river*; *nothing.*)

Shakespeare uses this technique in *Macbeth*, which begins with three weird sisters chanting that they will meet again, "when the battle's lost and won." A riddle they chase with another: "Fair is foul, and foul is fair." Our curiosity is hooked. How can a battle be lost and won? How can foul be fair? Racing ahead, we discover: Every battle is lost and won, because every battle has a winner and loser. To the loser, the result is foul, and to the winner, fair.

The riddles of *Macbeth* were serially recited by one of history's great communicators, Abraham Lincoln. Lincoln adored Shakespeare. On August 17, 1863, at the height of the American Civil War, he sat upstairs in his White House office, surrounded by honey-tinted battle maps, and declared: "I think nothing equals *Macbeth*. It is wonderful." Three months later, on November 19, he used Shakespeare's riddle method in what would become his own most famous speech, the Gettysburg Address:

> Four score and seven years ago our fathers brought forth
> on this continent, a new nation, conceived in Liberty, and
> dedicated to the proposition that all men are created equal.

What's the riddle? The riddle is America. A land dedicated "to the proposition that all men are created equal." A land where men are enslaved, creating inequality.

In *Macbeth*, the suspense generated by the weird sisters' riddles turns them into sources of *what if* thinking, prompting us to join Macbeth in co-imagining his next steps. And Lincoln's riddle does the same, stirring us to dream of future freedom:

> We here highly resolve that these dead shall not have died
> in vain—that this nation, under God, shall have a new
> birth of freedom—and that government of the people, by
> the people, for the people, shall not perish from the earth.

Give your audience a riddle and they will experience a similar vision of a future answer, joining you to make a story of tomorrow.

———

NIKE'S AD COMBINES ALL THREE Shakespearean techniques:

1. The ad starts in the middle of Walt's jog, halfway across the bridge.

2. Walt is an exception to the rule of young athletic models: He's a balding octogenarian.

3. Walt is a riddle: Why, at his age, when he should be taking it easy, does he run seventeen miles every morning? Seventeen miles! Every morning! At his age! "People ask me," he drawls, "how I keep my teeth from chattering in the wintertime." His grinning answer: He leaves his teeth behind, in his locker.

My analysis of the Nike ad excites the company's execs. But to turn it into communications of their own, they ask two follow-up questions.

First, they want to know how they can control what the audience imagines. It's all well and good, the execs say, to spark people to have a vision of the future. But how can you direct that vision? How can you ensure that your audience sees what you want them to see?

I reply: The only way to achieve control is with fear. There's no controlling imagination. This answer greatly disappoints the execs. But they cheer up when I explain that they don't need to control their audience to succeed like the Nike ad. The ad doesn't work by programming viewers; it works by stirring them to imagine a shared purpose. That shared purpose is why people buy Nike footwear. Not because Nike instructs them to but because they feel close, connected, bonded to Nike. They want to take Nike on their next adventure, just doing it.

To deepen that sense of purpose, use a fourth Shakespearean technique: End with the beginning. Or in other words, finish by telling your audience *why*.

Why is what the brain storythinks after it encounters a middle, an exception, or a riddle. That *why* becomes the launching point for the *what if*, which is to say, the future that the brain embarks on next.

You cannot control the *what if*. But you can shape the *why*, which is what the Nike ad does when it ends by explaining the runner's motive: "Just do it." This explanation answers the mystery of *why* the runner goes on his seventeen-mile run every morning, rain or shine. The runner runs because of his attitude: *Action beats doubt. So take the first step toward your goal—now.*

Nike didn't need to end on this particular *why*, but it's effective. It connects with the brain's core drive to grow. It reminds us of our human potential to go beyond old preconceptions, like Shakespeare's characters do when they break archetypal rules.

We get parallel reminders from Lincoln, Angelou, and sci-fi. Sci-fi reminds us *why* we dream: to create new futures, unlocking the potential of today. Angelou reminds us *why* we reflect on our biography: to discover what's exceptional within us, unlocking the potential of our individuality. Lincoln reminds us *why* America was founded: to give us all the chance to live free, unlocking the potential of our humanity.

As I say this, the execs nod attentively—but take no notes. In fact, they don't pick up a pen during our entire meeting. This, I think, is because the execs have good memories. But actually, it's because they're not interested in sci-fi, Angelou, or Lincoln. All they want is a quick formula for leveraging imagination into effective marketing.

Here's the formula I give them:

1. Prompt your audience to wonder *why*.

2. Explain why, answering their question for them.

3. Shut up, allowing your audience to imagine *what if*.

You can do (1) by beginning in the middle (like Shelley), by disrupting an existing narrative (like Angelou), or by posing a riddle (like Lincoln). You can do (2) by providing an explanation that strikes your audience as one they'd have imagined themselves, if they'd had more time. You can do (3) by restraining yourself. Don't try to tell your audience what to do next, after the ad is over. Sit back and let their imagination do the work. That work—much more than anything you say—will drive their future behavior.

In short, hook people's curiosity, halting them in wonder, then start them in a new direction by providing an explanation that reveals a fresh potential within them or the world.

Or, shorter: Get your audience to imagine a question, then answer it better than they can.

THE EXECS' LAST QUESTION IS: How about internal communication?

Internal communication is often seen as a kind of marketing. It is not. Marketing is for an external audience: customers, clients, collaborators. It produces engagement, encouraging more people to incorporate your story into theirs. Internal communication is for an in-house audience: your team. It produces alignment, ensuring that everyone is following one plan.

Internal communication is thus the inverse of external communication. It goes inward instead of outward, seeking cohesion instead of dissemination. So it employs the inverse story structure. Rather than starting at the *middle* and encouraging the audience to imagine the *end*, it starts at the *end* and encourages the audience to imagine the *middle*. Which is to say, it instructs people on where they need to go but empowers them to figure out the path.

You can achieve this via one more Shakespearean technique: *Commander's Intent.* The technique is discovered by Hamlet during a long speech in which he tells a group of actors exactly what to do—then tells them exactly what not to do. These are the two most counterproductive forms of internal comms: the first robs your team of agency, sapping their ability to adapt to situations you did not foresee; the second puts your team in a negative headspace where they don't trust their own intuitions. Hamlet manages to rescue his comms, however, by informing the actors that their "end" is to hold a "mirror up to nature." With this *end* in mind, the actors successfully improvise the *middle*. Forgetting their commander's micromanagement, they nail the performance by heeding his intent.

Three centuries later, the effectiveness of Commander's Intent would be dramatized on the world's stage by another legendary communicator: Winston Churchill. Churchill was prime minister of Britain during World War II. And he was also an admirer of *Hamlet*. In fact, he was such an admirer that he memorized Hamlet's "mirror up to nature," the whole speech, start to finish. The speech's example of a precision *end* proved useful to

Churchill on many occasions, including his darkest hour as prime minister: the retreat from Dunkirk in June 1940, after Hitler's army had invaded France. To stall Hitler's momentum and bolster British morale, Churchill knew that he had to retake the initiative. So he issued a short internal communication to the British army, ordering the development of "specially trained troops of the hunter class." This order led to the formation of the British Commandos, a group of soldiers who exchanged conventional military drills for new training methods. In place of parade formations, they hiked mountains, rode on zip lines, stalked rabbits, and boxed blindfolded.

None of these training innovations were in Churchill's order, yet they worked exactly as he wanted. On March 4, 1941, the newly minted Commandos launched a surprise raid on the German-occupied Lofoten Islands of Norway. There they captured the rotors and codebooks of an Enigma machine, the top-secret encoder used by Hitler's army. The captured materials helped the British decipher Hitler's internal comms, impacting battles from the Atlantic to North Africa and propelling the Allies to retake Dunkirk—and the rest of France.

Churchill's communication set these events in motion because his precision about his *end* (specially trained hunter-soldiers) allowed his subordinates to use their own imaginations to develop the *middle* (mountain hiking, zip line riding, rabbit stalking, blindfolded boxing). That *middle* fulfilled Churchill's intent in ways that extended beyond his direct sphere of control—indeed, so far beyond that they reached past the 1940s British army to influence the United States a decade later. Part of the *middle* was to ditch standard military helmets for berets the color of oak leaves, giving rise to Commando headgear that was adopted in 1954 by the unconventional soldiers of U.S. Army

Special Forces. Which is why U.S. Army Special Forces now call themselves Green Berets.

Inspired by their Churchillian roots, the Green Berets have a three-step formula for Commander's Intent. Step 1, tell your team the goal of their mission (that is, the story's end). Step 2, explain the *why* of their mission (that is, the story's beginning). Step 3, close your mouth, leaving your team to invent the middle themselves. This defines the strategy without constraining tactics (see chapter 2), allowing your team to use their initiative to do what you intend, not just what you literally say.

Failed internal comms—whether orders delivered by military commanders, directives issued by CEOs, or instructions given by parents—are usually blamed by the communicator on the audience. *My soldiers didn't listen. My team couldn't execute. My kids weren't able to focus.* This is rarely true. In most cases, the communicator departed from the Green Berets' Churchillian formula. The communicator either wasn't clear about the goal or wasn't clear about the *why.*

If your internal comms aren't working, start by making sure that you haven't given your team two (or more) goals. Sometimes this error is obvious: A communication literally tells a team to run in multiple directions. Often it's more subtle: A communication contains an order that contradicts a previous goal. This is a symptom of reactive management. It reflects a failure on the part of the communicator to determine the main goal. (See chapter 1.) Without that determination, communication has failed before a word is uttered.

The second-most-common error is to provide a goal without a *why,* so that when an unexpected obstacle (or opportunity) arises, your team isn't able to anticipate what you would do, creating hesitation, inertia, or disconnected extemporization.

Effective communicators don't blame their audience. And they don't obsess over word choice, hand gestures, or speaking from the chest in a deep voice. There are endless words, gestures, and voice tones that can work. The ones that work best are ones that come naturally to you, because they are your unique style—the style that you are comfortable with and that others recognize as your honest form of self-expression. Beyond that, style in comms is not essential.

What *is* essential is being consistent about a single goal—and articulating *why* that goal matters. With this method, your team's performance won't be programmed. Like a Commando op or a live Shakespeare production, it will emerge through improvised responses to shifting conditions. But if every team member understands the main objective and the global motive, the story will hang together, advancing your plot to the end.

SINCE THE EXECS AREN'T NOTETAKERS, I ask them for a business card. On the back, I write down the formulas for effective communication:

> *External Comms = Inspire a Question, Then Answer It*
> *Internal Comms = One (and Only One) Goal + Why*

Thanking me, the execs take the card and hurry off—except for one exec who lingers, making small talk. Until abruptly, he gets serious. His comms hitch, he confesses, isn't at work. It's at home. He's great at sales and directing teams, but when he leaves the office, he can't seem to communicate with his spouse, his children, his parents, his siblings.

Normally, the exec is poised and eloquent. Yet as he describes his failure to connect with his family, he avoids my gaze and fumbles his words, apologizing for speaking incoherently. What he's now saying he hasn't previously articulated. Not to his wife—or even himself. I'm the first person he's told about his personal struggles. For some reason he can't explain, he feels that he can talk to me.

When the exec divulges that he's never expressed himself like this before, I discern what's gone wrong with his family conversations. They're missing communication's final ingredient: trust. Trust comes from being candid, always, about what's happening in your life. If you don't have trust, you can express yourself perfectly without anyone hearing. Your listeners will comprehend yet not believe, prompting them to respond superficially—if at all. What sounds like a dialogue is actually you monologuing to yourself.

The remedy can be found in one last comms tip: *Before you open your mouth, commit to sharing the full and honest story of your life.* This tip originated many decades ago in a humid valley near the central highlands of Vietnam. At the heart of the valley sat a village of ironwood dwellings thatched with palm leaves. During the early twentieth century, the village bustled. Bicycles clattered down red dirt lanes, cabbage gardens flowered green and purple, and children played in the shade of banyan trees. But in the 1950s, civil war came, bringing death. Afraid, everyone fled for their homes. Even the pigs were corralled indoors, snouts wedged tight in bamboo pens. The squeak of water pumps ceased and sugarcane pastures wilted in the heat.

To restore the village's busy vitality, the U.S. Army dispatched an A-Team of Green Berets on a security mission. The mission's goal was to protect the villagers from the violence that had interrupted their daily routines, so the A-Team operated as a police unit, guarding thoroughfares and arresting armed looters. Yet the Green Berets soon noticed: No matter how many patrols they ran or rifles they confiscated, the old life did not return. The villagers stayed huddled inside, doors locked and windows shuttered. The streets remained vacant of everything but the banyan trees.

This made the Green Berets realize: Law enforcement was not enough. For villagers to leave their houses and mix freely, they couldn't just be safe. They had to *feel* safe. In addition to physical security, they needed emotional security.

Emotional security requires more than the absence of active threats seen by the eyes; it requires the absence of potential threats foreseen by the imagination. That absence brings a prospective serenity that's crucial for the maintenance of societies—and also for individual development, as illustrated by a favorite fact of Green Berets. The fact concerns another Vietnam denizen: tadpoles. Tadpoles hatch in the spring and fatten for months in rice paddies and hibiscus ponds until they're large enough to transform into frogs. But—here's the favorite fact—if tadpoles find themselves in a foreboding habitat (like a creek with traces of past predation or a lake getting shallow from evaporation) they cut short their swim time, turning more quickly into frogs. This is smart: Frogs are better than tadpoles at taking care of themselves. Yet it has a trade-off: Frogs that grow up faster also grow up smaller. By condensing their tadpole phase, they abbreviate the weeks they have to eat, to rest, to get big. Even though their accelerated metamorphosis keeps them alive, it makes them into little frogs.

The same thing happens to human children in emotionally insecure environments. Unsettled by premonitions of bad times ahead, they mature rapidly, learning to fend for themselves. This early adulthood helps them survive but starves them of youthful hours to feed their hearts and dreams, crimping their horizons. As a Green Beret medic puts it to me: "Kids born into fearful homes are more likely to use alcohol and become gang soldiers or sex workers. They're less likely to read books and become artists or leaders. And you just wonder: What if they'd been in a place that let them grow big?"

In the case of the Vietnamese village, the source of emotional insecurity was the Green Berets themselves. To the villagers, the Green Berets were strange men, heavily armed, with unknown motives. Their peacekeeping was appreciated, but the village had received the same protection from earlier warlords, and eventually, they knew, the bill came due. So even though the villagers were unhurt now, they worried: What rapacious payment might these Americans demand in coming days?

To reassure the villagers, the Green Berets shifted their mission goal to emotional security. They laid down their guns. They distributed sweet potatoes and chewing gum. They bowed to village elders, exchanging pleasantries. None of it worked—until one Green Beret found a way to deepen conversation. He observed that although the villagers were nervous to share their opinions, they listened closely when he relayed personal anecdotes about his childhood in the hills of western Georgia, where he'd lived with his mother on a dairy farm outside a one-store town. And gradually, the villagers' listening turned into sharing. They related tales about their own upbringing and the history of their valley, laughing and reminiscing.

As this trading of stories took hold, the Green Berets discovered: The more completely and honestly they shared their biographies, the more completely and honestly the villagers did too, creating a circle of trust that helped restore civil society. Villagers left their doorsteps to chitchat, pigs trotted out of their pens, and children returned to their games. Temples reopened, followed by markets and schools. Out of communication had come community. Or as the Green Berets termed it, *rapport*.

You can build the same rapport across social divides, whether you're in a faraway village or at your own kitchen table. Simply ask yourself: *What facts about my life am I afraid to share?* Then commit to sharing those facts, being candid about your biography. Lay the groundwork for candor by using the techniques we learned in chapters 3 and 6 for integrating past grief and shame into your personal narrative. To be honest with others about our life, we must first be honest with ourselves.

For this method to work, you don't need to share every hard fact about your life. In fact, you don't need to share *any* hard fact. You simply have to be willing to share, if it comes up naturally in conversation. That willingness shows that you're a person who possesses what Green Berets refer to as *authenticity*.

Authenticity isn't something the brain can detect. But the brain is very good at detecting a lack of authenticity. The lack reveals itself when a person acts evasively or defensively in conversation, dodging difficult topics or rejecting them. You won't do that dodging if you've committed to publicly acknowledging the difficult truths of your life. You will instead be calmly open, encouraging others to feel safe doing the same. The result will be a space of authentic connection where trust grows organically.

"This would be a great tip to share with our sales force," the exec muses.

Sure, it would be. But the tip's real purpose is to create the dynamic that has allowed the exec to voice, for the first time, his desire to fix things with his family. He feels that he can express that desire to me, not because I possess special insight into his life but because I've been trained by Green Berets to make peace with my own biography, creating a zone of emotional security where closeness can form between strangers.

The tip's real purpose is, in short, to produce communion. Communion, as Shakespeare discovered (see above), is the deep essence of communication. You'll know its presence when you feel interpersonal warmth, or as Green Berets prefer, *love*. Love begins when you meet someone willing to hear your full story, including the parts you wrestle to admit to yourself. Love flourishes when that someone reciprocates by revealing their full story. And love fades when the mutual disclosures end. Maybe we stop listening, or maybe we quit being transparent. Either way, the circle of trust is ruptured, and we retreat into our separate narratives. For affection to return, we must mingle our life histories again.

The formula for love works for every human relationship, whether it's romantic, familial, or collegial. All it takes is a willingness to share your entire life story. Many of us struggle to develop that willingness. Ashamed of our past or afraid of being judged by others, we conceal or dissemble. Yet as the Green Berets learned in that banyan tree village, the world is full of opportunities for authentic togetherness. To discover them, start by telling your story to yourself, honestly and completely. Then commit to sharing it. Not with everyone, not at first. But with people who aren't evasive or defensive. This will establish emotional security. And in its bond of love, you'll find true communication.

9

COACHING

Unleash the Rookie Like the Football
Champs and Dr. William Osler

They were the world's best football coaches, their fingers fat with championship rings. Yet they still lost sleep over their profession's most basic question: How do you guide your players to reach their full potential?

When I met the coaches, they were wrestling with the thorniest version of the question: the rookie quarterback. The rookie quarterback oozes promise. He has the skill to elevate his team— and the game. He can innovate, adapt, and lead. He can think faster than tacklers and improvise touchdowns, turning busted chalkboard tactics into upset victories.

But also: The rookie quarterback is an accident waiting to happen. He can spook, get tunnel vision, or melt under the lights. He can squander his gift through overconfidence or its opposite: self-doubt. He can be lazy, incurious, or indifferent to his teammates. He can invent as many new ways to lose as he can to win.

The coaches wanted my opinion: How should they handle the rookie? Should they give him a limited playbook, protecting him from mental snow? Or should they treat him respectfully but tough, like he was a veteran?

I knew nothing about football, but I'd learned how to coach rookies from Special Operations, which has a simple rule for on-boarding new talent. The rule is: *Unleash the rookie.* Or in other words: Let the rookie go through the playbook to pick the plays that excite him—then release him to run those plays however he sees fit.

My recommendation startles the coaches. They mull it momentarily. Then they double-check: This rule *really* brings out the rookie's full potential? Absolutely, I say. But that's not why Special Operations uses it. They use it because it brings out the best from everyone on the team. Including the coaches.

I FIRST HEAR THE RULE from an Army pilot.

She's in the 160th Special Operations Aviation Regiment, aka SOAR. The regiment flies a variety of aircraft, mostly helicopters like the stealth Black Hawk and the AH-6 "Killer Egg." It lifts wounded soldiers from alpine peaks, sets fast-roping Green Berets onto submarine decks, and speeds ski-masked Operators on hostage rescues. Its pilots brave extreme weather, usually at night, with hostile gunshots shattering their windshields. They swagger: *We can get you anywhere in the world, plus or minus a second.*

The pilot has an air of immaculate cool. Life on the ground is obviously beneath her. Although she's too polite to say it, I can tell from her languid calm that she's feeling less than stimulated by our conversation. Her heart rate looks to be about five beats per minute.

Our meeting isn't about rookies. It's about how experts get better, because most experts don't. Instead of engaging in continuous ascent, they reach the top—then flatline. The pilot calls this the paradox of expertise: "The paradox is that an expert is a learner who doesn't learn. To become an expert, she had to learn. But an expert is someone who knows. And when you know, you don't need to learn. Meaning that the expert has mastered a skill—*learning*—that she's now wasting."

"But you've figured out how to escape the paradox?" I ask.

The pilot nods. "The secret is: You let the rookie fly."

"How do you let the rookie fly?"

"I take leave of my mind, that's how I do it." The pilot chuckles at her own joke, then continues. "Here's how it works. First I recruit a rookie as my copilot. Then I hand the rookie the controls on a difficult mission, the kind I would find challenging."

"Isn't that dangerous?"

"It can be. But an older pilot, he told me once: *We gotta train our replacements. Or else we'll be doing this the rest of our lives.*" She chuckles again. "That was another joke. We *wish* we could do this the rest of our lives."

I get that letting the rookie fly makes the rookie better. But what I don't get is: "How does that make *you*, the expert, better?"

"It does it in a way I never expected. And it took me a good time to get there. At first, I was on the rookies, tight, correcting them every instant they did something I wouldn't. But after a while, I let the rookies go. And that's when they surprised me."

"They surprised you by doing smart things you wouldn't?"

She laughs. "Sure, once in a while a rookie does something clever, and I pick up that trick for myself. But that's not what I'm talking about. I'm talking about when the rookie gets you into some mess you never imagined. They get aggressive, fly outside their abilities, and before you know it, they've chained together so many mistakes that you can't go back and correct them."

"What do you do then?"

"You *run with* the rookie's mistakes. Instead of trying to undo the error chain, you embrace it. When you do that, you force yourself to find a new way forward, one you've never done before. It's a reality break, like you're flying outside your mind. You don't know how you do it, but you do. Afterwards, when you play it back in your mind, you realize you invented a new trick, in real time."

I imagine myself in a helicopter cockpit, with the alarm lights blinking because my rookie copilot has made sixteen errors simultaneously. "That must be terrifying."

"It is, the first time it happens. But then you realize: *I can handle this.*"

"So you let the rookie take the controls again?"

"That's right. After my heart calms down, after a couple clean flights, I let the rookie fly into another storm. And this time, *I let him fly longer.*"

"You let him fly longer?"

"That's the key. If I saved us from crashing last time, I figure: I had room to spare. And now I'm better than I was then. Because of that experience, I've improved. So I can let the rookie fly longer, chaining more mistakes together. That pushes me closer to my own limit. So when I take back the stick, I *really* have to fly out of my mind."

I imagine myself back in the helicopter as the alarm lights are blinking—*and I'm continuing to let the rookie fly.* More danger indicators are flashing, more warning bells are ringing. But still I keep my hands off the controls, letting the rookie create more problems.

If this sounds nuts to you, it also sounded nuts to me. But then I heard the same thing from other experts.

"Here's how I do it," I'm told by a Hollywood showrunner. She runs a half dozen TV series collectively budgeted in the hundreds of millions of dollars. "I'll give a junior writer control of an episode. Or even of a whole story arc. Then I let them go. I don't correct them, even if I see them making a mistake. I let them go until they've almost crashed the show."

"And then you take over?"

"Yes, but the key is *I don't go back in time and reverse their decisions*. I push forward, owning their choices. I change as little as possible."

This reminds me of the pilot: *You can't undo the rookie's mistakes, because you can't fly backward in time. If you could, you'd reverse and do it your way, not learning anything. But because you have to go on, you challenge yourself to do something new.*

"And that method," I ask the showrunner, "forces you to draw on your full expertise?"

"More than that—it *increases* my expertise. It makes me a better writer."

I ask other showrunners. They agree. One adds: "Same thing when I work with actors. At the start of my career, I used to hate it when an actor objected to a line. I'd think: *Actor, do your damn job and speak what I tell you!* Now, I love it. I let the actor write his own line. And then if we get in a jam during filming, I reach in and save it."

I go to Miami and talk to sales agents with multibillion-dollar portfolios who say: "My best deals have come when a rookie went in some wacky direction, offering clients a deal that didn't exist. To save the deal, I had to find a way to deliver what the rookie promised. When I did, I didn't just close the deal. I increased my own powers. I started seeing new places to make sales that I never saw before."

I go to San Francisco and talk to software magnates who extol the virtues of hiring young programmers. "When we put inexperienced coders on a team, it makes everyone better. We don't try to control the rookies. We encourage their free spirits. That busts through walls in our thinking, inspiring fresh directions."

I go to New York and talk to flight instructors who do a version of SOAR training. "To be clear, I'd *never* do it in an actual aircraft. But in a simulator? Sure. I let the rookie make all kinds of mistakes. Then I take the controls and see: *Can I land the plane?* That shows the rookie: *Don't ever give up.* There's always something you can find, within yourself, to save the aircraft. And every time I do it, it makes me a better pilot. That's the truth. I hope I never end up in an emergency in a real aircraft. But if I do, I believe that I've grown my skills to handle it."

THIS METHOD TAKES ADVANTAGE OF the biological structure of the neuron. The neuron isn't shaped like a wire, running in a straight line from point A to point B. It's shaped like a tree, with a trunk (the axon) that splits into multiple branches (the synapses), allowing it to go from A to B or C or D . . .

This is the same shape as your imagination. (See chapter 2.) The sameness is not coincidental. The neuron's branching anatomy enables your imagination to generate forking actions, making the future a forest of possible stories.

And that's not all that the neuron's shape allows your imagination to do. While your imagination is running neural branches forward, it can jump past those branches to a future destination. From that destination, it can extend neural branches backward . . .

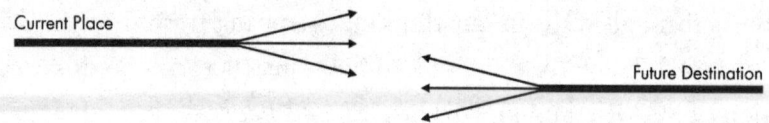

Current Place

Future Destination

. . . until one of the backward branches hits a forward one, and—*voila!*—you've discovered a plan for achieving your goal.

This is what happens in the SOAR pilot's brain when she hands over control. She's not just anticipating all the different ways the rookie could fly ahead. She's also reverse branching from her future target, the landing zone, searching for intersections between the forward trees and the backward.

The same storythinking method is used by earthbound creatives, as I discover from studying improv. Improv is a form of theater where actors spontaneously act out scenes, reacting to one another. The best teams, at hallowed improv institutions like the Groundlings and the Upright Citizens Brigade, are a mix of experts and rookies. Why? Because as one of the experts informs me: "A show needs two things: a creative beginning and a strong ending. Without the beginning, no audience cares. Without the ending, no audience claps."

The creative beginning comes from the rookies. The rookies are good at flying beyond their own abilities and getting into trouble. That trouble is what you want at the start of an improv show. It creates an impression of spectacular danger, exciting the crowd and getting the adrenaline pumping. But if the show goes on like that too long, it wanders, chaotically, until it runs out of gas. To stop this from happening, the more experienced members of the improv team gradually take control, guiding the show to its landing. Which they do by jumping forward to an imagined ending—then plotting back, in branches, until they find a branch that intersects with one of the branches that a rookie is creating.

You don't need to be in a cockpit or live onstage to trust your brain to do this. The fact that it works in both places should, however, give you confidence: You can risk it.

But wait, you might be thinking. *Isn't this a technique for experts? How do I know if I'm one of those exceptional creatures?* You know by running a simple diagnostic: Hand control of what you're doing to a rookie. If you experience intense apprehension when you do this but get more relaxed the more the rookie flies into the unknown, then you're an expert. That's because you have to work hard initially to restrain your caution— but can rapidly draw on your brain's storythinking powers to anticipate answers to the problems that the rookie is creating.

If you feel less relaxed the more the rookie flies, then you're not an expert yet. You need more practice to imagine at the speed of life. And if you feel relaxed at the thought of handing over the controls in the first place—congratulations! You're the rookie! Whoever gave you the controls, make sure they're in the cockpit before you do anything else.

All of us are expert at something. If you think otherwise, spend an afternoon mentoring a child. They'll immediately pick up on things that you are good at. You might think those things are no big deal. You might think that anyone could learn them. Well, thinking like that is the mark of an expert.

—————

I'M SAYING THIS TO THE football coaches when they interrupt me. They point out that I haven't addressed their core concern: What's best for the rookie? Instead, I've explained what's best for them, the coaches.

I agree. That's exactly what I've been doing. Because I don't believe that the coaches' core concern is what's best for the rookie; they'd love to trade him for a robot quarterback they could program to do exactly as instructed. Which reveals: The coaches' core concern is handing over control.

That's why I've shared the SOAR pilot's technique of unleashing the rookie. It demonstrates that the path to coaching success isn't control. It's trust. Trust in your own coaching experience. To coach your best, you have to believe: Whatever the rookie mucks up, you can unmuck. The more you trust, the more you relax, and the more you relax, the more you unleash your intuition, adapting to the unknown like a Special Operator.

But let's say that I'm wrong about the coaches' root concern. Let's say that their top priority really is the rookie's long-term growth. The best coaching method remains: Unleash the rookie. Army Special Operations has confirmed the effectiveness of this method with legions of rookies, and there are countless other examples of its success, not just in improvisational occupations like Hollywood and sales but in highly regulated professions like manufacturing, engineering, and medicine.

As an example from manufacturing, there's Robert Noyce, the 1950s Silicon Valley chip builder who paved the way for Woz and Jobs (see chapter 1) by handing million-dollar electronics projects to recent college grads. As an example from engineering, there's the Apollo space program, which used Noyce's electronics to land Neil Armstrong on the moon (see chapter 7) by staffing its mission control with engineers whose average age—according to NASA historian Sandra Tetley—was twenty-six.

And as an example from medicine, there's Dr. William Osler. Osler was born in 1849 on Midwestern Canada's agricultural wetlands. Over the next seventy years, he became history's most effective teacher of physicians, training thousands personally and tens of thousands more through his changes to medical education.

Medical education prior to Osler was a system of cautious control. Students learned in lecture halls, where they memorized the ideas of previous generations. Which is why, year after year, century after century, medicine barely evolved.

Osler changed this with two simple innovations. First, he sent medical students into the hospital wards. Rather than memorizing old cures, they were given their own patients—and asked to heal them. Second, Osler told medical students: *Listen to your patient.* Instead of looking for answers in textbooks, young doctors opened their ears, relied on their intuitions—and were saved from crashing, when necessary, by their instructors.

Osler, in short, unleashed the rookies.

To spread his new curriculum, Osler penned an 1892 textbook, *The Principles and Practice of Medicine*, which became a med school staple, from San Francisco to Shanghai, for more than four decades. One of the textbook's readers was a young Canadian student, Frederick Banting, who enrolled to study medicine at the University of Toronto in 1912. Two decades later, Banting made a pilgrimage to Osler's old Oxford home. By that time, Banting had himself become an eminent physician. He'd spearheaded the discovery of insulin, rescuing millions of diabetics from death, a feat for which he was awarded the Nobel Prize. Yet despite all his professional expertise, when Banting thought of Osler, he still experienced a giddy thrill: "To have been in the same house, slept in the same bed, bathed in the same tub, shaved by the same mirror, talked on the same veranda, viewed the same books and pictures as Sir William Osler fills one with an inspiration that puts sleep to flight."

The same inspiration was felt by thousands of early-twentieth-century doctors whose imaginations were unleashed by Osler's innovations. Alongside Banting, those doctors revolutionized health care, dramatically increasing the rate at which new cures were developed and implemented. Leeches, milk injections, and cocaine were replaced with flu vaccines, blood banks, and antibiotics, increasing life expectancy from forty-six to sixty-five and ushering in the future of modern medicine.

That future is waning in our time, due to math-minded insurance providers and their focus on control: control of cost, control of doctors, control of patients. You can, however, still witness the power of unleashing the rookie in your own coaching, mentoring, or parenting. Empower the individuals in your charge by letting them go, not to abandon them but to get out in front, improvising a flight plan to guide them to a new landing zone.

That's how they reach their full potential. And how you reach yours too.

10

LEADERSHIP

Go Self-Reliant Like Wayne Gretzky and Nikola Tesla

You were born to lead.

I know this because of who you were in the beginning, a thousand centuries ago. Your tribe was barely a dozen, most of them children. At thirty, you became the eldest. And when hunger came, it fell to you to lead through winter to new hunting.

You are descended from generations who passed this test. And you can pass it too. But right now, you are failing because your nature has been hidden from you. Your whole life, you've been taught that you need education. *Education* is a Roman word that means "to be led." It means that you were born to follow.

Education is our modern way. Never in history have humans spent so much time in classrooms, passing school tests instead of life ones. In school, you are told that you inherited a head full of unreason. The unreason comes in many forms: emotion, bias,

ignorance of the facts. Because you are so inherently unreason-
able, school can do only so much to correct you. Still, you submit
to the correction out of fear and shame, hoping it will make you
into someone better. The longer you hope this, the deeper you
distrust your nature. You surrender the power of self-assessment
and rely on institutional validation, losing your internal direction.

As you march toward graduation, you are told that the highest purpose of human life is to be a leader. This resonates with
your spirit. You imagine leading teams—maybe even companies
or countries. But when the time comes to walk at the front, you
falter. You have been ingrained with the habits of a follower, so
leading feels unnatural. Self-conscious, you doubt yourself, and
the people around you sense it, losing faith in your abilities. You
carry on, emptily giving orders that are mostly ignored. Eventually you retire, glad to be free of the incessant self-questioning—
and relieved to see that the person who takes your place falters too.

THIS IS NOT JUST YOUR story. It is a common tragedy. Most
would-be leaders, whether they are twenty-two-year-old platoon
commanders or gray-haired CEOs, fail.

The failure occurs in three main ways. First, there are the
would-be leaders who get spooked, reacting too slowly, soliciting
excessive advice, and trying always to do the safe thing. Second,
there are the would-be leaders who get angry, attempting to impose their will on life's changing tides, shouting and blaming and
intimidating, burning out their teams before getting swallowed
by their own inability to adapt. Third, there are the would-be
leaders who get disorganized, distracted by minor drama, launch-

ing initiatives then contradicting them, spinning fast and going nowhere.

And these failures aren't the real catastrophe. The real catastrophe is the few leaders who succeed. The vast majority of them believe that their success is due to special powers of intelligence, empathy, self-control, or perception. They think that they were born with rare gifts that other people lack. So even in their triumph, they perpetuate the myth of born to follow.

How did a primeval species of leaders become a modern culture of followers? According to the Romans who coined *education*, the turning point was the decline of tribal militias. In those militias, heroes led by example, running first to challenges. But then came the rise of empires, and emperors did the reverse of heroes: They stood in the rear and commanded subordinates forward.

The same imperial mindset lies at the core of modern business, which runs on the logic of management. *Management* is a medieval term that means "to steer a horse," and its goal is the same as an emperor's: to influence other people's behavior. The influence can be gentle, like an experienced hand who heeds a stallion's instincts to better control it. Yet it is always about getting the animal to do what the rider wants.

In modern business schools, this steering is often styled as a source of leadership. Most basic is *authoritative leadership*, or telling others what to do. More nuanced is *participative leadership*, or working collaboratively to build consensus. Most prized is *transformational leadership*, or converting people to a shared mission in which they exit their egos to fight for a bigger dream.

But none of these are leadership. They are all still management. Management is exerting influence to guide processes and outcomes. Maybe you achieve that result via clear direction (authoritative). Maybe via active listening and empathetic negotiation (participative). Maybe via inspirational persuasion and charismatic motivation (transformational). All those techniques can produce movement, but none of them—or any other management technique—will produce gains until you do something more fundamental: figure out where you want to go.

That figuring out is leadership. Leadership is taking the first step into tomorrow. It's grabbing opportunities that other people dismiss or don't see.

This root distinction between management and leadership is why no amount of managerial training will ever produce leaders:

- Management trains you to monitor others, but leaders have their eyes on the future ahead, not the legion behind. Like their tribal ancestors, they lead by example. They know: If the path works, others will follow.

- Management trains you to stick to the data, but leaders realize that in changing times, data inhibits adaptation. The highest statistical probability is less likely to work than a fresh possibility, because the numbers have already been outdated by life.

- Management trains you that a supreme decider must be put in charge, but leaders understand that teams of autonomous planners do not splinter into chaos. They extend insights and reinforce breakthroughs.

Managers seeks orchestrated harmony. Leaders seek spontaneous self-direction. Management culminates in benevolent autocracy. Leadership, in respectful democracy.

While leaders are born, managers are produced by education. There were no corporations in the wilds where we evolved. Management emerged instead out of the ancient imperial tax system of accounting. Its purpose was and is to make sure that the numbers add up, whether by abacus, punch card, or digital computer. That's why statistics, finance, and lean productivity remain the core of MBA programs, the summit of management training.

If you want to be a manager, keep going in school. If you want to be a leader, return to the beginning.

IN THE BEGINNING, LEADERS ARE innovators. They see the future, faster. They show the way by spotting the exceptional first.

Next, leaders are resilient. They get stronger from setbacks and smarter from failure. They use honest memories of personal triumph to process the real pain of grief and shame, developing antifragility.

Next, leaders are decision-makers. They know when to push hard on the plan—and when to pivot, fast.

Next, leaders are communicators. They create a new narrative of the future—and spread it. That's why the same brain regions that go active in storytellers go active in successful startup founders.

And finally, leaders are coaches. They unleash the talent in their organization. They don't try to control, influence, or manage. They let the rookies fly.

Leaders, in short, combine the five skills of the preceding chapters. They have united intuition, imagination, emotion, and commonsense, going full Primal.

But as I discover from embedding with U.S. Special Operations, there's one more skill that leaders must possess. It is: self-reliance.

SELF-RELIANCE WAS DESCRIBED IN 1841 by the New England literary sage Ralph Waldo Emerson:

> Whoso would be a man, must be a nonconformist. He who would gather immortal palms must not be hindered by the name of goodness, but must explore if it be goodness. Nothing is at last sacred but the integrity of your own mind.

In other words: Do not worry about the crowd. Follow your own inner rule. This will shock society. They will judge you an eccentric or a menace. They will fear your independence and pity your wasted talent. They will warn that you have gone astray—and are trampling their fences. But you are not lost. You are finding yourself.

In time, people will recognize this. They will see that you have passed the test of your own conscience, and they will honor you with their vote. As Emerson says: "Absolve you to yourself, and you shall have the suffrage of the world." When that happens, you will not just be leading yourself. You will be leading everyone else.

This is what Special Operators mean when they call themselves unconventional. They break the law not out of impertinence but out of reverence. They know that the law is groupthink, fear, and inactivity. It is the rule of the times, not the rule of all time. To find a deeper commandment, Operators leave the road for the hills, keeping their own compass.

It will feel strange to leave the party for your own path. But it is your nature. You entered the world self-reliant. This is easy to overlook, because as children, we seem dependent. But children are possessed of profound autonomy. They don't ask for permission. They run ahead, guided by their own spirit, not caring what people think. They live emotionally and intellectually free. Without trying, they lead.

That self-reliance fades as we age, becoming self-conscious. We fret over how we appear to others. We worry about what the world makes of our behavior. Such concern is not always bad. It can motivate striving for the greater good. But in our modern world, it has become overwhelming. Unlike in ancient days, when villages were pockets in the wild, society is now everywhere, leaving no room to breathe outside. Our species crams the globe, and when people aren't with us physically, they're on our screens, draining away the hours once used for personal reflection.

Yet even though it's harder today to be a leader, it's not impossible. Human nature has not changed, as you can see from the long walk.

THE LONG WALK IS A training exercise developed in the 1950s by the British Commandos. (See chapter 8). In the 1970s, it was adapted by classified U.S. Army units to cultivate self-reliance.

The long walk starts when you are placed in unknown wilderness. You then set off alone to reach a far-off destination. Unlike in a traditional military task, no one observes your journey. You have no companions, no superior, to say whether you are headed in the right direction. You must make your own path through strange terrain, trusting your intelligence. If you arrive, you are honored as a leader.

The long walk is what Operators call *simple not easy*. Like keeping a promise or moving on from a mistake, it's straightforward to understand in theory but hard to execute in practice. So hard that almost no one succeeds. Some get disoriented, others injured. But the vast majority simply quit. They cannot handle the stress of being their own guide. Overcome by self-doubt, they turn back, seeking the security of an outside opinion. They would rather be told that they have failed than live in the uncertainty of their own progress.

The same clamor of nerves afflicts us all when we dare to venture by ourselves in unfamiliar directions. These ventures require us to assess, without data or external counsel, whether we're headed in the right direction. They are our own long walk. And on it, we struggle. We set out full of energy but grow increasingly doubtful. Questioning ourselves, we slow our pace, double back, and halt at crossroads.

That halt is typically permanent. If we stall during an independent enterprise—whether it's starting a business, launching a scientific initiative, or embarking as an artist—we become less likely to attempt again. And if we make a second attempt, we usually quit faster. We have lost faith in our capacity to forge ahead solo. Our brain has decided: *I am not self-reliant.*

It's possible, however, to reverse that decision. When Operators fail the long walk, they're given an opportunity to perform a "recycle," where they learn to activate the mental power known as *vision*. Vision comes from imagination, which looks beyond the now, glimpsing potential futures. (See chapter 2.) Vision grabs one of those futures, claiming it as our destination. It's the tomorrow that we pursue. It's the possibility that we commit to making real.

By setting our ultimate goal, vision bolsters self-reliance.

Like an internal compass, it gives our brain the assurance that we know where we're headed, encouraging us to go on rather than asking for help. That's why Operators who activate vision improve at the long walk: The success rate for Operators who recycle is higher than the success rate for first-timers.

To activate vision, the recycle employs a simple mantra: *Vision can be coached but can't be cautious.* Let's break it down, starting with the first part: coaching.

COACHING, AS WE SAW IN chapter 9, unleashes the rookie. This method is highly effective for activating vision, as the Operators illustrate by walking me through coaching's proving ground: sports. They point to Richard Williams, the father of Serena Williams, who released his thirteen-year-old daughter's independent foresight by pulling her out of a regimented tennis academy. They describe the way that Pelé, Michael Jordan, and Joe Montana were coached to see—then seize—future possibilities. And they share the inside story of the Great One, Wayne Gretzky.

Gretzky was a hockey player with such powerful vision that he became revered as a prophet. When Steve Jobs unveiled the iPhone at the 2007 Macworld Expo, he explained its prescient electronics by saying:

> There's an old Wayne Gretzky quote that I love. "I skate to where the puck is going to be, not where it has been." And we've always tried to do that at Apple.

Gretzky was so good at winning the race to the future that his opponents suspected he had mystical assistance. Gretzky knew otherwise:

Some say I have a "sixth sense." . . . Baloney, I've just learned to guess what's going to happen next. It's anticipation. It's not God-given, it's Wally-given.

Wally was Gretzky's father. And also Gretzky's coach. It was Wally who taught Gretzky anticipation. To explain how, Gretzky acted out a typical training session from his childhood:

Wally: "Where's the last place a guy looks before he passes?"

Me: "The guy he's passing to."

Wally: "Which means . . ."

Me: "Get over there and intercept it."

Here, Wally coaches Gretzky to peer inside his opponent's head. And he does so by teaching Gretzky to see inside his—Wally's—head, anticipating his thoughts before he speaks them:

Wally: "Which means . . ."

Me: "Get over there and intercept it."

In our computer age, coaches often treat anticipation as a math equation: *Forecast the puck's vector by analyzing the angle of your opponent's eyes.* By coaching this way, they don't unleash the rookie. They *program* the rookie, making logic's mistake of thinking that the future can be predicted, when the best that life allows is the imagination of possibilities that you bring to pass through your own actions. Read Gretzky's words and you will see: He never says that he computes the puck's trajectory. Instead, he calls anticipation a "guess," a product not of algebra but of creative conjecture. That's because Wally didn't coach by treating Gretzky like a robot. Wally provided broad strategic direction—then released the controls and let Gretzky fly.

This coaching technique is why Gretzky became more than a duplicate of Wally. As Gretzky got older, he realized that he couldn't rely on Wally's eye-watching trick: Good players didn't always look before they passed the puck. But because Gretzky had been unleashed instead of programmed, he was able to use his imagination to extend Wally's method. He saw that every player had distinct tells—aka exceptional information—that indicated the plans inside their minds. From the distinctive flatness of Howie Morenz's stick blade, Gretzky intuited how the late great played, and in a game, he did the same with multiple players simultaneously. Keying in on their unique traits, he envisioned the story of the game's coming seconds.

Gretzky achieved this without Wally. He'd developed his own vision, becoming self-reliant.

You can learn vision like Gretzky did: from a coach. To get that coach, seek out a mentor with expertise in your chosen field, whether it's sport or engineering, business or politics. If you don't know where to look for a mentor, start by connecting with people who've recently retired from your dream job. They're no longer working full time, so they'll have some spare minutes to talk. And they'll also have a lifetime of experience to share.

Yet no matter how experienced your mentor, don't forget: *Go where experts can't say no.* (See chapter 8.) Listen to your mentor when they tell you that your plan won't work. But don't look to them to tell you what to do. Seek the path yourself. Activate intuition to see exceptions to current rules. (See chapter 1.) Use imagination to extend those exceptions into possible futures. (See chapter 2.) Draw on emotion to determine which future resonates for you. (See chapter 3.)

Your mentor will want you to develop this independence. Because a good mentor will do for you what Wally did for Gretzky: activate your vision. That vision will carry you beyond your mentor's expertise—and beyond everyone's, including your own. Which brings ·us to the second part of the Operators' rule for activating vision: Don't be cautious.

"CAUTIOUS ISN'T LEADING," THE OPERATORS tell me bluntly. "It's following."

I'm not on board with that statement. I believe leadership can—and should—be cautious. After all, not-cautious leadership is reckless leadership. And reckless leadership wastes sweat and blood on long shots and daydreams, sacrificing the good of the team for the commander's thoughtless whims. If there's one quality I want, always, in a leader, it's care for the team. I want to know that my leader is protecting my interests, putting my future first.

The Operators agree. In fact, they could not agree more violently. Which is why, they say, they don't want cautious leaders. "Cautious leaders mortgage the future. They kill your tomorrow by safeguarding their today."

To prove it, the Operators take me to Pineland, the lunar jungle where they train recruits to activate intuition. (See chapter 1.) In Pineland's early days, the Army noticed: After recruits learned to spot exceptional information, they detected threats and opportunities with equal accuracy—yet they did not treat the threats and opportunities the same. When recruits spotted a threat, they usually acted on it. When they spotted an opportunity, they almost never did.

I am fascinated by this discovery. "The recruits reacted faster to threats than opportunities?"

"Yes. Much faster. They responded to threats immediately. But when they saw opportunities, they hesitated. In fact, they hesitated so long that they usually didn't act until the opportunity had passed."

"Why? What was stopping them?"

"They got cautious."

"But why?"

"The most common explanation they provided in after-action reviews was that they were 'thinking critically.' And by thinking critically, they convinced themselves that the opportunity was too good to be true."

Now I understand. Critical thinking comes from logic, which doubts anything not proven by data. Since new opportunities have no track record, they're discounted.

"It makes you feel like you're being safer," the Operators observe. "But really, it's a fatal error. By pausing for more intel instead of seizing opportunity, you deprive your team of a foothold in tomorrow, dooming them to die when time ticks on. That's why we call it mortgaging the future."

Pursuing unproven opportunities is the definition of leadership. Leadership exists to take the next step into the future. If you don't take that step, you're not leading. You're following the data. And following is an action that your team can take without you.

"How," I ask the Operators, "did you train recruits to act on the opportunities they saw?"

"We sped up their vision by giving them a little reading."

"Reading?" I'd been expecting something more high-tech.

"Yeah, reading. We'll show you."

The Operators usher me down a steel elevator to an underground library, built from poured concrete and lit with cheap fluorescent bulbs. Its metal bookcases are stacked with black folios of mission scenarios. The scenarios look like ones I've seen in Army history archives. But there's a twist: They're from wars that haven't happened.

"Made-up wars?" I ask. "You speed up vision by reading fiction?"

"Not any fiction. *Realistic* fiction. These are wars we believe can happen in the near future."

Taking a black folio from a shelf, I see that it's filled with fictional but realistic examples of exceptional information: innovative weapons, irregular enemies, original tactics. These singularities leap the brain from *middle* to *beginning* to *end*, prompting the recruits to glimpse potential tomorrows. (See chapter 8.) The glimpses are often so vivid that recruits jump out of their library chairs. They have been launched—literally—into imagining future plans and strategies.

Different future plans and strategies resonate with different readers. This often makes readers worry that personal bias is blinding them to better options, but within imagination's zone of possibility, all options are viable. What matters is who acts most assertively to make their vision happen. Rather than trying to weigh the pros and cons of every possible tomorrow, it's more effective to dash hard and fast for a tomorrow that fits with your life narrative. If that tomorrow is invalidated by new events, abandon it instantly. Otherwise, keep dashing.

This speed of action is facilitated by the underground library's commitment to realistic fiction. The fiction creates a speculative space where recruits feel liberated to seize on possibility, practicing the mental mechanics of vision. Meanwhile, the realistic nature of the fiction limits magical thinking, so that like practicing acrobatics in half gravity instead of none, it helps the training transfer to the world outside.

The transfer is evident when recruits return to the field. They continue to react rapidly to new threats. Yet now they also react rapidly to new prospects. They have unshackled their vision from critical thinking, outrunning previous facts to grab future opportunities.

Make-believe stories having this real-world effect? It might seem incredible, maybe even fictional. Yet the history of business schools shows: The same training can benefit other would-be leaders.

WOULD-BE LEADERS ARE EVERYWHERE, MORTGAGING the future with their caution. That caution is a global product of modern education, but nowhere is it more directly counterproductive to leadership development than in business schools, where it has produced the initiative suppresser known as "define the problem."

"Define the problem" is a logical technique devised in early 1900s America by Frederick Taylor and Alexander Hamilton Church, the founders of modern management theory. Modern management theory is based on the premise that good managers don't simply enforce existing processes; they improve those processes by identifying and eliminating inefficiencies. The more accurately managers can pinpoint an inefficiency—that is, the better they can "define the problem"—the more rapidly they can arrive at a quantifiable solution.

During the first decades of the twentieth century, this focus on logical problem-solving became the foundation of Harvard's MBA program—and also of industrial psychology, the precursor to organizational psychology. After World War II, it was established as a mainstay of international manufacturing, from automotive to electronics, by Homer Sarasohn and Charles Protzman's 1949 textbook *The Fundamentals of Industrial Management*:

> As engineers and management people, we are convinced that the logical approach to determining what changes are needed and the benefits to be derived from them stems from the use of . . . five steps. They are:
>
> 1. Define the problem precisely.

During the later twentieth century, "define the problem" was pushed deeper into global industry by consulting firms such as McKinsey—and also by design thinking, which instructed managers to (1) define the problem and (2) ideate a solution through progressive iterations.

There's nothing inherently wrong with "define the problem." It's a fine way to tweak and troubleshoot factory assembly lines. Yet it has become a systemic drag on leadership development because it is misrepresented by design thinkers, organizational psychologists, and corporate consultants. Instead of being advertised as what it is, a management tool for optimizing current systems, it is marketed—across the world's top business schools—as a driver of innovation. This pitch has sold a lot of MBAs, but at a cost: It restricts the future to being an updated version of the present, constraining enterprise and limiting initiative.

To uncover innovation's real source, let's flip the method of McKinsey, Frederick Taylor, and *The Fundamentals of Industrial Management*. Instead of looking at how modern industry oils its existing machinery, let's look at how it was invented in the first place.

Modern industry and its corporate leaders—Apple, SpaceX, Nvidia—sprang from the enterprise of engineers such as Alexander Graham Bell, Robert Goddard, and Claude Shannon. Bell pioneered the telephone, ushering in the communication age. Goddard pioneered the liquid rocket, ushering in the space age. Shannon pioneered electronic computing, ushering in the digital age.

These feats took vision—and like the vision of the Operators at Pineland, it was nurtured by stories. In the cases of Bell, Goddard, and Shannon, the stories were science fiction. Bell devoured Jules Verne and memorized the Shakespearean tales that inspired *Frankenstein*. Goddard was obsessed with H. G. Wells's *The War of the Worlds*. Shannon's love of sci-fi was lifelong; in his twilight years, he was copying out passages from Robert Silverberg's *Lord Valentine's Castle*.

By immersing themselves in science fiction, these engineers engaged imagination, which, as we saw in part I, has two connected functions:

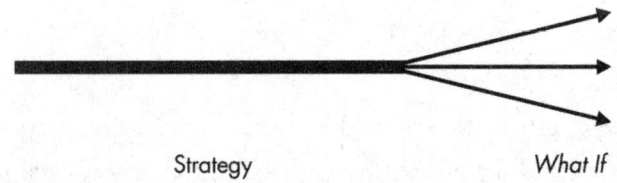

Strategy   What If

First, imagination multiplies *what if*. As Shannon put it: "Like a science fiction writer, I'm thinking, *what if*." Second, imagination helps *define the strategy*. (See chapter 2.) Goddard said after reading *The War of the Worlds*: "I imagined how wonderful it would be to make some device which had even the *possibility* of ascending to Mars." This possibility became Goddard's grand dream, the bigger intent that concentrated his rocketry work.

Imagination's first function is the one most associated with entrepreneurial leadership, yet the second is equally crucial. Like "define the problem," *define the strategy* hones our purpose, but instead of confining us to logical probabilities, it launches us after a single long-term possibility. It operates, in short, as a source of vision. By clarifying our big goal, it helps us determine which opportunities fit with where we're headed, so that instead of second-guessing, we jump fast. The result is a smart incaution that emboldens us to grab strange treasures. Strange treasures aren't always gold; life brims with glitter. What gets us duped, however, isn't a lack of critical thinking. It's a failure to sharpen our individual strategy. That sharpening makes our vision less like anything that other people could fabricate—or that could happen accidentally.

Bell, Goddard, and Shannon weren't the only industrial pioneers who used imaginative stories to define their strategy. History bursts with examples—dozens, hundreds, thousands. But one is enough to illustrate how powerfully story can unbridle vision, leaping us quicker when prospects appear. That example is Nikola Tesla.

TESLA WAS BORN IN 1856 on the borderlands of the Austrian Empire. As a child, he hunted frogs through forests of black pine. In his twenties, he dropped out of university and immigrated to America, where he invented a revolutionary electric motor.

Prior to Tesla, the electric motor had been an exotic gadget. It ran on direct current (DC), which could be transmitted only about a mile, limiting it to a few urban hot spots. Yet Tesla saw: This geographic constraint could be surmounted by switching from direct to alternating current (AC). AC could be conducted at high voltage over long distances, making it available to everyone, everywhere. Electricity would become an everyday convenience, powering kitchen appliances and filling homes with light. All that was needed was a cheap and reliable AC motor.

A prototype of such a motor had been developed in 1879 by physicist Walter Baily. Successive rounds of tinkering had, however, yielded no significant advances. Tesla's teachers concluded that a practical AC motor was impossible. Tesla's idol—Thomas Edison—declared DC to be the future.

Tesla defied this consensus. He began by rejecting Baily's prototype—and, in fact, by rejecting *all* prototyping. Prototyping, like "define the problem," shifts the focus of engineering from innovation onto iteration. And iteration, as Tesla pointed out, can only refine existing systems. It cannot blaze a trail to new ones.

To do that trailblazing, Tesla looked beyond logic: "We have, undoubtedly, certain finer fibers that enable us to perceive truths when logical deduction . . . is futile." Like Gretzky, he imagined the future: "When I get an idea I start at once building it up in my imagination." And like Bell, Goddard, and Shannon, he accelerated his vision with narrative fiction. He read Shakespeare. He recited Serbian epics. He memorized the plays of Johann Wolfgang von Goethe.

Goethe, as we saw in chapter 5, was the second name on

Einstein's list of modern innovators, the link between Shakespeare and scientific revolution. And in February 1882, Goethe's fiction prompted Tesla to envision a new strategy for taking electricity mainstream:

> I was enjoying a walk with my friend [Antal Szigeti] in the [Budapest] City Park and reciting poetry. At that age I knew entire books by heart, word for word. One of these was Goethe's *Faust*. The sun was just setting and reminded me of the glorious passage: "The glow retreats . . ." As I uttered these inspiring words the idea [for the AC motor] came like a flash of lightning.

To experience that flash yourself, start, like Tesla, with Goethe's *Faust*. In the "glorious passage" Tesla quoted on his walk, a mind rotates the earth while its body stands still:

> The glow retreats, done is the day of toil;
> It yonder hastes, new fields of life exploring;
> Ah, that no wing can lift me from the soil
> Upon its track to follow, follow soaring!
> A glorious dream! though now the glories fade.
> Alas! the wings that lift the mind no aid
> Of wings to lift the body can bequeath me.

While imagining that turning without turning, Tesla had a vision of a motor that performed the same action: a mind (i.e., a magnetic field) rotating while its body (i.e., its metal casing) stood still. This was the AC motor Tesla built—the motor that spins the wheels of modern industry.

Tesla did not build the motor immediately. To settle on a precise blueprint, he had to explore many potential *what ifs*. Those *what ifs* were, however, now joined in his mind to a defined strategy: *a rotating magnetic field in a stationary metal casing*. Like Goddard when H. G. Wells's *War of the Worlds* focused his imagination on building a Mars-seeking rocket, Tesla had seen where he was going, and with his destination clarified by Goethe's story, he knew which opportunities to seize. Two months after his flash of inspiration, he hopped from Budapest to Paris to hone his engineering skills at an Edison dynamo factory. In 1884, he sprang across the Atlantic to join Edison's New York Machine Works, where he learned the business of selling electricity. Until, in 1885, he split from Edison to strike out on his own.

When Tesla departed the world's most powerful electric company, his former colleagues branded him a crank, and, unable to secure financing for his inventions, he dug ditches to pay for his dinner. But Tesla's vision guided him through this destitute period. While grinding out a living as a repairman, he persuaded a telegraph exec and a patent attorney to rent him a lab at 89 Liberty Street, in Lower Manhattan. And when the lab opened in April 1887, he anticipated exactly what equipment to stock: *Wire coils to produce the rotating magnetic field, laminated iron to make the metal casing, brass bolts to hold it all together. . . .*

A few months later, he connected the coils to an iron rotor. Rushing in where logic feared to tread, he'd forged his revolutionary motor.

TESLA USHERED IN THE ELECTRIC age by doing what leaders do: Imagine a story, then live it. This can seem a mystic feat, but it has a primal recipe: Mix vision with self-reliance. Vision jumps ahead to see a route that self-reliance walks, making dream reality.

You can lead your own original age by using the same recipe. It's simple. But it won't be easy. You will have to leave the safety of consensus, hazarding dark country. So how do you know that you are ready? How do you know that you can press forward on shifting ground, grabbing the chance that others doubt?

Operators know by using a self-assessment they call *Covert Victory*. A covert victory is a victory that you hold secret because you don't feel the need to bond or brag. It's the successful mission that your own children will never know about. It's the heroes' wall in the compound where the U.S. Army's most classified unit trains, the wall that contains no names.

To run *Covert Victory*, ask yourself: When you succeed, can you keep it private? Or do you feel the need to tell others? Do your acts of courage and charity feel real only when you broadcast them to the world?

If you do a hard thing, congratulations. If you attain greatness, congratulations. But if those congratulations mean something to you, you're still dependent on outside voices to tell you that you're on track. To discover your inner compass, you need to keep defining your strategy: What's the goal that sets you apart from the people around you? What's the destination that you would choose above any other? What's the possibility that you would sacrifice everything to achieve?

Find the answers by building your bookshelf, like Bell, Shannon, and Goddard. Sharpen your imagination with realistic fiction. Look beyond patterns. Anticipate horizons.

And after the flash of clarity arrives, keep inspiration going. Don't be the leader who falls into believing that the rest of the world was made to follow. Instead, when you see someone else preparing for their long walk, remember who you were at the beginning, a thousand centuries ago. You were not a horse to be managed, a problem to be defined, or a computer to be programmed. You were a free original, an intelligence acting faster than precedent.

The initiative you displayed back then became the collective origin of our species, the mutual inheritance guiding each new generation through winter's night. And that mutual inheritance reveals: You're not the only one who's born to lead. Everyone you meet is.

So coach their self-reliance. Kindle their vision. Be like Wally to Gretzky, Goethe to Tesla. Lead the next leader into the future.

Beauty, the world seemed to say.
And as if to prove it (scientifically)
wherever he looked, beauty sprang instantly.
—VIRGINIA WOOLF

PART III

PRIMAL SCIENCE

11

MOTO

From the Biological Big Bang to William Shakespeare

The sky is clear, the breeze is calm, and the air tastes like nitric oxide.

It's June 2021, in the North Carolina bogs of the Army's Fort Bragg. I've been advised—*strongly*—to wear sunglasses. Not to block the glare. To stop the horseflies from eating my eyes.

I'm at Bragg to visit a covert training site. I've been in many other covert training sites, so I'm expecting a playground of pricey tech: virtual reality simulators, waterless recuperation baths, algorithmic heart monitors. But the site is not that. It's the opposite: aggressively primitive. Its corridors have the feel of a 1970s student co-op: haphazard furniture, ambient sweat, people roaming round half dressed. There are spartan sheds linked by crumbling tarmac. There are driftwood pits where gladiators wrestle. There are temples built from dead helicopters.

In the dirty heat beside the temples, I greet a group of military men and women. I do not know their names. I know only that they are Special Operators.

Over the days and months that follow, I will learn that the Operators are legends within their community. They come from 1st SFOD-Delta, the U.S. Army's elite direct-action unit. They come from the British SAS, the world's first special operations outfit. They come from Canada's Joint Task Force 2, the U.S. Army's Green Berets, and the U.S. Navy's DEVGRU. And they come from another Army unit I am not cleared to name.

These are the Operators you've encountered over the previous chapters. For me, however, it's the first time I've met them. They're guarded but friendly. They've heard that I come bearing a gift: a new science to help them act smart when chaos hits and logic breaks.

Over this book's remaining pages, I'll give you the science that I shared with them. To lay it out, I'll tell two stories. The second, in chapter 12, will be the story of how I discovered the science of Primal. The first, in this chapter, will be the story of Primal itself: how it emerged in prehistoric times and why it has been exiled from our modern world.

PRIMAL INTELLIGENCE IS POWERED BY the animal neuron, which evolved in the Cambrian oceans more than five hundred million years ago. That era has been called the Biological Big Bang because life diversified explosively, generating fresh species that gobbled up resources—then took to gobbling up each other. The resulting competition intensified life's age-old concern: *Eat.* And it added a new, no less pressing concern: *Don't get eaten.*

The first concern, *Eat,* is the origin of logic. The second,

Don't get eaten, is the origin of story. Here's how those two origins transpired:

- To eat, the brain developed the power to see food. It did so through neurons that detected light, switching on and off. That switching is how transistors work. And like transistors, the neurons ran symbolic logic. They inducted data through the eye and identified spatial patterns that correlated with nutritious meals, operating computationally.

- To not get eaten, the brain developed the power to act creatively. It did so through neurons that were mechanically different from transistors. Instead of absorbing data, those neurons innovated behavior, escaping predators by initiating surprising movements. Such movements were most effective not when they were random but when they anticipated the eater's intention, investing evasion with maximum precision for minimum effort. And such movements were also most effective when they chained together reinforcing actions, so that rather than thrashing haphazardly, they proceeded with fluid coherence and gathering momentum.

These dual functions of intelligence evolved, in tandem, over the next half billion years. Each now makes up a large share of our modern human brain:

- The symbolic logic function birthed our visual cortex, which is an extraordinarily powerful computer, capable of rendering megabytes of sensory data into three-dimensional

images. In time, it also birthed higher-order algorithmic functions—arithmetic, deduction, interpretation—
powering brain regions that can add, make arguments,
and handle certain language elements (e.g., nouns and
adjectives).

• The creative action function birthed our motor cortex,
which enables the fingers of surgeons, the hips of athletes, and the arms of dancers to discover movements
that heal injuries, elude tacklers, and delight audiences.
In time, it also birthed mental processes such as causal
and counterfactual cognition (i.e., thinking *why* and
what if). Those processes now power brain regions that
handle verbs (the language element beyond symbolic
logic) and that drive the hypotheses of scientists, the tactics of soldiers, the imaginations of engineers, the plans
of entrepreneurs, the strategies of politicians, and the
narratives of storytellers.

These two functions make our brain different from computers. Unlike computers, our brain doesn't think only in data and
abstractions. It *can* think in data and abstractions. But it can
also think in exceptions and actions, allowing us to spot emergent opportunities and initiate new technologies.

When I explain our brain's two functions, one of the Operators frowns. "You say computers can't think in actions. But what
about this?" She shows me her laptop. On its screen is an AI-
generated animation of a galloping horse. "Isn't this an action?"

That's a great question. And the answer is: Yes and no. Yes,
the horse is performing an action—galloping—in our brain, and
no, it isn't performing an action in the computer. To unriddle this

paradox, let's tease apart the mechanical difference between logic and action. Logic is one thing equaling another (A = B). Action is one thing *leading to* another (A → B). The distinction can seem trivial, but it's so fundamental that logicians from Aristotle to Bertrand Russell have acknowledged that logic can get no closer to action than if-then statements, which are often conflated in human conversation with A → B but which are actually correlation, or in other words, A = B. This is why AI thinks in webs of correspondences, i.e., patterns, while most human intelligence is thinking in chains of causes, i.e., narratives.

(If the difference between logic and action is unclear, here's an example. Since logic is A = B, computers process events as equations, so to an AI, *if fire then smoke* means *fire = smoke*. And since the terms on either side of an equation are interchangeable, it also means *smoke = fire*. This interchangeability works in semiotics, because if there's fire, that's a sign of smoke, and if there's smoke, that's a sign of fire. But when translated into motion, it violates physics. In the real world, *A → B* is not the same as *B → A*, any more than *fire → smoke* is the same as *smoke → fire*. The former states that fire causes smoke. The latter states that smoke causes fire. Which is to say: The former is physics, while the latter is hallucination. When our brain hears *if fire then smoke*, our neurons can convert it into *fire → smoke*. But an AI can know only *fire = smoke*, conflating physical action with magical thinking.)

Because computers think in A = B, the horses that seem to gallop across the laptop are not, in fact, acting. Their action is an illusion created by the screen cycling through frozen horse snapshots, like a hand flicking the pages of a cartoon flip-book. And crucially, that illusion can't be perceived by the computer, only by us. By thinking A → B, we can imagine horses galloping, and when we see those horses on the laptop screen, we can imagine something else: that the computer perceives the horses galloping too. The computer, however, can see the horses only as static images, which means that when an AI tries to generate moving animals, the best it can do is mix and match old snapshots of A = B. It can't create original A → B.

How can our brain invent actions that computers can't? Is it because we possess a mystical power, like consciousness? No. The explanation is entirely mechanical.

OUR BRAIN THINKS A → B through motor intelligence. Motor intelligence can be abbreviated as *moto*. It runs on a nonlogical brain machine: the synapse.

The synapse is a junction between two neurons. It was discovered by the world's first neuroscientist, Santiago Ramón y Cajal, at the end of the nineteenth century. Viewed by microscope, it appears to be a gap, a fact that prompted an eminent group of twentieth-century scientists, the Sparks, to hypothesize that the synapse worked like an electronic switch. An electronic switch can be as simple as a semiconductor (aka a transistor) inserted into a circuit, and one elementary kind of semiconductor is a gap. The gap interrupts the circuit, keeping it "off"—unless the electricity is cranked high enough to lightning bolt across, turning the circuit "on." This off/on mechanism can, as Claude Shannon discovered in 1937, run logic's three operations: AND-OR-NOT. And due to the engineering marvel of the metal oxide semiconductor (or MOS) transistor, it now powers all—*all*—the algorithms of AI.

If the synapse worked like a MOS transistor, the human brain would think like AI, cogitating in bytes and mathematical equations. But because of the Nobel Prize research done by neuroscientist John Eccles in the 1950s, we know that the Sparks were wrong. Neurons do not connect via lightning bolts. They connect instead via protein transmitters and other physical machinery. When neuron A extends a path to neuron B, that's not a MOS transistor thinking A = B. It's a synapse thinking *A leads to B*, or in other words, A → B.

(*But couldn't you digitally simulate that synapse with computer software, thereby programming MOS transistors to think like neurons?* This question is often posed to me by AI engineers and cognitive scientists. And the answer is another "Yes and no." Yes, you could build a digital simulation of a neuron. But no, that simulation could not replicate the neuron's A → B function. To unriddle this second paradox, remember, as we saw back in chapters 1 and 2, that A → B evolved to process exceptions, aka unknown causes. And unknown causes cannot be simulated by a computer. The software would therefore be able to simulate the neuron in a vacuum, yet it could not simulate the neuron in action. *Wait. Why couldn't you program an unknown cause into the neuron simulation, enabling it to model the neuron in action?* To do that, a human programmer would need to formulate the cause as a mathematical algorithm. Which is to say: The actual neurons in the programmer's brain would have to perform the task of analyzing A → B into A = B, turning an unknown cause into a known equation. The equation could then be simulated by the computer, but at that point, the computer would not be operating like a neuron. Rather than doing the synapse-work of imaginative conjecture, it would be doing the transistor-work of calculating correlations. In short, a computer simulation of a neuron could operate only as a system closed to the exceptional information that the neuron evolved to process. Like the horses galloping on the laptop screen, the digital neuron would thus be a symbolic representation that lacked the physical mechanisms to perform its ostensible function, making it an A = B that looked like an A → B but could not do A → B.)

A → B isn't better than A = B. Yet it's often more useful, which is why it exists in the brain. Ever since the visual cortex evolved, hundreds of millions of years ago, the brain has had the option to go completely A = B, junking moto and thinking in pure logic. But it hasn't. It has retained A → B because moto can act smart in ways that logic can't. Moto runs on feedback, allowing it to operate with low (even no) information, taking the initiative and imagining futures with no precedent. Often, moto's experimental method generates new art, new science, new technology. Always, moto's bias toward action maintains a healthy psychological momentum that helps the brain overcome setbacks and push through uncertainty.

Moto is largely insentient. We're not aware of the action sequences that our neurons use to drum rhythms, write letters, slice bread. That's why artists, auto mechanics, and other physical practitioners often can't articulate how they move their limbs. Instead, they say: *Just watch me and imitate.*

Yet even though we're not usually conscious of moto, we can consciously train it, enabling our brain's motor regions to produce more creative, targeted, and effective actions. Our tool for doing this is story.

STORY IS A SEQUENCE OF actions: *This event caused that event, which caused another event.* When we imagine a story, we draw on our brain's power of moto, because moto is the mechanism that generates new actions. And just as moto can inspire story,

story can impact moto. If we use story to imagine a strategic goal (see chapter 10), that goal can focus moto to invent paths to get there; if we use story to review our past (see chapter 6), that review can activate moto to process old anxieties into new SOPs.

When we employ story in these conscious ways, we're story-thinking, or to be more technical, we're engaging narrative cognition, which differs from deduction, interpretation, critical thinking, and the rest of logic. To tease apart the difference, count the number of symbolic representations in this picture:

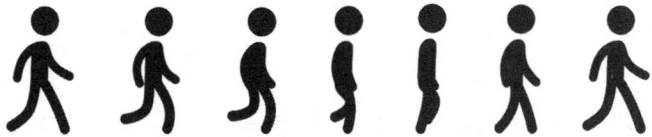

Now look at the same picture and imagine it as a single person walking. The first operation (counting symbols) is logic; the second (imagining action) is narrative.

By learning to distinguish logic from narrative, you can un-riddle many of the brain's mysteries, including the difference between simple consciousness (your awareness of these words) and self-consciousness (your awareness that *you* are reading these words):

- Simple consciousness is spatial and sensory, reflecting its origins in vision. (This relationship between sentience and seeing is why we close our eyes to sleep.) Simple consciousness is thus logical.

- Self-consciousness is temporal and imagined. It begins with the awareness of our self continuing in time, or in other words, with the awareness that our now has come from our past. That's a mental story of cause → effect. Self-consciousness is thus narrative.

This is perhaps the profoundest example of how our brain is a computer—and also more. To wake up, becoming aware of the world, is to think like an algorithm. But to become self-aware, discovering our own personal history and purpose, is to do what AI cannot: think in story.

That's how storythinking works in the brain. Now let's explore how it works in life.

STORYTHINKING HAS SHAPED HUMAN LIFE for hundreds of millennia. It's what enabled our Neolithic ancestors to invent tools, plan hunts, and imagine gods. But we can summarize its place in human life—then and now—via a single story: Shakespeare.

Shakespeare binds together the book you've been reading. Pieces of that binding have been marked in earlier chapters, like when Einstein identified Shakespeare as the source of scientific creativity. But those pieces only hint at the full story, which is that all this book's pioneers—of innovation, resilience, decision-making, communication, coaching, and leadership—developed their powers of intuition, imagination, emotional intelligence, and commonsense by reading *Hamlet*, *Othello*, *Antony and Cleopatra*, and the rest of Shakespeare:

- Steve Wozniak said of Steve Jobs: "From the day we met, he was talking about important people like Shakespeare. That have really changed humanity forever."

- Maya Angelou said: "I met and fell in love with William Shakespeare."

- Carl von Clausewitz's personal library consisted of military treatises—and Shakespeare's *Dramatic Works.*

- Abraham Lincoln asserted: "Some of Shakespeare's plays I have . . . gone over perhaps as frequently as any unprofessional reader."

- Nikola Tesla adored Shakespeare, as did his rival, Thomas Edison, as did Edison's other rival, Alexander Graham Bell, who was taught to recite Shakespeare by his grandfather, a former Shakespearean actor.

- Ralph Waldo Emerson declared that while the greatest works of philosophy were "conceivably wise," Shakespeare was "inconceivably" so.

- Albert Einstein listed Shakespeare as a prime example of a creative naturalist, the model for modern chemistry, medicine, and physics.

- Ludwig van Beethoven viewed Shakespeare as his "idol."

- Neil Armstrong's classmate said: "By the time we were in high school . . . he could quote from most of Shakespeare."

- William Osler's first book purchase was the Globe Shakespeare, which he loved so much that he donated a copy of Shakespeare's First Folio to Oxford University.

- Benjamin Franklin secured a copy of Shakespeare's complete works for the Library Company of Philadelphia, where any American colonist could read it.

- George Washington quoted Shakespeare's *Henry V* to his Army on November 1783, celebrating his soldiers as a "band of brothers" whose labors produced exceptional happenings: "events which have seldom, if ever before, taken place on the stage of human action."

- Horatio Nelson referred to his junior commanders as his Shakespearean "Band of Brothers."

- Charles Darwin remembered how he "used to sit for hours reading the historical plays of Shakespeare."

- Thomas Paine taught himself to write by imitating Shakespeare.

- Dwight Eisenhower recalled that the highlight of high school was acting as the hero in a Shakespeare play.

- Robert Noyce acted Shakespeare at his college dramatic society.

- Marie Curie inherited *Hamlet* from the Polish Romantics Adam Mickiewicz and Juliusz Słowacki. "Since my childhood I have had a strong taste for poetry, and I willingly learned by heart long passages."

- Winston Churchill memorized Shakespeare whole, as the actor Richard Burton discovered to his consternation when he tried to play the role of Hamlet at London's Old Vic, only to be confronted by Churchill sitting in the front row, reciting every line in concert.

- Virginia Woolf's Septimus Smith, the shell-shocked veteran whose scientific eye for beauty provides the part III epigraph, read Shakespeare avidly.

- Vincent van Gogh rhapsodized: "My God, the beauty of Shakespeare! Who is as brilliantly obscure? . . . But of course, reading Shakespeare can make you shocking to others, and without wishing harm, offend society with your unconventionality."

Shakespeare awakened the intelligence of these artists, scientists, and leaders by rejecting the logical mindset of medieval schools. That mindset had begun its rise in twelfth-century Italy when John of Venice reconstituted Aristotle's ancient proof that logic (and its powers of induction, deduction, and interpretation) could be distilled to the three mechanical functions AND-OR-NOT. From there, logic became both the glory and the shortcoming of the universities of the European Middle Ages. In those universities, medieval physicists and psychologists acclaimed AND-OR-NOT as the ultimate intelligence, the mind of God, yet for all that they inducted, deduced, and interpreted, they achieved no great insight into the workings of nature or the brain. The insight didn't occur until the Renaissance, when rebel artisans and experimenters (such as Leonardo da Vinci, Galileo, and William Harvey) rejected logic and rediscovered intuition, imagination, emotion, and commonsense. At the time, no scientific explanation existed for these mental powers, but Shakespeare perceived that they came from story. Story ran on exceptional information, a phenomenon marked in *Hamlet*: "As a stranger give it welcome." (See chapter 5.) So Shakespeare filled his plays with exceptions, strange and stranger: the astute madness of Lear, the gorgeous wrinkles of Cleopatra, the noble delinquency of Falstaff. His characters acted innovatively, not statistically. They broke old patterns, creating original rules.

This rebirth of story didn't go unchallenged. Shakespeare

died in 1616, and over the next hundred years, the Renaissance was supplanted by the Enlightenment. The Enlightenment prided itself on being an age of reason, and in search of mathematical laws of science and morality, it dusted off the logic of the Middle Ages. *Hamlet* was dismissed as savage. *Othello* was censored. *King Lear* was rewritten to follow eternal principles of justice. Shakespeare's eye for life's exceptions was shuttered.

Yet not forever. During the eighteenth century, the intuitions of the Renaissance were resurrected by lonely souls like poet-artist William Blake. Born in West London in 1757, Blake apprenticed for seven years as an engraver then enrolled to study painting at the British Royal Academy, where logic-minded instructors attempted to program him in "abstraction, generalizing, and classification." To which Blake retorted: "To Generalize is to be an Idiot." So out of step was Blake with the Enlightenment that he was deemed a lunatic. But while Blake struggled to endure poverty and scorn, he took strength from Shakespeare. Shakespeare reminded Blake of what he was at birth: "I have recollected all my scattered thoughts . . . and resumed my primitive and original ways." Shakespeare revealed the real path to science: "What is now proved was once only imagined." Shakespeare showed that poets not logicians were the seers of the future: "Poetic Genius . . . [is] the Spirit of Prophecy."

That spirit of prophecy abided in Blake. Just as Blake foresaw, Shakespeare was revived. The revival came in the early nineteenth century—first in Germany, then England, and finally, across Europe. The French painter Eugène Delacroix—whose murals later inspired van Gogh—raved: "There's been a general invasion! Hamlet raises his hideous head; Othello's dagger punctures conventional theater." This puncturing of conventional theater was carried on by many brave nonconformists, none more spectacular than American actor Charlotte Cushman. Boston-born in 1816, Cushman sang as a teen in Mozart's sentimental opera before pivoting to Shakespeare. During the mid-1830s, she performed in *Othello* and *Macbeth* to packed crowds in Albany, New Orleans, and Manhattan, until at the age of twenty-two, she booked a show at London's famed Haymarket Theatre.

The Haymarket handed Cushman a stock Enlightenment script: a comic redo of *Romeo and Juliet* in which the star-crossed young lovers escaped tragedy to live happily ever after. Cushman was appalled. What right did the Haymarket have to change Shakespeare's story? The Haymarket replied that it had every right. Shakespeare was dead—and his story was too unusual. The public preferred generic narratives and clichéd positivity.

Cushman refused to perform anything but Shakespeare's exceptional ending. The Haymarket threatened to replace her—but she was unbowed. Eventually, the Haymarket caved. Victorious, Cushman doubled down on her unconventional staging by casting herself as Romeo.

Audiences loved it, applauding the performance's singularity. *The Times* enthused:

> It is enough to say that the Romeo of Miss Cushman is far superior to any Romeo we have ever had. The distinction is not one of degree; it is one of kind. For a long time, Romeo has been a convention. Miss Cushman's Romeo is a *creation*.

Charlotte Cushman had grasped Shakespeare's core insight: What makes a story work isn't its fidelity to formulas. It's how it breaks the rules.

Thanks to rebels like Cushman, Delacroix, and Blake, Shakespeare became the most popular playwright of the nineteenth century, powering the upstart movement known as Romanticism. And in the early twentieth century, there came another Shakespearean revolution: the overturning of neoclassical economics.

Neoclassical economics had emerged from the application of Enlightenment logic to financial markets. Its great creation was *Homo economicus*, a statistical approximation of the average person. *Homo economicus* always behaved logically, prompting neoclassical economics to predict that markets always did too. The problem was: Markets didn't. So when government finance ministers consulted *Homo economicus*, banks failed and recessions ensued.

In the early 1900s, the limitations of neoclassical economics came to the attention of a math whiz who counted Shakespeare in his "holy trinity." The whiz was John Maynard Keynes. Impressed by Shakespeare's narrative approach to psychology, Keynes infused economic theory with nonlogical mechanisms—such as "price stickiness"—which acknowledged the influence of human imagination upon markets. That influence meant that finance ministers needed more than calculators. They needed commonsense. And the fast path to commonsense was to read Shakespeare. Shakespeare's story mind had grasped the art of practical decision-making. (See chapter 7.) Which is why, as Keynes recorded in his 1930 *A Treatise on Money*: "Shakespeare . . . died rich."

Storythinking was again in the ascendant. Its primal powers had returned to power new poetry, science, and business. But in the middle of the twentieth century, logic staged a comeback.

THE COMEBACK'S ARCHITECTS WERE A group of statisticians known as the programmers.

The programmers worked in the 1930s and 1940s for the U.S. Departments of Labor, Commerce, and Defense. They assigned precise numerical values to everything: An acre was worth twenty-four bushels of corn, a high school degree was worth five hundred dollars, a bomber was worth one thousand infantrymen. Then the programmers came up with logical ways to increase those numbers. They designed farms that grew more crops, textbooks that communicated more information, factories that built more flying fortresses. And they called it *optimization*.

No one paid much notice to the programmers until 1943. That year, the word *optimization* appeared in twice as many popular publications as the year before. The next year, the same thing happened. And the next year and the next. In fact, *optimization* continued increasing in popularity, right down to the present day. It's now ubiquitous in business, manufacturing, technology, finance, health care, sports, advertising, media, and education.

Why did all this begin in 1943? That year was when the first general purpose electronic computer—ENIAC—was built. And the computer made us all into programmers. We now value data and its children: social science, surveys, analytics. We have learned to think in demographics, averages, the betting odds. We strive to serve more customers, build more products, earn more income, cure more patients, win more games, find more information, sell more merchandise, attract more viewers, train more students—and do it faster, cheaper, easier.

This algorithmic way of life can do impressive things. Yet it has an obvious limit: Optimization can improve existing products and processes but it cannot create original ones. No matter how big the computer or ingenious the programmer, logic cannot invent new tech, new markets, new art, new business. Or so commonsense suggests. But in our modern world, the programmers have overturned commonsense. They have claimed that their computational method can do more than optimization. They have claimed that it can do innovation.

This contradicts what logicians themselves have claimed for more than two millennia, back to the time of Aristotle. Innovation creates what's new, while logic calculates what's true, and there's nothing new about the truth. Truth is timeless; one plus one has always equaled (and will always equal) two. That's why logic was embraced by medieval theologians, who shuddered at novelty as a crime against God. That's why the first European to champion innovation—Machiavelli—remains a byword for untruthful behavior.

And from Aristotle onward, logic wasn't just seen as morally opposed to original thinking; it was also recognized as being mechanically incapable. Logic works by crunching data into trends and averages, using the past as a guide to what is typical—even archetypal. Its core function was thus viewed by classical logicians as the contrary of creativity. Creativity fabricated the unprecedented while logic solidified precedent.

What changed? What prompted our modern world to think that logic could power innovation? The shift was driven in the mid-twentieth century by American psychologist J. P. Guilford.

During World War II, Guilford worked with the U.S. Army, where he encountered ENIAC. Amazed by ENIAC's aptitude at math, Guilford became convinced that all intelligent behavior could be reduced to computer protocols, and in the 1950s, he proposed that innovation was a combo of two such protocols: divergent thinking and convergent thinking.

Divergent thinking is random. It arbitrarily associates old ideas to produce new ones. When done at scale—in team brainstorming sessions or with computers—it can produce long lists of novelties.

Convergent thinking is logical. It refines the results of divergent thinking via pattern finding and prototype iteration. When fed the novelties produced by brainstormers or computers, it can identify ones that fit the model of past successes, eliminating illogical misfires and identifying high-probability breakthroughs.

This two-step protocol for computing new ideas became known among Guilford's followers as *ideation*. And it was embraced by the programmers. Over the later twentieth century, they incorporated ideation into businesses and schools, where it became the foundation of design thinking and managerial troubleshooting. Then in the twenty-first century, the programmers fulfilled Guilford's ultimate dream: coding ideation into computers. The result was generative AI.

Generative AI has been hailed as the future of innovation. But it will never revolutionize the rules of art, technology, or anything. You can establish this via commonsense: Generative AI is far more random and far more logical than we are, so if ideation were the secret to invention, AI would have obsolesced us already. And you can also debunk the programmers by tracing the history of the brain's evolution, as we have done over the previous pages. That history reveals that AI is, at best, half intelligent. It lacks the mental hardware that the animal neuron evolved more than five hundred million years ago to invent action. It is half our gray matter accelerated and the other half lobotomized. It has no commonsense, imagination, or emotion. So it will forever be incompetent at innovation—and at strategy, communication, and leadership.

To run those special operations, we need the part of our neuroanatomy that thinks A → B. And to run those special operations better, we need to do like Albert Einstein, Vincent van Gogh, Maya Angelou, Steve Jobs, and this book's other Shakespeareans. We need to hone our primal power of thinking in story.

THAT'S THE THEORY I SHARE with the Operators. Intrigued, they offer to test it. The theory holds up. In January 2023, the Army awards me a medal for "groundbreaking research."

When I bring home the medal, my family is astonished. Most surprised is my mum. "Explain to me: How did you get on with those military men?" she inquires, doing her best to sound more curious than judgmental.

She has her reasons for being judgmental of military men. Her father was a British army colonel who avoided fighting at the Battle of the Imjin River during the Korean War, preferring the peacetime barracks life of boot polishing, spit-shine drill, and mustache measurement. It was a program of regimented, empty discipline that clashed violently with my mother's temperament. As a willowy young girl living on a German NATO compound, she unleashed anarchy by releasing the village pigs across her father's immaculate parade ground. Later, when her father tried to control her by throwing away her books—*They're giving you ideas*, he discerned—she ran off to become a nurse, tending to gas-blind World War I veterans in Florence Nightingale's old wards.

"I partnered with the Army," I say, "to help Operators act smarter in the fog of combat . . ."

"Oh, please!" she cuts me off. "I'm your mother. I know you! You can't harm a fly—you cried, when you were a little boy, after you saw me squash an ant that ran across my kitchen table. You made me promise never to kill another ant again. You're too soft-hearted for war. So tell me straight: How did you and the Army manage to work together?"

Okay, here's the answer. Special Operations and I share an unconventional belief. We believe that to activate the parts of the human brain that are smarter than a computer, it's necessary to venture beyond modern psychology into a science more ancient and imaginative.

Maybe you'd like to join that venture. If so, I'll share the story next chapter.

12

STORYTHINKING

Pixar, William James, and the Science of Singular Minds

M y unconventional research into human intelligence started in the late 1990s, two decades before I met U.S. Special Operations. In those days, I worked in a University of Michigan Medical School neurophysiology lab researching the synapse—the A → B machine that generates original action. On a hand-made microscope rig held together by rolls of tape and mismatched screws, I plugged glass instruments into individual synapses to track what they were thinking. Then I engineered mutant synapses, changing their machinery to make them think differently.

This method of studying the brain was very different from the method used in psychology experiments. Those experiments weren't conducted on lone mutants. They were conducted on hundreds of average people. Or rather, they were conducted on hundreds of individual people who were mathematically synthesized into one average person, producing a standard model of how everyone typically thought.

This mathematical modeling struck me as clever but misleading. I could believe that the more brains you piled up, the more they looked the same. But I could not believe that they *were* the same. And I found support for my belief one afternoon when I discovered, on a gently rusting shelf at the back of the lab, a little green pamphlet titled *A Naturalist's Field Guide*. Handmade in the 1960s by a college instructor on an early photocopier, it employed a mix of splotchy typewriter and elegant sketches to explain the science of natural history.

Natural history dates to ancient researchers like Pliny the Elder (see the Introduction), but its modern reputation was established in the nineteenth century when Darwin used it to discover evolution by natural selection (see chapter 5). Its method is deceptively simple: Sit in nature, waiting patiently for things that grab your curiosity. Curiosity is sparked in your brain by the unexpected—a new species, an original behavior, or some other exception to biology's known laws. Keep your eyes on that surprise, watching where it comes from, what it does, and how it interacts, learning the bigger story of the exception and its role in the environment.

When I read about this method in the little green pamphlet, I was enchanted. Here was a science that worked the opposite of statistics. Instead of being distantly impersonal, it cultivated an intimate "feel for life" that was acquired, like wisdom, through long years of patient dwelling. And although natural history started small and proceeded slowly, it was as ambitious and far-reaching as any scientific enterprise. By treasuring the local, it illuminated the global; by starting with unique characters, it grasped the plot of the greater whole. This was how I wanted to study the brain, unearthing its secrets. Why had I never heard about natural history before?

I soon got an answer from the lab director, a slender man with a boyish mien, a genius for science, and a habit of expressing himself with uncompromising bluntness. Plucking the pamphlet from my hands, he tossed it in a trash chute. Natural history, he told me, was dead.

The dying had begun in the wake of Einstein. His enormous fame had infected biologists with "physics envy," the desire to do research with the infallible rigor that the general public associated with mathematics. The result was the rise of big-data ecology (where scientists crunched spreadsheets to produce algorithmic models) and of cognitive science (which treated neurons as transistors performing Bayesian computation). This statistical approach to science made natural history seem outdated, and it had another more directly destructive consequence: It mass-produced itself. Where decades of painstaking fieldwork were required to train a natural historian, mathematical biologists could be manufactured via a single statistics course. Equipped with a hundred-dollar calculator and a knowledge of standard deviations, they could study butterflies, oceans, emotions, or anything: It was all the same because it was all numbers. And even more efficiently, mathematical biologists did not need to travel much—or ever. They could exist at their desks, crunching data collected by automated sensors, speeding out articles for prestigious science journals, and pushing the labor-intensive work of natural history to the margins—then to extinction.

That, the lab director said, was the tragic tale of natural history. But while the tale he told was true enough, it was not the whole story. After recovering from my dismay at the little pamphlet's destruction, I slipped away to the medical school's library. Planting myself at an old oak table, I read about natural history's rise and fall, which my brain digested into three short narratives:

1. In the early nineteenth century, the electromagnetic laws that inspired Einstein's physics were discovered by Michael Faraday—without math. Faraday preferred to operate, as the natural historians had done, by patiently developing a "feel" for nature. Nowadays, that feel would be regarded as a gateway to irrationality and pseudoscience, but Faraday was a conscientious researcher who knew what he was doing, and his findings were upheld by the elegant mathematical equations of James Maxwell, leading to the advent of modern electricity—and later, quantum theory.

2. In the late nineteenth century, Harvard professor William James helped inaugurate modern psychology—without statistics. His method was to closely study individual cases, developing a feel for the human brain. This study led to breakthrough insights about free will, consciousness, and spirituality—all of which have been validated by the cross-checks of later mathematical researchers.

3. In the twentieth century, a neuroscientist set up a lab to study mutant synapses. The neuroscientist had no time for graduate students who wanted to rapidly capture data and crank out papers. But he had endless patience for training a young researcher to develop a feel for how brain cells worked. The neuroscientist was my lab director, and the young researcher was me.

These three narratives reveal natural history's deeper scientific root: naturalism. Naturalism is the careful observation of natural rarities. It's driven by curiosity and also by imagination, because in addition to recording what physically happens, the naturalist must speculate creatively on the unseen physical mechanisms that cause the happening. That creative speculation produced the nineteenth-century revolutions that yielded modern biology, modern physics, and modern psychology. And although it rejects the brute generalizations of statistics, it is not contrary to math. It is complementary, generating hypotheses that can be tested by later calculations.

Moved by the stories of Faraday and James, I decided that I would become a naturalist. I would probe the mysteries of human intelligence by studying brains that excelled at low-information processes—imagination, emotion, commonsense, intuition—that couldn't be discovered by the statistical methods of modern psychology. I would set up a lab like the one where I had trained, except that instead of studying the singular intelligence of individual synapses, I would study the singular intelligence of individual brains.

But how? How could I research individual brains in the same way that I'd learned to research individual synapses? Mulling it over as I brewed a batch of altered DNA, I had an epiphany: A brain was a group of synapses, which was a group of A → B, which was a group of actions. And a group of actions was a narrative. The brain thus thought in narrative. To understand the powers of human cognition not explained by computation, I should probe the mechanics of story.

This was the theoretical breakthrough that led, in time, to everything in the book you now hold. To repeat the key insight: *The brain thinks in narrative, so we can discover how the brain operates by studying the mechanics of story. In addition to using microscopes to anatomize neurons, we can advance brain science by using intuition and commonsense to analyze novels, myths, and plays.* But while this was my theoretical breakthrough, it took many years to make practical gains. That's because I knew lots about microscopes and neurons—and almost nothing about novels, myths, and plays. To take the next step in my research, I needed to learn how story worked.

If I were a psychologist, my plan to do this would have been to look for general story rules and archetypal patterns. I wanted, however, to explore the unique processes of individual brains, taking the nonstatistical approach of a natural historian. Rather than running populational studies on typical myths and block-busters, I needed to observe an exceptional producer of narra-tives, spending years embedded with an original novelist, auteur filmmaker, or other innovative story maker. But what story maker would grant me that access? Who would permit a neo-phyte practitioner of an old-fashioned science to pry into their most private crevices?

It was then—on a snowy midnight walk home from the med school lab—that I struck upon the notion of studying Shake-speare. I hadn't read Shakespeare since I was assigned him in ninth grade, and I hadn't connected with him then. In fact, I'd viewed him with dislike: I was raised to think of myself as a Scot whose ancestors had been colonized by the English empire and forced to read *Macbeth.*

Still, I was familiar with Shakespeare's legend: Country boy with little education goes to the big city and transforms the world, inspiring later generations to revolutionize art, science, technology, medicine, and politics. And I knew that Shakespeare had not achieved all this by thinking in math. He had excelled at intuition, imagination, emotion, and commonsense, becoming one of history's great masters of the brain processes that I wanted to investigate.

Could I learn from Shakespeare what was special about human intelligence? Yes, I thought. I could if I was patiently curious, immersing myself for years in his exceptional creations. And if I struggled at first—or even at length—that would be okay. Like the cadavers that the medical school used to train its first-year doctors, Shakespeare could never be harmed or offended, no matter how clumsy my probing.

Had the little green pamphlet not resonated so deeply with me, this plan might have seemed ridiculous. But it did not seem ridiculous. It seemed exciting. So off I went to Yale to get a PhD in literature, bringing my lone copy of Shakespeare: a paperback *Henry V* from high school.

When I left the lab, many of my colleagues in neuroscience and psychology warned me that I was wasting my life. But they would change their minds because of what happened next.

WHAT HAPPENED NEXT DID NOT happen fast. Guided by my years of studying atypical brain cells, I went weird science on Renaissance literature, startling my Yale professors and amusing my fellow students. I was urged by senior faculty, on two separate occasions, to exit the PhD program.

But over time, my unconventional background worked to my advantage. It allowed me to read literature differently from my classmates, seeing things that they did not. And eventually it guided me to a simple but original theory about Shakespeare: He had devised a method for inventing stories that worked. He was more than a great wordsmith who crafted beautiful language.

He was a nimble innovator who changed the narrative—and kept on changing it.

After Yale, I spent a summer at the New York Academy of Medicine, then accepted a position at the newly formed Humanities Institute at Stanford, where I had no responsibilities except to show up twice a week to give the university Shakespeare lectures. One day, after I delivered a lecture with the title "If You Can Create a Story That Works, You Can Change the Future," I was asked by a student if I had seen any Pixar movies. Those movies, she said, were doing what I said Shakespeare had done: telling new stories that succeeded. They weren't based on traditional Hollywood formulas like the hero's journey. They were original and effective, earning prestigious awards and big box office.

Fifteen minutes later, I picked up my office phone and called Pixar, which had established its studio just across San Francisco Bay. I told Pixar my theory about Shakespeare, and they extended me an invitation to their story department. In the archives, I learned the rich and wild natural history of movies like *Toy Story*. And I realized: My student was right. Pixar was indeed using a version of Shakespeare's method. It was rejecting standard plots in order to risk experimental story structures like that of the soon-to-be-released *Up*.

Then, abruptly, Disney purchased Pixar. Disney executives made assurances that nothing would change, but we all knew otherwise. The bulk producer of narrative formulas had taken over a unique biome, like the Death Star swallowing a coral reef. The life inside might be preserved, but not alive. It would be a neuron in formaldehyde.

Needing a new ecosystem for my naturalism, I went south to Los Angeles, joining the faculty of the University of Southern

California and doing research with the Academy of Motion Picture Arts and Sciences, an organization of Oscar-winning writers, producers, and directors. They were intrigued by my theory and encouraged me to test it by writing screenplays. The first one was reviewed by the talent agency CAA and sent back with the assessment "This writer has no talent." I returned to my theory and kept trying. A few months later, I wrote a script that sold to a major studio. More sales followed. I worked on projects with Sony, Paramount, Universal, even Death Star Disney. I worked in film, I worked in TV, and I worked in theater with authors and actors from the Royal Shakespeare Company to neurodivergent community playhouses.

Until at last, I got my big break. Not in Hollywood. But in science.

THE CALL CAME FROM PROJECT Narrative, the world's leading academic institute for the study of stories. Headquartered far away from Los Angeles and other glamorous hubs of media and publishing, it sat inconspicuously at Ohio State University. Guided by the conviction that stories were cocreated with audiences, it had embedded itself in the American heartland, ground zero for popular taste.

Project Narrative funded me to start a lab, fulfilling my dream and expanding my research. I gained recognition for my theories about how stories work in the brain, reuniting with my colleagues in neuroscience and psychology. And in addition to continuing my study of the imaginations of writers, I began to explore the unique intelligences of engineers, entrepreneurs, doctors, and leaders. During my time in the Bay Area, I had made connections at Apple, Google, and Facebook. In Los Angeles, I had worked with Amazon and Netflix. At Project Narrative, I linked up with health care giants like Cardinal Health; fashion titans like Gap and Victoria's Secret; big insurance agencies like State Farm; fast-food chains like Wendy's; shoe companies like Nike; blue-chippers like Lockheed Martin and General Electric; and fast-growing startups like Faire and Indeed. I met venture capitalists and hedge fund investors, government research labs and artistic nonprofits, lumber consortiums and pet spa operators.

At first, these organizations wanted my help with marketing. I agreed, but only if I was allowed inside their strategy and operations. The organizations balked. What did strategy and operations have to do with marketing? All three, I said, were story. Strategy was the story of what the organization wanted to do, operations was the story of what the organization was actually doing, and marketing was the story of what the organization wanted people to think it was doing. In successful organizations, the three stories aligned. In dysfunctional organizations, they diverged, creating inauthentic marketing.

Persuaded, the organizations gave me access, and as I poked through their shining C-suites, I noticed that the executives fell largely into three tribes:

1. *The classic rationalists.* They believed in rational-choice theory and quantitative economics. They were students of management, which they saw as a universal science that enabled its disciples to run any business. Dish soap, TV shows, health care: All were digits that could be crunched into quarterly earnings reports.

2. *The rational humanists.* They stressed the importance
   of empathy and ideation. They had an affinity for design and quoted behavioral economists like Daniel
   Kahneman and Dan Ariely. They spoke of pain points
   and typical users. They believed in personality tests and
   demographics.

3. *The AI futurists.* They saw that computers processed
   data faster than humans, and since they viewed data as
   the key to smart choices, they concluded that it wouldn't
   be long before computers replaced human leaders.

These tribes viewed themselves as rivals, but they all shared
the same basic model of intelligence: rational decision-making.
And for the most part, they believed that they possessed a greater
capacity for rationality than other people. Other people were
trapped in bias, emotion, or incomplete data. Other people therefore needed to be better informed—or, when their irrationality
was intractable, to be manipulated into good decisions via incen-
tives, nudges, and an enlightened "choice architecture."

This, the three tribes believed, was where marketing came in.
Marketing deployed narrative to program people with the right
data or behaviors, steering the mob onto the path of reason. Tell
the correct stories and you could eliminate prejudice, boost well-
being, and get the world to buy your wholesome products, ushering in an optimized future of healthy politics, healthy ethics, and
healthy balance sheets.

This struck me as creepy. And it clashed with what I knew
about intelligence. Computers could not see the future, nor could
management or ideation. They all relied on data, and although
the three tribes viewed data reverently, treating it as an oracular

guide to decision-making, data is inherently backward-looking. Such hindsight can be useful when the future is the same as the past, as in the timeless world of math. But in the real world, things change, breaking data and its patterns. That's why our tomorrow doesn't lie in design; it lies (as Darwin saw) in the asymmetrical conflicts of biological evolution. That's why our tomorrow doesn't lie in management; it lies (as Pixar's executives saw) in leaders with vision. That's why our tomorrow doesn't lie in computers and their statistical brilliance; it lies (as Shakespeare saw) in human imagination.

My views on design and computers were politely ignored by the three tribes. But my assertions about leadership resonated. The execs had all experienced the power of vision. They knew that leaders needed to see beyond data into new futures. And they wanted to know: Could I help their brains create more strategies— more *stories*—that worked?

Yes, I said. To prove it, I asked the execs to explain their current products and operations. Then I told them future products and operations that Shakespeare might invent as sequels. My goal in these conversations was to encourage the execs to read Shakespeare. But this is not what happened. Instead, the execs offered to pay me thousands of dollars an hour to be a consultant. I was, they told me, a natural—at strategy, at tech, at health care, at management, at lumber, at pet spa operations, at venture capital. I had been born with the gift: an intuitive grasp of business.

When I heard this, I realized I had failed as a teacher. For I had failed to communicate the truth about myself. If there was one fact I knew with absolute certainty, it was that I was *not* a natural at business—or any other worldly activity. Any neutral observer will tell you: My instincts are atrocious. When presented with a novel situation, I inevitably blunder it. The only reason I survived to adulthood is because I'm a whiz at multiple choice. My ability to pick the right option from a list propelled me to scholarships at private school and college, and it also enabled my journey from neuroscience to Shakespeare. You might have been wondering about a detail I skipped during my earlier account of that journey: How, exactly, did a synapse researcher get into the world's top PhD program for Shakespeare? Well, dear reader, I hacked my way in, through a standardized test. The test was the literature GRE, a multiple-choice exam that spanned from *Beowulf* to *Beloved*. I hadn't read either book—or the thousands in between. But I'd taken many standardized tests and knew how to ace them. I began by getting my hands on old copies of the GRE. I analyzed them into diagrams and spreadsheets, like a statistician or a rational-choice theorist. In a few hours, I cracked their core logic, producing data tables that I uploaded into my memory. Then I took the test and got an extremely high score. Looking at that score and at my track record in science, Yale concluded: This kid knows *a lot*. The truth, as Yale was soon to discover, was that the kid knew nothing. I was simply an expert at ticking the right boxes, the human equivalent of a Shakespeare chatbot.

This is the secret I have been hiding from you. I don't dislike IQ tests and statistics because they have caused me personal harm. I dislike them because I am very, very good at them. So good that I can see their limits. So good that I can tell you, based on decades of personal experience, that brilliance at IQ tests and statistics does not translate into brilliance at life.

How, then, was I successful at advising CEOs on how to run their billion-dollar operations? Let me share with you what I explained to them.

I TOLD THE CEOS THAT my useful advice derived from the theory I'd developed at Yale and Pixar: *There's a method for inventing stories that work.* When I unveiled that theory, the business execs thought it was simply an insight into screenwriting, marketing, and other forms of storytelling. But it was much more.

Another term for *story* is *plot.* Another term for *plot* is *plan.* And a plan is a path through life. It's how we overcome setbacks and invent new medicines, new technologies, and new markets. It's imagination applied to practical problems and opportunities. It's the secret to success in business, engineering, and everything.

I knew this because of Shakespeare. Shakespeare didn't simply succeed as a writer. He succeeded at life.

Not at first, mind you. In the beginning, he was a nonevent. Born in 1564 in a rustic English town, Shakespeare married at eighteen and vanished at twenty-one. For seven years, he remained in obscurity. No records exist of his creative activities. Whatever he did, it wasn't deemed worthy of remembering.

When Shakespeare finally swam back into view, in London in 1592, it was to be accused of plagiarism. The allegation was harsh—but not unfounded. Shakespeare's writings from this time show no great uniqueness. They recycle tales from popular chronicles and ancient playscripts, and their style sounds so borrowed that many scholars believe that Shakespeare literally incorporated chunks from other authors.

Then catastrophe struck: In the streets outside Shakespeare's writing garret, bodies swelled with charcoal boils. It was the return of the Black Death, killer of millions across Asia, Africa, and Europe. To help contain the disease, Shakespeare's playhouse was shuttered. Yet even so, one in ten Londoners perished. Anyone with money fled the city. With no stages or paying customers, theater companies sank into bankruptcy or quietly disbanded.

This could have been the end of Shakespeare's career. Instead, the plague year marked the start of a revolution. Beset by financial uncertainty and civic volatility, Shakespeare found his individual voice, emerging as the visionary who inspired a billion imaginations. The plagiarist became an original. The follower of past trends became the leader of future generations.

Shakespeare didn't get there all at once. Yet his transformation was impressively brisk. He altered his business strategy, recruiting investors and devising fresh tactics for engaging the public. In short, he made new plans. And beneath those new plans was something even more potent: a *method* for making new plans. A method for shifting course, adapting to circumstance, and driving change. This method differed fundamentally from rational decision-making. In rational decision-making, you use data to pick the best option. With Shakespeare's method, you use imagination to create a *new* option. You don't select from known quantities; you dash beyond them.

This method became Shakespeare's great gift to posterity. Before it made its way to me, it powered the breakthroughs of Vincent van Gogh, Marie Curie, Steve Jobs, and the other leaders and innovators of the previous chapters. And although it might seem incredible that a writer of make-believe could have such a real-world legacy, it's no accident that Shakespeare passed along a method for making new plans. New plans, as we've seen, are new stories. If you can invent one, you can invent the other.

Which came first? Was it Shakespeare's ability to create plans that made him an innovative storyteller? Or was it his innovative storytelling that made him a creative planner? Because we know so little about Shakespeare's life, we can't say for sure. But we can make an educated guess. After Shakespeare was accused of plagiarism, he responded by penning *Richard III*, a play that has been praised for displaying his first strokes of originality yet is not, really, that original. Its core story is cribbed from Shakespeare's rival, Christopher Marlowe, a college dropout who dazzled 1580s theater audiences with heroic plays like *Tamburlaine* and *Doctor Faustus*. (See chapter 5.)

From Marlowe's plays Shakespeare borrowed the character of an ambitiously inventive plotter, and to create the plot of his own play, he then thought like Richard III, asking himself: *What would an ambitiously inventive plotter do?* After Shakespeare finished *Richard III*, he then kept plotting. He invented the stories of Hamlet and Cleopatra. And he invented the business stratagems that made his company wealthy. So the thin evidence of history suggests: Shakespeare learned to plot by reading a story about a plotter. That story activated his imagination, turning him into an effective real-world planner. Gratified by his subsequent success, he then paid it forward, creating new stories that activated the imaginations of his own audiences, training their brains to invent fresh strategies for thriving at life.

I shared this tale, many times, with the business execs. It never convinced them. They didn't believe that Shakespeare had given me a method for making new plans; they believed that I had been born with a gift for planning. And I couldn't blame the execs for being skeptical about the value of reading *Richard III*. I had been unable to coax them into experiencing what I had: the brain-changing effect of Shakespeare's narratives. As a result, the execs never improved their own powers of imagination. They simply borrowed mine.

But then, in the final act of this story, U.S. Army Special Operations came knocking.

WHEN I FIRST MET ARMY Special Operations, I thought they were long-haired commandos who kicked down doors to kill terrorists. They laughed and told me not to believe everything I saw on the internet. Their actual mission, they said, was to solve problems that no one else could. When I asked to know the specific nature of those problems, I was told that the problems could be just about anything: *When the American people can't fix something, they ask government, and when government can't fix it, they ask the Army, and when the Army can't fix it, they ask us.* To find a fix, Special Operators embed for years in foreign environments, using patient immersion to spot opportunities and generate strategies.

Special Operators are thus naturalists, like me. And like me, they have been led by their naturalism to emphasize the value of individuals—and to believe that imagination can invent plans that math and data can't.

Because of our shared method, Special Operations and I bonded quickly. And we also bonded over something else: the certainty that I was not a natural. Special Operations suspected this the instant they met me. And they confirmed it by rooting out another secret that I have been keeping from you—and that I would have kept hidden from everyone, forever, if the Operators had not brought it into the open.

The secret starts with my dad. Born in the green and pleasant land of England's Lake District, he had a brilliant, even beautiful, mind. But he never learned to cope with reality. As a young neurosurgeon working in a London hospital, he found himself overwhelmed with anxiety. His job was too exacting, too life-and-death. So he began prescribing himself pills to calm his worried thoughts. Other doctors noticed, an investigation was launched, and he was summarily fired.

Suddenly jobless, my dad panicked. He strolled into a British pharmaceutical company and claimed that he could help with sales. This was a lie. He knew nothing about sales. So when the company hired him, he went to work each day, locked himself in his office, and sat there blankly for eight hours before unlocking his door and returning home. After three months, the company discovered that he'd never opened his desk or operated his phone. They promptly fired him.

Searching for a fresh start, he accepted a job in America. He called my mum from New Jersey and told her that he'd bought a new house. She was shocked. She had a young child (me) and a pair of aging parents in England. She didn't want to pick up and move across an ocean to a place she'd never seen. My dad assured her that the new job and the new house would be only temporary. He turned out to be right, but not in the way that he meant.

For the next fifteen years, my dad lost job after job. Every time the phone rang, my mum tensed, thinking that it was him calling to say that he'd been fired. Usually, it was him calling because he'd made a mess at work and had locked himself in his office, racked with panic. On the weekends, he tried to forget the coming workweek—and really, his whole life—by drinking prodigiously. My mum responded with fury. She shouted to rouse my dad's dignity. She shouted to make him think of the children (I now had younger sisters). And eventually, she just shouted. My sisters and I would tremble upstairs in our beds as the house beneath erupted.

Then one day, my sister Joanna died. She went to sleep complaining of a headache and never woke up. The autopsy was inconclusive, but my dad blamed himself. He was a doctor. He should have spotted the symptoms. He should have saved her. Sick with guilt, he collapsed entirely. At work, he wrote poems to his dead child. At home, he sat for hours in the bath, washing himself endlessly. We all knew that the next time he lost his job, it would be for good. And then how would we survive?

Terrified, I devoted myself to school, earning a scholarship to a private academy with science labs and a classics department. I was painfully out of place on its charming Philadelphia campus: While other students drove luxury cars, I was dropped off by my dad (usually late) in his twenty-year-old Buick. Ashamed of my family's immigrant weirdness and having inherited my dad's un-easy relationship with reality, I began telling extravagant lies. I claimed to have learned to ski in the French Alps, to match my schoolmates who vacationed on the slopes at Vail. I claimed to have watched TV shows that didn't exist, because mine was the only family I knew without HBO. I claimed that my grandfather had invented a secret gadget that won World War II.

Nobody at school believed my lies. They regarded me with a mixture of pity and amusement. But I continued to excel at tests, and it soon became clear to my teachers that I would go to a good university. From there, they assumed, I would be fine. When I got to college, however, I was not fine. I did well in my classes but saw no purpose in them. I felt stuck at an unmagical Hogwarts, mastering arcane formulas that had no power outside the classroom. Disappointed by school's pretentious emptiness, I drifted aimlessly. Until one day, I met the recruiter.

The recruiter was a sergeant in the United States Marine Corps. He'd targeted my friend Chris, a general studies major who'd been one of the best high school runners in Iowa. Chris had already heard plenty about the military; his father had served in Special Forces during Vietnam. But I was fascinated by the recruiter. He had no fear and moved with absolute purpose. He was the opposite of my own dad.

When the recruiter detected my interest, he invited me to try out for Officer Candidate School down in Quantico, Virginia. Immediately, I said yes. Thinking this was his easiest sale ever, the recruiter drove me down to the processing station. I took a multiple-choice exam—the Armed Services Vocational Aptitude Battery—and got such an astronomical score that the recruiter couldn't believe it. I was his lucky strike, the perfect candidate, dropped into his lap.

We then went to do my fitness test. My recruiter considered this a pure formality. He knew that I was friends with one of the fastest humans in the Midwest, so he figured that I'd be a good runner too. I was not. I made it a hundred yards into the three-mile course and stopped. The recruiter dashed up, thinking I was hurt. But the only thing hurting was my lungs. I'd never run that far before.

I didn't reveal this to the recruiter. I didn't want him to know that I was renowned as the most incompetent athlete at my high school: weak, slow, awkward. It was only because sports were mandatory that I'd been admitted onto any of the teams. I'd show up at practices, flap at a few balls, then sit on the bench during games, reading a book. If the recruiter knew that, I thought, he'd stop recruiting me. So I pretended that I was simply out of shape. I told the recruiter that I'd been spending all my time in the library, not in the gym. I promised that I'd train hard. I promised that I'd pass the fitness test next time.

Not leaving anything to chance, the recruiter opted to train me personally. Three days a week, for three months, he woke me at dawn to go running and pump iron. To bulk me up, he put me on an eating schedule. He weighed me every Friday—and measured my chest and my biceps. Under his diligent care, my body transformed. I swelled to 185 pounds of muscle, with legs that could run for days. I remained as uncoordinated as ever, but so long as I was standing still, I looked (with my six-foot frame and buzzed blond hair) like a recruiting poster.

I retook the fitness test. I passed with flying colors. And I got a ticket to Quantico.

My flight landed on a humid summer morning. I unbuckled my seat belt and stepped into the aisle—when something smashed into my face. The man in the seat ahead had yanked his suitcase out of the overhead bin and onto the titanium glasses perched on the bridge of my nose. The glasses had been specially purchased, with the recruiter's approval. They'd been advertised as indestructible, a necessary quality for glasses that would be worn by me, a nearsighted klutz. But they were not, in fact, indestructible, as I discovered in that instant on the airplane. Under the hammer force of the falling suitcase, they snapped apart.

Stunned, I gathered up the broken fragments and fled the aircraft. Peering around blearily, I tried for a moment to piece together my shattered eyewear, before concluding that it was hopeless. What should I do? Was there an optometrist in the terminal? No, there was not, I learned to my dismay, squinting at the airport map, my panic rising. So what now?

When my recruiter had put me on the plane, he'd been clear about two things. One, walk directly from the plane to the airport exit, where a Marine Corps bus would pick me up. Two, do nothing—absolutely nothing—to draw negative attention. I decided that confessing that I'd destroyed my indestructible eyewear qualified as negative attention. So I did the only thing I could think to do. I tossed the busted glasses in a trash can, hiding the evidence. And I joined the line for the bus, blind.

When the bus arrived, I stumbled aboard, trying to hatch a plan. If I'd had any sense, the plan would have been to admit to someone, anyone, that I needed a new pair of glasses. But I was too ashamed of displaying weakness in that place of massive strength—and too scared of disappointing my recruiter, the surrogate father who had poured so much love into getting me here. So my plan became: Pretend you don't need glasses. Pretend you can see. Go through boot camp blind.

This was a very dumb plan. It ensured that, in the same way that I'd distinguished myself as the most incompetent athlete at my high school, I distinguished myself as the most incompetent recruit in my platoon. I was shown how to dress, shoot, and use a compass. But I couldn't see the instructors or their instructions. So I just guessed. And pretty much always, I guessed wrong. I ironed my camouflage hat into a heptagon, not an octagon. I loaded bullets backward into my rifle. I charged toward nonexistent targets.

After one of these comical missions, the boot camp medic noticed I was limping. He ordered me to remove my boot. My sock was damp with blood and my heel was grotesquely swollen. I had not reported these problems, assuming that they were normal wear and tear from days of hiking. They were, in fact, symptoms of cellulitis, a bacterial source of gangrene. I had failed to properly bandage a blister because I had spent the lecture on foot care doing my usual: feigning eyesight instead of actually seeing. The blister had become infected, and my foot was now so septic that the medic warned that it might be amputated. I was briskly evacuated to Walter Reed Hospital and pumped full of antibiotics. Luckily, I kept my foot. But that was the end of my time at boot camp.

My exit from the Marines was good for me. Back at college,

I discovered neuroscience, embarking on my strange and wonderful career. But while I was happy about how events turned out, I found myself unable to share the full tale of my boot camp fiasco. I told people that I'd mis-ironed my hat, misloaded my gun, and mis-bandaged my blister. But I laughed it all off as evidence of my innate lack of athleticism and general unfitness for military service. I never mentioned that I'd been functionally blind because I'd been too petrified to ask for replacement eyewear. Every time I thought back to that moment on the plane gangway with my smashed glasses in hand, I felt the same panic, the same shame, the same helpless incompetence in the face of an unexpected crisis. All those years later, and I still didn't know how to deal with the fact that I had acted so absurdly dumb. So I always pushed it from mind.

Special Operations uncovered the actual story. And when they did, I knew: My chance to do science with them was finished. Why would Operators develop advanced brain training with someone who'd flunked basic military instruction? Why would they research Primal Intelligence with someone who had demonstrated such a total lack of commonsense?

But the Special Operators were not fazed. They didn't care that I wasn't a natural. In fact, it made them more interested in collaborating. If the training worked for someone at my ability level, they figured, it must be legitimate. And as they informed me with self-assured grins, they weren't naturals either. Sure, they were often treated like they had been born with the gift. They'd accomplished remarkable feats, creating the impression that they were remarkable too. It was not so, they knew. They were ordinary people who'd done the extraordinary, aided by the right equipment. They had no trouble believing that my own success came the same way, so they asked to swap tools: *Whatever special know-how you have, you gotta hand it to the team. You gotta make yourself expendable, because at any moment, a bullet can take you out. Teach us your way of thinking, and we can carry on the mission for you.*

Thanks to the Operators, that's what I did. I got the know-how out of my head. I stopped being a fake savant and became a true teacher. I learned, at last, to do for others what Shakespeare had done for me: pass on a method for activating the brain's primal power to create new plans that work. With that method, you can adapt to change and win in chaos. You can create the future by seeing the possible faster. You can carry on the mission when the unexpected bullet comes.

That method is what you hold now in your hands, spelled out in this book's previous chapters—and summarized in the quick guide appendix that follows. It has worked for thousands of third graders, college students, MFAs, engineers, salespeople, doctors, teachers, athletes, MBAs, social workers, CEOs, and Special Operators.

And it can work for you.

PRIMAL SELF-ASSESSMENT QUIZ

Answer these twenty questions to diagnose your
Primal powers—and make a plan for growth.

SECTION I

I'm good at noticing people's unique strengths.

STRONGLY DISAGREE   DISAGREE   NEUTRAL   AGREE   STRONGLY AGREE

If something weird or unexpected happens, I rationalize it as random
noise or a distraction.

STRONGLY DISAGREE   DISAGREE   NEUTRAL   AGREE   STRONGLY AGREE

I have a strong track record of spotting new trends before they
become popular.

STRONGLY DISAGREE   DISAGREE   NEUTRAL   AGREE   STRONGLY AGREE

When I see someone act strangely, I generally conclude that there's
something wrong with them.

STRONGLY DISAGREE   DISAGREE   NEUTRAL   AGREE   STRONGLY AGREE

The more I see of the world, the more I realize that there is to discover.

STRONGLY DISAGREE   DISAGREE   NEUTRAL   AGREE   STRONGLY AGREE

SECTION II

When life changes, I immediately envision new options.

STRONGLY DISAGREE   DISAGREE   NEUTRAL   AGREE   STRONGLY AGREE

I often struggle to reach my long-term goals because I don't see a clear path to get there.

STRONGLY DISAGREE   DISAGREE   NEUTRAL   AGREE   STRONGLY AGREE

When something happens, I can quickly list many possible reasons why it occurred.

STRONGLY DISAGREE   DISAGREE   NEUTRAL   AGREE   STRONGLY AGREE

If I don't know the answer, I rapidly seek outside guidance.

STRONGLY DISAGREE   DISAGREE   NEUTRAL   AGREE   STRONGLY AGREE

I am relaxed when my plans fail because I know that I can improvise.

STRONGLY DISAGREE   DISAGREE   NEUTRAL   AGREE   STRONGLY AGREE

SECTION III

When I feel grief or shame, I value them as sources of positive growth.

STRONGLY DISAGREE   DISAGREE   NEUTRAL   AGREE   STRONGLY AGREE

Looking back on my life, I have often drifted without a strong sense of direction.

STRONGLY DISAGREE   DISAGREE   NEUTRAL   AGREE   STRONGLY AGREE

I rarely get angry but am always assertive.

STRONGLY DISAGREE   DISAGREE   NEUTRAL   AGREE   STRONGLY AGREE

I would like to be a leader but generally feel more comfortable following.

STRONGLY DISAGREE   DISAGREE   NEUTRAL   AGREE   STRONGLY AGREE

When something (or someone) is harmful for me, I immediately remove it (or them) from my life.

STRONGLY DISAGREE   DISAGREE   NEUTRAL   AGREE   STRONGLY AGREE

SECTION IV

In familiar situations, I immediately repeat what worked in the past.

STRONGLY DISAGREE   DISAGREE   NEUTRAL   AGREE   STRONGLY AGREE

I need a lot of information to make smart decisions.

STRONGLY DISAGREE   DISAGREE   NEUTRAL   AGREE   STRONGLY AGREE

If I'm anxious, it's always because something unprecedented is happening.

STRONGLY DISAGREE   DISAGREE   NEUTRAL   AGREE   STRONGLY AGREE

When circumstances change, I stick to my routine.

STRONGLY DISAGREE   DISAGREE   NEUTRAL   AGREE   STRONGLY AGREE

I am exceptionally good at making financial investments.

STRONGLY DISAGREE   DISAGREE   NEUTRAL   AGREE   STRONGLY AGREE

SCORING

1. For all four sections, score the odd-numbered questions (1, 3, and 5). If you answered "Strongly Agree," write +2 next to the question. If "Agree," write +1. If "Disagree," write -1. If "Strongly Disagree," write -2.

2. For all four sections, score the even-numbered questions (2 and 4). If you answered "Strongly Agree," write -2 next to the question. If "Agree," write -1. If "Disagree," write +1. If "Strongly Disagree," write +2. (In other words, score the even questions the *opposite* from the odd.)

3. Add up your numbers from each section.

4. Section I is *Intuition*. Section II is *Imagination*. Section III is *Emotion*. Section IV is *Commonsense*. (For more, see the chart on the next page.)

5. Rank your sections from highest score to lowest.

6. Your highest section is your *leading Primal power*. Your lowest is your *limiting Primal power*.

7. Your scores are relative not absolute. They rank your Primal powers in comparison to each other not in comparison to other people's. With practice, your scores can grow.

Intuition	**Imagination**
I_N	I_M
Power to spot exceptions to rules	Power to invent new plans
Drives opportunity-discovery and "empathy" (really, curiosity)	Improvises effectively and creates strategy
Logic misunderstands as pattern recognition	Logic misunderstands as ideation— or as magic
Emotion	**Commonsense**
E_M	C_S
Power of personal direction	Power of analyzing the situation
Grows from good experiences and bad	Matches your action to the nature of the times, maximizing your effectiveness
Logic misunderstands as a tool for knowing others when it is really for knowing yourself	Logic misunderstands as statistical

PRIMAL ABILITIES

Innovation. Intuition + Imagination. *Create the future, faster.*

Resilience. Emotion + Imagination. *Grow stronger from pain and smarter from failure.*

Decision-making. Imagination + Commonsense. *Make the right call, even with limited information.*

Communication. Commonsense + Emotion. *Meet your audience where they are—and connect them to where you are.*

Life Purpose. Emotion + Intuition. *Find the ultimate reason for your existence.*

Coaching. Intuition + Commonsense. *Help others maximize their potential.*

Leadership. Imagination + Intuition + Emotion + Commonsense. *Change the world for the better.*

Generally, you grow fastest when you target your limiting Primal power. But you can also grow by targeting a desired Primal ability. So, if you want to get better at Communication, focus on improving commonsense or emotion, starting with the one at which you score lowest. For training exercises, see the Appendix. For further training, go to operationhuman.com.

PRIMAL QUICK GUIDE

Your brain learns fastest when theory is combined with practice, or in other words, when you understand *why* something works at the same time as you experience *how*. To deliver *why-how*, the previous chapters have been written in story, because story joins understanding to experience, communicating the big picture while immersing the brain in the feeling of living it. To distill *why-how*, this quick guide pairs theoretical overview with practical exercises, allowing you to flip between textbook reading and getting your hands dirty, speed-training Primal.

PRIMAL ACTIVATION: THEORETICAL OVERVIEW

- Life is volatile and uncertain, requiring low-information intelligence. That intelligence is driven in our brain by narrative cognition, aka thinking in story.

- The most important story is the story you think to yourself about yourself.

- Your story maximizes your intelligence when your past is integrated and your future is branching, giving you a defined strategy and unlimited tactics:

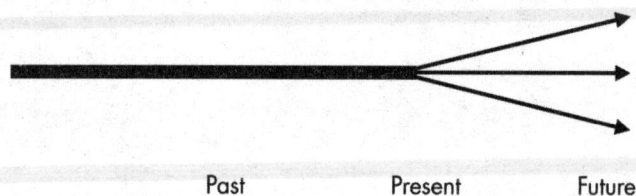

Past   Present   Future

- This story is your life plan, because *plan* is another word for *plot* is another word for *story*. Your life plan is the source of all your other plans, which drive everything from your career and your relationships to what you eat for dinner.

- To make your plans as effective as possible, your brain has evolved four primal powers: intuition, imagination, emotion, and commonsense.

- Intuition sparks plans; imagination shapes plans; emotion sustains plans; commonsense selects plans.

- Intuition comes from spotting exceptions to rules. To spot exceptions, delay *Why* and focus on surprising *Who*, *What*, *When*, *Where*, and *How*.

- Imagination turns intuition into plans. To imagine more flexibly, seek new *why*s. To imagine more precisely, restrict yourself to one top goal.

- Emotion assesses your personal story. Grief signals that you're divided between two worlds, diminishing your impact; shame, that you're split into two people, diminishing your purpose. Anger signals that you see only one future path. Fear signals that you don't see any plausible future path. Dumb pride and maverick gratitude reveal what's special about your fight, strengthening your *why*.

• Commonsense is knowing when you don't know. It reveals when your environment has fundamentally shifted, invalidating your old plans. To tune your commonsense, eliminate past anxieties by updating your standard operating procedures. Then go Now + 1, focusing on your next task and no further into the future.

• Framed in terms of your story:

    • Intuition initiates your story by revealing what's exceptional about you and the world.

    • Imagination grows your story by developing your exceptionalism into an integrated past and by developing the world's exceptions into a branching future.

    • Emotion maintains your story by revealing when your past is fragmenting or your future narrowing.

    • Commonsense directs your story by helping you choose which future branch is best for your current situation.

• Your four primal powers are stronger together. Imagination makes commonsense nimble; commonsense makes emotion effective; emotion makes intuition purposeful; intuition makes imagination perceptive. That combined strength lives inside all of us, waiting to be awakened.

PRIMAL ACTIVATION: PRACTICAL EXERCISES

When deciding which exercises to do, follow this commonsense rule: *On easy days, target your weaknesses; on hard days, your strengths.*

Intuition

• Get an old photo from a distant place with unknown people. What could you do in the world of the photo that you can't do in your life now? (If this feels too simple, pick a newer photo from a nearer place with more familiar people.)

• List people who are *creative.* Congratulations. You've just thought like a computer, using a keyword for fast memory search. Now think like a child, remembering (or discovering) a specific story of when every individual person on your list was creative. Repeat with other mental tags and labels: *wise, generous, strong . . .*

• Find two people who excel at exactly the same job: server, salesperson, surgeon. How do they do the job differently from one another? What work situation could each handle that the other couldn't?

Imagination

• What unlikely hitch could interrupt your day? (If it's a hitch you've experienced before, you've just failed the exercise: You're reliving the past, not imagining the future. To succeed next time, start by focusing on a piece of exceptional information.) Once you've imagined a hitch, shift gears and imagine an unlikely opportunity.

- List your top three goals for the year. Rank them. Now forget goals 2 and 3. (You've just defined your strategy.)

- Select a routine task. Do it differently today. Tomorrow, do it a third way. (You've just branched your tactics.)

Emotion

- Anger is a gun. Prevent accidental discharge by learning to use it intentionally. First, engage anger by imagining that something precious is under threat. Then disengage anger by recalling, in vivid detail, a time when you adapted your plans on the fly. Repeat this process, training yourself to cock anger fast—and quickly clear the chamber.

- What scares you? How has that fear led you to copy others instead of being yourself?

- Remember a sacrifice that made you proud. What can you do to earn that pride again? (If you don't know, review the specifics of what you sacrificed—and why.)

Commonsense

- Choose something you've succeeded at. What three rules would you give someone to guide them into becoming as good as you? (You've just identified your standard operating procedures.)

- Recall a moment of bad luck. Imagine it happening again. If you get tense, remind yourself that luck is out of your control—that's why it's luck. Repeat until the tenseness goes.

- Think of everything that could go wrong this week—then narrow your focus to everything that could go wrong in the next few seconds. Feel your anxiety grip the moment.

For more Primal Activation exercises, go to operationhuman.com/more.

PRIMAL APPLICATION: THEORETICAL OVERVIEW

- Innovation starts with intuition and is advanced by imagination, which is accelerated by doubling down on anomalies; by leaning into the tension between the *why* of an existing rule and the *what if* of an exception; and by eating your enemy.

- Resilience is more than grit and perseverance. It requires purpose and flexibility, which come from trading optimization for antifragility.

- Antifragility is generated by combining optimism with Planner not the Plan.

- Optimism is not *I will succeed*. Optimism is *I can succeed*.

- Planner not the Plan is *Don't plan to improve the plan; plan to improve the planner.*

- The best decisions match the newness of your plan to the newness of your situation, going where experts can't say no.

- To communicate your vision, prompt your audience to imagine a question, then answer it better than they can.

To communicate instructions, give your team a single goal and tell them *why*.

- Coaches always let the rookie fly—and never let the rookie crash.

- Leadership is strategic vision plus self-reliance.

- Strategic vision is creating and communicating a story of the future.

- Self-reliance is acting in a way that you are proud of—without feeling the need to tell anybody. This is known as *Covert Victory*.

PRIMAL APPLICATION: PRACTICAL EXERCISES

Innovation

- Revisit a failed initiative. Relaunch it, doubling down on its most original element.

- Identify a conflict between yourself and your family, your community, or your organization. What rule of theirs are you violating? What new rule preserves the spirit of their rule—while allowing you to do what you do?

- Study something you find threatening. How can you incorporate one of its core characteristics into your life without compromising yourself?

Resilience

- What possible victories could you achieve this year?

- Recall a fight you had—that made a relationship stronger.

• What life goal can you let go—by achieving it another way?

Decision-making

• Give each of your life rules this test: What situation would require you to abandon it?

• Identify a working routine. Make a plan to improve it. Don't use the plan.

• Pick a problem you're having. Ask friends for advice. Implement the piece of advice that makes you exactly as anxious as the problem does.

Communication

• Select a topic. Write down everything you know about it on a deck of note cards. Arrange the note cards in an order that stimulates people to read all the way through the deck. (Hint: Start with a surprise, then follow with plot twists, using wonder to generate curiosity.)

• Get a partner. Provide them with a goal (e.g., "Acquire a banana") and a *why* (e.g., "Because your one-year-old likes mashed banana"). Ask your partner for a plan to achieve the goal. If the plan sounds good (e.g., "Go to the nearest grocery store"), give your partner a reason that the plan won't work (e.g., "The store is out of bananas"), and ask your partner for a second plan. If the second plan sounds good (e.g., "Go to another grocery store"), give your partner a reason why the goal is impossible (e.g., "There's a global fruit shortage, so no bananas can be found in any store"), and ask your partner for a third plan. If the third plan sounds good (e.g., "Buy a sweet potato, because mashed sweet potato is similar to mashed banana"), then congratulate yourself! You've communicated effectively. (If the first plan is no good, work on providing a clearer goal. If the second plan is no good, work on providing a goal that is only a goal and not also a path to that goal, i.e., only *what* should be done and not also *how* it should be done. If the third plan is no good, work on providing a more specific *why*.)

- Review your life for an uncomfortable fact. In your next conversation, prepare to disclose that fact—but don't, unless it comes up naturally. This will make your conversation partner more likely to reveal facts about themselves, building trust.

Coaching

- Identify a task that you perform with low (not no) anxiety. Declare yourself an expert.

- Get advice from someone who knows less than you. Take the advice—and make it work.

- Pick a problem that you've solved to your satisfaction. Ask others how they'd solve it. Refrain from judgment when they solve it differently.

Leadership

- Remember a childhood dream you had. What version of that dream could you achieve in the next five years?

- Envision a life goal that's possible but not probable. What's the first step you can take toward it now?

- Do something good. Don't take credit.

PRIMAL SCIENCE SUMMARY

- Storythinking = Intuition (which detects exceptional information) + Imagination (which speculates *why* and *what if*)

- Emotional Intelligence = Treating fear and anger as signals to get more tactically creative and treating grief and shame as signals to get more strategically integrated

- Commonsense = Using tested plans in familiar situations and original plans in changing times

- Antifragility = Optimism + Planner Not the Plan

- Primal = Storythinking + Emotional Intelligence + Commonsense + Antifragility

- Logic = Induction + Deduction + Interpretation + Math

- Artificial Intelligence = Logic

- Human Intelligence = Logic + Primal

ACKNOWLEDGMENTS

Thanks to Tom Gaines for the invisible hand; to Kelly Green for helicopter jumping; to Angela Samosorn for showing the way; to Richard McConnell for exceptional information; to Kenneth Long for catalytic wisdom; to Greg Bunch for seeing futures faster; to Preston Cline for tacit knowledge; to Brittany Loney for no hero like you; to Clare Murphy for the infinite story; to Toby Lester for business infil; to Ed Croot for unconventional leadership; to Nick Dockery for operational vision; to Earl Plumlee for first-step plans; to Christopher Haviley for Robin Sage; to Trent Upton for the dojo; to General Beagle for driving change; to Jacko for killer humility; to Tom Spooner for the integrated life; to Sanny for legendary intelligence; to Swick for effective curiosity; to the unit for antifragility; to the other unit for sending me; to the covert victors for self-reliance; to Mike Benveniste for running the lab; to Erik Larson for busting AI; to Pat Enciso for getting elementary; to Kelly Wegley for improving school; to Trent Bowers for saying yes; to the National Council of Teachers of English for big creativity; to the American Camp Association for big character; to the Academy of Motion Picture Arts and Sciences for rewriting reality; to Paul Dayton for natural history; to Chuck D for black steel in the hour of chaos; to Gary Goldman for story university; to Lawrence Manley for Shakespeare; to Edward Stuenkel for brain science; to Jim Phelan for Project Narrative; to Carolyn Savarese for strategic genius; to Megan Newman for intuition; to Hannah Steigmeyer for commonsense; to Elisabeth Koyfman for imagination; to Tracy Behar for target close.

And to Sarah for Just Bloom.

FURTHER READING ON PRIMAL INTELLIGENCE

Fletcher, Angus. 2021. *Wonderworks: Literary Invention and the Science of Stories*. Simon & Schuster.

Fletcher, Angus. 2022. *Creative Thinking: A Field Guide to Strengthening Your Creative Core*. U.S. Army Command and General Staff College.

Fletcher, Angus. 2022. "3 Exercises to Boost Your Team's Creativity." *Harvard Business Review*, March 24.

Fletcher, Angus. 2022. "Why Computer AI Will Never Do What We Imagine It Can." *Narrative* 30: 114–37.

Fletcher, Angus. 2023. *Storythinking: The New Science of Narrative Intelligence*. Columbia University Press.

Fletcher, Angus. 2024. "Shakespeare Didn't Brainstorm: Why Literature Proves That There's More to Intelligence Than AI." In *Routledge Companion to Literature and Artificial Intelligence*, edited by Genevieve Lively and Will Slocombe. Routledge.

Fletcher, Angus, and Mike Benveniste. 2022. "A New Method for Training Creativity: Narrative as an Alternative to Divergent Thinking."

Annals of the New York Academy of Sciences 1512 (1): 29–45. https://doi.org/10.1111/nyas.14763.

Fletcher, Angus, and Mike Benveniste. 2024. *Narrative Creativity: An Introduction to How and Why.* Cambridge University Press.

Fletcher, Angus, Preston Cline, and Matthew Hoffman. 2023. "A Better Approach to After-Action Reviews." *Harvard Business Review,* January 12.

Fletcher, Angus, Patricia Enciso, and Mike Benveniste. 2023. "Narrative Creativity Training: A New Method for Increasing Resilience in Elementary Students." *Journal of Creativity* 33 (3): 100061. https://doi.org/10.1016/j.yjoc.2023.100061.

Fletcher, Angus, and Thomas L. Gaines. 2021. "The Limits of Logic: Why Narrative Thinking Is Better Suited for Modern Combat," *Modern War Institute,* October 19.

Fletcher, Angus, Thomas L. Gaines, and Brittany Loney. 2023. "How to Be a Better Leader amid Volatility, Uncertainty, Complexity, and Ambiguity." *Harvard Business Review,* September 28.

INDEX